Harvest the Bitter Root

Harvest the Bitter Root

Terror, Love & Border Justice in Civil War Missouri

Joseph F. Dwyer

OVERRIDE

MMXIV

Copyright © 2014 by Joseph F. Dwyer
ALL RIGHTS RESERVED

ISBN 978-0-9907145-0-7

Printed in the United States of America
First Edition

for bulk sales of *Harvest the Bitter Root*
and for author interviews & book signings
PLEASE CONTACT: joseph.f.dwyer@att.net

Revenge… is like a rolling stone, which, when a man hath forced up a hill, will return upon him with a greater violence, and break those bones whose sinews gave it motion.

JEREMY TAYLOR

Acknowledgments

TO MY WIFE, Christine Ann Dwyer: For a lifetime of love and forbearance in all our endeavors. She stands behind me when I need support. She stands in front of me if I need protection. She stands at my side so that we may face adversity together. She is my best friend. Chris read the manuscript, tasked with focusing on textural enhancement. Her input proved invaluable as she assisted with insights and developments on meanings and nuance.

To my friend, Larry Rothenberg: Avid adventure reader, outdoorsman and sportsman: Larry's critiques helped me focus on sections of this manuscript where supplemental explanations were required. His enthusiasm for the story inspired me to work more intensely toward continuous improvement.

To my friend, William Appelquist: Individualist, problem solver and man among men: Bill embraced the concept of this story from the very beginning. His feedback was insightful and continuously on target. I hold Bill's validation in high regard for many of the manuscript's action details.

To my friend, Mary Rothenberg: Artist and enthusiast of the creative process: Mary's interest in this project provided additional impetus. Mary insightfully identified helpful parallel and complementary currents in the text.

ACKNOWLEDGMENTS

To my friend, David Pasquale: Fearless and adaptive nonconformist, in a world devolving toward consensus by committee. He is a trusted comrade and insightful sage with the ability to bring issues into perspective. His story and personal example are key components underpinning Harvest's individualist narrative.

To my editor and friend, Frank Martin: A man of repute, through vision, experience and achievement. He embraces the Quest and shares his unique perspectives with those having the audacity to challenge and resilience to adapt. Goals require focus. Frank marshals efforts with determination to claim realization, perception and accomplishment.

To my granddaughter, Harriet Everett: Sensitive soul, interactive collaborator and interpretive artist. Thank you for the contribution of your homestead cabin drawing.

JOSEPH F. DWYER

Introduction

THE AMERICAN CIVIL WAR did not erupt in 1861 as reported in history books. The fighting first began in 1854 when Congress passed the Kansas-Nebraska Act. This legislation focused on whether newly admitted states would allow slavery via popular vote. The politicians looked at a paper map and assumed their course of action correctly balanced electoral power, but the Missouri populace along the Kansas border viewed the law as an unwarranted intrusion into their lives.

In the Northeastern United States, the slavery debate increased in scope and intensity. Thousands of fervent abolitionists flooded into the Kansas - Missouri border region, after receiving funding from the Massachusetts Immigrant Aid Company. They viewed their mission as a crusade from God and exhibited passion for freeing all slaves immediately. Although most were well intentioned, they prepared no workable plan for what to do with the slaves once liberated.

These newcomers did not understand the local culture. They considered the area overrun with evil and avarice. They viewed slavery as the dominant practice and assumed all white men were slave owners or pro-slavery sympathizers. Nothing could have been further from the truth. More than 90 percent of the white population did not belong to the slaveholder class. Most were God-fearing, hard-working dirt farmers and townsfolk, many living day-to-day on the margins of survival. The residents lived by a code of self-reliance where overcoming adversity barely received a second thought.

INTRODUCTION

Slave ownership by wealthy landholders had been a reality for generations. The folks who grew up in the midst of that institution did not contemplate its rationale or ethic. Third and fourth generation Missourians did not lecture other people on what to do or how to live their lives through judgmental predisposition.

Nevertheless, in 1854, after generations of self-sufficiency, vast numbers of Eastern and Northern opportunists stood at their doorstep in the newly established territory of Kansas. Missourians saw this influx as an invasion of the homeland their ancestors earned through toil and bravery. War appeared inevitable. The rich hired mercenaries to safeguard their property and fight their battles. The poor did their own fighting and dying. Tragically, no one imagined there would be so much of both.

The combatants were almost exclusively mobile cavalry units from the regular Army and partisan military contingents. Battles were small, intense and worst of all, frequent. The killing was up-close and personal. The recurrent skirmishes left little time for preparation. The character of the countryside and the mobility of the cavalry units meant fighters needed to be prepared at all times and capable of using traditional and untraditional weapons. Once out of ammunition, combat options diminished significantly. Fighters, who did not own a sword, were required to use their empty rifle, or any available tool, to attempt beating an adversary to death.

On the border, casualty expectations were 100 percent and taking prisoners was infrequent. Experienced combatants fought to the death. They understood capture would result in torture, inevitably followed by execution. The countryside lay littered with the savaged remains of partisans from both sides.

INTRODUCTION

Their souls may have eventually found their way to Paradise, but their bodies became carrion to vultures and coyotes. Their names were soon lost to memory. The only thing their families knew with certainty was that they never returned home.

Terror was the operative norm. Mutilations, such as scalping and dragging, emerged as accepted practice. Such brutality encouraged men to fight with a complete lack of regard for human life. The commanders of both the Northern Jayhawkers and Southern Bushwhackers possessed charismatic personalities tainted with extreme moral corruption. These men continually demonstrated the expertise to elevate degradation to an art form. Opposing sides made concerted efforts to raise the intensity of revulsion; intending to force their opponents to back away in horror. The tactic was not successful for either camp. Once blood spilled, neither side backed down. Reprisals spawned counter-reprisals and the spiral of butchery became unstoppable.

Harvest the Bitter Root

1
1863 - Western Missouri

PREDAWN

"Dead?" sputtered Nathan with his lips parted slightly. The boy sucked in a sharp breath and clenched his stomach as if punched. Nate took a quick look in the direction where Ussher's eyes seemed focused.

He continued, "You really think so? Jimmy, our Jimmy? He wasn't drinking or nothin' before he left. Said he'd be back in an hour, two hours most, and that horse of his is fast, lightning fast, and Jimmy, well… he's been riding since he was three. I heard Big John sayin' that we're gonna' need Jimmy and that horse for… A Big Ride, he called it."

Nate's anxiety caused him to speak rapidly and shift his skinny frame side-to-side. For the past 16 months, he lived on the edges of existence. After losing his family to the war, he felt as if he had become little more than a nuisance to everyone with whom he came into contact. Jimmy was the exception. He always treated Nate with regard. Jimmy shared everything until Nate could get belongings of his own. Those items were most often leftovers from dead men unclaimed by the other fighters. In all his 14 years, no one had shown him more kindness, including family. Jimmy was Nate's best friend and acted as his adopted older brother.

"And I also heard…"

"Shut up!" snapped Ussher, his voice barely perceptible but unconditional. Those piercing eyes transferred their intensity from the grassland to Nate, who now was startled even further. "Just shut your goddamned mouth. Use your brain for once. Look out there. Look hard. What can you see? What do you hear?"

* * * *

It took Nate a moment to disengage eye contact with Ussher. It made him feel vulnerable to look away. He was afraid Ussher could peer inside him and understand how upset he actually was at that moment. He liked being with this man. He was decent toward him, although his ways were harsh and his voice was often severe. Nate pushed his gaze beyond Ussher and across the field to the gradually brightening horizon. Although positioned downwind, he did not suspect anything, and no discernible movement caught his eye. It had been a long quiet night, and he was God-awful tired. He inhaled a breath and did his best to clear his mind of fatigue. Although still in darkness, Nate shielded his eyes with both hands as he looked for movement along the seams and shadows of the landscape in front of him. Everything looked normal and no threats appeared obvious.

It astonished Nate how Ussher never became drowsy. Nate could not remember if he had ever seen him sleep. Obviously all men need to rest at one time or another. Ussher was not an exception in this matter but he did not seem to want others to notice this aspect of his human side. He always volunteered for the late watch. The night seemed to bring out anger from deep within him. Nate occasionally observed Ussher squeeze his eyes tightly shut while sucking in a silent, mournful breath. It was as if he were struggling to expel a dream or memory from his mind. Although curious about his manner, Nate chose not to question the motives behind Ussher's behavior.

Inevitably, daylight returned, the security vigil ended, and the daytime sentries took up their positions. Most mornings Ussher disappeared into the forest, seeking personal solitude. He walked straight away from camp. Then, a short distance from the perimeter, he stepped effortlessly off the path and vanished into the background.

Ussher possessed a knack for vanishing, which is distinctly different from hiding. Hiding is a fixed action, defensive by nature, and subject to bursts of startled energy. Those attempting to hide use their surroundings as a barrier. Barriers are easy to define and understand. As a result, they draw attention and heighten watchfulness. Boulders, trees, fence lines, and such are common structures known to be locations used by those wishing to hide. When men see these structures, they instinctively believe that opponents may be waiting in ambush. Therefore, these features draw the focus of adversaries, even those who only possess minimal survival knowledge.

Vanishing is interactive. There is a difference between standing beneath the cover of a shadow and stepping inside the shadow itself. Knowing how to move inside allows the body to adapt to the light gradients and diffuses the silhouette into the landscape. Those with skill immediately determine the usefulness of a particular shadow and weave seamlessly inside. Once in place, they remain motionless and wait for advantage. Opposing combatants usually look from object to object. They sweep from one fixed feature and proceed to the next. The searcher's eye makes adjustments from structure to shadow and then back to light. This allows a scout, standing motionless where the shadow begins, to go unobserved. The ability to conceal in plain sight offers immeasurable advantage to those possessing the skill. The stationary aberration of one masked by dappled light exceeds the visual acuity of those searching for enemies thought to be hiding behind forest structure.

The essential companion to conceal in plain sight is the ability to mask your proximity from those you want to avoid or intend to ambush.

The main component of this skill is avoiding eye contact with the enemy. The eyes are portals of hostile intent, generating their own power. They extract information from the environment for the brain to process and assimilate into decision-making preparedness. Intense focus often causes those targeted to experience quivers of misgiving and energizes neck hairs with static. Fighters often sense the feeling of impending danger, causing them to become more cautious and watchful.

To counter and control this awareness force, skilled woodsmen rely on their peripheral vision for close observation. They focus on inanimate objects near the individual they are watching. The energy from their gaze bypasses the target while still collecting necessary decision-making information. This practice lessens the likelihood the observer will be detected. Few scouts possessed the ability to utilize this tactic. Fewer perfected the technique to the competency level Ussher achieved.

Nate recalled one recent early morning, shortly after first light, when his curiosity overruled his caution. He waited less than half a minute and then followed Ussher into the shadows. He came up with a story, more like an excuse for his action, in case Ussher became angry over the intrusion. The tree branch Ussher pushed aside still appeared to be moving as Nate followed him in. As soon as he stepped under the canopy, Nate paused a moment and allowed his eyes to focus, expecting to see Ussher. To his surprise, there was nothing to see. He looked in every direction, but Ussher was gone, seemingly evaporated. He listened carefully but heard nothing but birds and crickets. The event both impressed and unnerved him. It was like being on speaking terms with a ghost.

* * * *

"I said, 'Look hard. What do you see? What do you hear?'"

Ussher repeated the order using a deliberate, menacing tone to provoke the boy's vigilance. After allowing his thoughts to wander, Nate gave Ussher his full attention. In spite of his youth, he sought to appear competent and in control. He wanted men to think of him as loyal and trustworthy. Nate hated sentry duty. He dreamed of the time he might receive a scouting mission, like the kind Charlie Hawkins assigned to Jimmy last night.

Following Ussher's directions, Nate searched the landscape intently. The only thing he saw was vacant backdrop. He doubled his efforts, but he still came up empty. He could feel Ussher's expectation but he did not have anything to offer.

"Mr. Ussher," he finally confessed, "I'm sorry, but, I don't see nothin' and I don't hear nothin'."

Ussher remained stone quiet. Nate knelt down silently and continued peering into the empty distance. He watched Ussher shift his eyes slightly, and then noticed them relock onto something distant. Ussher pulled the hammer back on his Henry rifle. It clicked and set with lethal intention.

"Son," he finally responded, "For the first time tonight, you and I agree. There is nothing to see and nothing to hear, and THAT seems to be the immediate problem. Now, go wake

Hawkins and the others. This camp ain't no secret to those Jayhawkers anymore."

2

The Jayhawkers

TYLER AND HIS JAYHAWKER RAIDERS guessed right; just free the horse and allow him to run. A good one returns home and this one looked exceptional. They followed the young mount for more than an hour. Because of his speed, they lost sight of him on two occasions. Fortunately, the trail was moist so clear prints marked a path easy to pick up and follow. When they reckoned they were almost on top of the Bushwhacker camp, the Raiders dismounted. They secured their own horses behind cover and followed on foot. Jack Mingo took the lead. Born with one-half Pawnee blood, he was the best tracker Tyler ever recruited. His skills would be useful in the pre-dawn half-light.

Earlier, Mingo impressed everyone with his sense for detecting trouble. He peered out over the top of the campfire at the line of horses the Raiders secured between two trees. The horse Mingo looked at most intently was his own. He rode a distinctive blue roan, Mustang-Spanish mix. In the three years since he acquired the horse, Mingo learned to observe its reactions closely. Although the horse was never skittish, it was observant and responsive to changes in the environment. It stared keenly at anything that caught its attention visually or by scent. The animal's intensity was infectious and soon caused other horses to pick up the cue and search in the same direction

Mingo's horse indicated.

This night, his horse concentrated on a point ninety degrees to Mingo's right. He did not look in the direction of the horse's interest and gave no indication of his growing suspicion to others. He knew that any word of alarm, no matter how calmly stated, was likely to make his comrades turn and look in the direction of the problem. Such movement could alert the enemy of his detection. This situation would attain better results if he handled the problem in his own way.

Mingo finalized the exact location causing his horse such concern. He grabbed his gun and ran north without saying a word. Everyone looked at each other, asking, "What the Hell is going on?" Five minutes later, he came back pulling a tied-up young prisoner with him. The kid bled from his temple where Mingo hit him with the butt of his rifle. The Raiders knew those damn Bushwhackers were all around. In this part of the country, you could be a half-mile from a small band of the enemy and never realize it. Earlier, Tyler set up sentries but none of those lazy assholes noticed the enemy scout moving in their midst.

* * * *

The Raider's interrogation of Jimmy had been aggressive and undisciplined. They were loud and abusive. They grabbed and pulled him in different directions. Several Raiders questioned him at the same time. The tactic confused Jimmy and frustrated them. Combining confusion with frustration often creates an emotional disconnect that turns into unintended consequences. The confusion caused Jimmy to lock down his mind and block the inquiring voices. He stared at the ground, vowing never to disclose information to these Kansas sodomites.

From the Raider's point of view, their frustration was aggravated from their inability to locate Missouri militia contingents. They wanted the opportunity to extract retribution for recent setbacks, with the additional bonus of collecting posted bounty money. Very soon, their dissatisfaction progressed to beating. It quickly escalated because that is the essential nature of beating. It takes on a dogged life of its own and does not cease until the aggressors are satiated, exhausted, or the victim dies.

Blow-by-blow, Jimmy's strength diminished. Reality became unreal. Blood and sweat obscured his vision and breathing from inside a broken rib cage was no longer possible. Intuitively, he understood there was only one escape. He accepted his inevitable fate and willed himself toward that final release. The pounding thunder from blows to his head progressively attenuated into a subtle beehive of humming and the waves of nausea subsided. Just before death reached out to take him, the shock and trauma paused to allow Jimmy a moment of quiet. For some reason, he noticed his flickering shadow illuminated by the campfire. He wondered if it would vanish once he passed. As a faint prayer departed through his broken teeth and bleeding lips, Mercy quietly descended and enveloped Jimmy into her arms. She opened the gateway to transcendence, allowing the pain to dissolve and agony to evaporate. Total anguish restructured into stillness and sublime peace.

Jimmy's suffering ended two minutes before the Raiders realized he was dead. They continued to compete for a better position to inflict additional kicks or punches into the young scout. They jostled and swore at each other for being in the way. After a while, they became conscious of Tyler repeatedly yelling at them at the top of his lungs. "He's dead," he screamed. The men looked at Tyler, then at Jimmy, and finally at each other. The rage in their eyes gradually transformed into vacancy. One-by-one, they drifted to neutral areas to settle down. None of them previously thought about killing Jimmy. They were only interested in beating him because it felt good to beat someone. Now that the pounding was over, the men no longer felt good about anything. They drifted into the exhaustion that inevitably follows a large expenditure of adrenaline.

Tyler regretted killing the young scout so quickly. He may have possessed some useful enemy information. Then again, with Mingo along, tracking down and mopping up the remaining opposition scum was a virtual certainty. Besides, those Missouri bastards had been stealing and sniping at his men for several days. Three of his Kansas Raiders were dead. Two more were trying to heal up. Once his men saw the captured scout already bleeding, it just sent them into frenzy.

To make matters worse, that kid had a real smartass mouth on him. Thought he was being a real man, acting defiant and all. Tyler thought about the scout's death with a faint reflective smile. Jimmy proved himself surprisingly tough for someone so young. Even ripped apart as he was, there was no pleading and almost no tears. As he watched his Raiders, Tyler worried some. The upcoming fight might be intense, and the ride back to the Harris ranch would take a couple hours. He was concerned his men had worn themselves clean out, while beating and kicking that kid to death.

Tyler quickly refocused on the upcoming fight. His Employer, Talbot Harris, paid a $30 bounty for every Bushwhacker, dead or alive. He promised to pay $500 for the life of the man carrying his stolen Henry rifle. After daybreak, the Jayhawkers planned more payback against the Missouri Militia, especially for the son-of-a-bitch who carried the Henry.

The weapon possessed a unique report from that of a Springfield or Sharps rifle. It was a combination of exploding gunpowder and splitting air. You could always tell when a wound came from a Henry. It made a smaller hole than the minie ball, but it penetrated deeper or traveled through the body. Before leaving the Harris ranch, Tyler promised his boss that his rifle and the Bushwhacker scalp of the man who took it, would both adorn his saddle on the return trip. He might even do this scalping himself since he did not intend to partake in the assault.

* * * *

Unless caught by surprise, Tyler never participated in the up-close fighting. From his point of view, he was too valuable to the mission to risk injury. His job, as he saw it, was to assemble the correct number and right type of men for the assignments given to perform. The fact that most of his missions essentially involved the same tasks, and the individual ability of available men remained constant, did not matter to him. The men in every patrol understood that Tyler led from behind. It did not matter much if they bought into his story of self-importance. Each of the raider partisans was essentially in this fight for money or revenge. Too much time had passed and too much blood spilled. There was no longer any concern for something trivial, like fighting for a cause.

* * * *

Tyler reflected a little and decided it was necessary to demonstrate he had no problem getting into the shit. He pulled out his skinning knife and strode over to the lifeless form of the young scout, which was lying face down.

Tyler straddled Jimmy's body and shouted, "Death to all these fuckers."

He pulled the head backwards by the hair and placed his boot on the base of Jimmy's neck. After cutting a deep semicircle gash across the forehead, he jerked hard with a backward motion. As Jimmy's scalp tore and separated from his head, Tyler spit on the corpse and held the bloody trophy high for all to see. "Yeah, that's the way you do it."

With that action, Tyler issued a clear notice to all the locals. They needed to understand he was as dangerous as any partisan leader in the area. Bloody Bill Anderson, that Bushwhacker menace, wasn't the only one who knew how to strike terror into the hearts of men.

A scalp was as good as a corpse and a mutilated rebel body was a clear warning to the Bushwhacker lowlifes who dared oppose the new order taking control. Old Man Harris now owed him a $30 bounty. With any luck, none of his Jayhawker comrades would realize he intended to keep the entire amount for himself.

3

Ambush

USSHER CALCULATED correctly. Nate took five minutes to wake the men. He needed to be quiet and move quickly without frightening the horses and alerting the enemy that the militia was ready for their attack. He knew to nudge Charlie Hawkins first and do so with great care so he would not become loud or belligerent.

Hawkins was exceptionally foul-mouthed, even for this rough-and-tumble militia group. He resorted to coercion and ridicule whenever anyone dared disagree with him. Both Jimmy and Nate were often targets for random abuse whenever Hawkins felt the need to exert his perceived authority. Since the abuse did not appear life threatening and neither boy was kin, Ussher refrained from intervening.

* * * *

There was already bad blood between Ussher and Hawkins.

Martin Vaughn, one of Quantrill's original commanders, reluctantly appointed Hawkins leader of a scouting party. Except for Ussher, who was 12 years his senior, Hawkins, at 24, was the oldest in the group. He was a capable fighter and enjoyed taking charge, but Ussher doubted Hawkins would live long enough to attain the skills required to lead men effectively.

Vaughn also recognized Hawkins' tendency to be immature and impulsive. With Hawkins standing next to him, Vaughn asked Ussher to join a scouting foray, to keep things focused. Ussher was a reluctant member of the militia and never sought an active leadership position. While chewing on a blade of Indian grass, he listened attentively to Vaughn's request. He knew of Hawkins' past actions in the field and that he often confused escaping disaster with tactical success.

After a long pause, Ussher agreed to help, for the sake of the mission and men, but he stated his conditions of participation with clarity.

"I ain't taking any shit from this hothead," Ussher's voice punctuated his resolve. "And no taking unnecessary chances, like shooting without first trying to investigate the whole situation."

Ussher made hard eye contact with Hawkins to stress the point. Hawkins held his ground and smirked. He stepped assertively in front of Vaughn and raised his brawny arm, pointing an index finger at Ussher's face to emphasize his own point.

He retorted confidently, "I know who you are, and what you are, old man. You just make sure that your sorry ass can keep up with the rest of us."

Ussher feigned departure then suddenly walked toward Hawkins, who quickly braced himself. He advanced forward, and then through the space Hawkins occupied. His left shoulder struck hard against the left shoulder of Hawkins as he walked on and away. The jolt spun the ruffian 90 degrees. Hawkins immediately appeared pissed off and began to pursue the departing older man.

"I guess you're lookin' to get your ass kicked, you redneck shit," Hawkins bellowed as he started his pursuit.

Ussher allowed Hawkins to grab his arm and spin him around. As Ussher's body squared up to confront the incensed thug, a blade flashed followed by a howl of pain, fear, and wounded disbelief. Hawkins found himself dazed and looking up at an equally confounded Vaughn. His left temple pulsated with pain and his chin bled profusely.

With one lightning movement, Ussher unsheathed his knife, struck Hawkins across the forehead with its hilt, and with the return motion, slit open his chin. Ussher bent over and put his face menacingly close to that of Hawkins.

"This old redneck shit, could've placed that cut across your throat just as easy," Ussher's voice rasped evenly, without emotion.

Hawkins remained stone silent and did not attempt to look

at Ussher. He felt relief when Ussher withdrew from his menacing stance and stood back up. Ussher looked at Vaughn and then pointed at Hawkins.

"Better muzzle your dog and teach him to show some respect. Being big ain't no salvation for being stupid, and he's gonna' get people killed. He just walked into an unnecessary ass kickin' from a little bump on the shoulder. I don't give a shit if he dies, but I'd hate to see our boys shot down because he don't think before gettin' himself into a losing situation. A real leader never gets baited into a fight so easily or signals his intent so clearly."

Vaughn raised both hands with palms extended in Ussher's direction. "I know. I got it. I'll take care of it right now."

Vaughn turned to Hawkins and yelled, "Get your ass up".

Hawkins arose awkwardly holding his left hand against his temple and his right hand against his chin.

Vaughn ordered, "Apologize to this man."

Hawkins hesitated.

Vaughn screamed in his face, "Apologize."

"All right," Hawkins expressed through a terse exhale. Without making eye contact he mumbled, "I apologize."

Vaughn yelled into his ear, "It's Mr. Ussher."

Hawkins desperately wanted to take a rag with cold water and place it against his bleeding chin. Using only his hand did not stop the blood. He sucked in a breath.

"I'm sorry, Mr. Ussher, I was pure stupid and I apologize."

Hawkins was aware enough of his situation to include a tone of sincerity. There was nothing else to say. Ussher looked at Vaughn.

"Leave it be," he said, waving his hand and turning away.

From that moment, a new dynamic emerged from their

encounter. Hawkins maintained a respectful demeanor and Ussher reciprocated by tolerating him on a day-by-day basis.

* * * *

Ussher relocated himself to higher ground and into a flanking position facing the incoming Jayhawkers. He counted eight. Seven of them advanced in a low crouch. From the way they moved, he knew immediately these men were not hunters. They were probably cowhands, more used to sitting in a saddle looking for strays than stalking the countryside searching for enemies.

Hunters are all about the details. They are alert to natural signs, apparent in both reality and perception. In the wilderness, success comes from a combination of intelligence and sensory giftedness. The environment changes constantly. What is evident in sunlight is unresolved in the shadows. Scents in warm weather change character when the temperature cools. The sounds of the forest alter, hour-to-hour, as the humidity changes. Every day brings new lessons. A true woodsman never stops learning. A hunter's capability is rooted in a lifetime of experience in the wild. For an elite few, it produces a survival skill mirroring natural instinct.

Ussher immediately recognized the lead Jayhawker scout as a true hunter and woodsman. He covered the ground using a zigzag approach, sweeping the terrain for signs of danger and advantage. He kept his body low and traveled decisively. His actions were smooth and practiced. Ussher noted the specifics of his movements and the unique, balanced pace he maintained. His approach was distinctive from other fighters in his experience. If he were a betting man, Ussher might wager the scout's bloodline contained Indian heritage.

His trained eye and experienced mind quickly analyzed that this opponent was an effective and resourceful fighter. Men of this caliber were rare. Ussher instantly admired and respected his ability. In better times, he would enjoy sharing a cup of homebrew with him. He reflected on the benefits such an encounter might offer. Exchanging tracking and trapping information with a huntsman of this quality would be a privilege. This assessment of the Jayhawker scout led Ussher to finalize his decision and focus on his immediate task.

This man needed to be the first to die.

4

Battle

As Nate awakened the members of the small militia party, each man guessed danger was imminent. This kid would never disturb them if the situation were not life threatening. Each sought to clear the sleep from his head as quickly as possible while voicing the same questions, "Where? Which way?"

Nate pointed in Ussher's direction while the four men grabbed their weapons and fanned into a small defensive semicircle. Ussher had earlier instructed the Missourians to keep a fifteen-foot distance between each man. This separation prevented a sniper from shooting one man and easily setting his sights on the next fighter. Ussher realized the importance of this move, especially if the enemy possessed repeating rifles. The Missourians discussed and practiced this tactic and knew to wait for Ussher to make the first move.

Nate went to the horses, still saddled from the previous night. As silently as possible, he checked the cinch straps in case the riders needed to mount their horses on the run. This used to be Jimmy's responsibility until he received his scouting assignment. Nate prayed he was going to be able to do the job as good as Jimmy. Failure could result in punishment, which could be anything from a beating to expulsion from the camp. It was getting near daybreak, and the sky cleared. Very soon, everyone involved would be able to see everyone else. The whole situation was sure to turn into a brutal, bloody pox.

* * * *

As Ussher waited for whatever fate this morning would bring, he thought about Jimmy, "Our Jimmy," as Nate liked saying. He regretted he had not opposed Hawkins' idea to send Jimmy to shadow the Kansas raiders.

The young man acted thrilled when Hawkins issued the understated order, "Hey Jimmy-boy, get up on that horse of yours and take a ride for me. After that ass kickin' we put on those Hawkers yesterday, they might be out looking for us and thinking about payback. See what those Kansas pricks may be up to and get back to me, okay?"

The older militiamen reinforced Jimmy's enthusiasm with mock admiration. They chimed in with, "Way to go, boy! Now you're moving up with the men". "Jesus boy, you're 16 years old. It's about time you started doing your part."

Fact was, none of these men wanted to take any chances in the darkness themselves. They each remembered their own eagerness at Jimmy's age but now they knew better. Experience taught that nighttime was dangerous and dying alone, surrounded only by enemies, was a terrifying situation to contemplate. Besides, they were in the fifth day of scouting and fortune favored their side every step. They recently talked about that very point and felt sure their luck was about to run out. An ass screwing from Providence seemed inevitable.

Just before Jimmy rode out, Ussher caught him by the arm as he mounted his horse.

He cautioned, "No need to be stupid. Keep your distance. You have good eyes so there's no reason to get too close. Those Kansas Raiders are snake-mean and will open up your neck just for fun".

"Yes sir," Jimmy responded, barely able to suppress a smile. "I'll be careful, sure."

Ussher saw the spark in his eyes and heard the excitement in his voice as Jimmy ruffled Nate's hair. Nate beamed back with pride as he watched Jimmy vault into the saddle. Ussher knew in his core that Jimmy, our Jimmy, felt the invincibility that comes with youth. He was blind and deaf to the plausibility of danger and the significance of caution.

Since Jimmy's disappearance, Ussher was angrier with himself than with Hawkins, but right now, he needed to put those concerns aside. He had to concentrate and take care of business, and the business-at-hand was releasing the demonic action named Killing.

Most men never realize Killing is not an isolated act. Unleashing such a malevolent spirit and allowing it to thrive in your midst is an action of consequence. A prudent man would never enter a room filled with vipers but never give a thought about shooting at an enemy and initiating lethal retribution.

Killing demands the full attention of the fighter and easily becomes insatiable. Once unleashed, combatants need to keep its destruction moving forward so it does not turn back and devour its author. Killing is an erratic force, whose path is unpredictable. It is an irrational and volatile tool to use only in the most desperate situations.

* * * *

Ussher sighted-in the Henry rifle onto Jack Mingo's lean torso. He briefly pondered a head shot, but recognized the report from the Henry would cause Mingo's men to fix on his position and start shooting in his direction. If he missed the head, Mingo would gain cover and ensnare Ussher in crossfire. As he slipped on an old leather glove for protection against barrel heat, Ussher decided to target Mingo's body and allow the .44 caliber round to do its deadly work.

As he advanced, Mingo bypassed Ussher by only 35 yards. Through sheer luck, his zigzag running moved him away from the location Ussher used for cover. Mingo crouched behind a low rise and assessed the militia camp in the pre-dawn light. In an instant, he analyzed several facts. He observed four men, already arrayed defensively. Damnation! Mingo recognized they carried single shot rifles and some possessed side arms. He saw a thin boy working the cinch straps on the saddles, and counted six horses.

Ussher felt he could almost read Mingo's mind as he tallied one more horse than there were riders. With all the horses saddled, Mingo reasoned there was one fighter unaccounted. He surveyed left then right, and saw nothing. He started recalling every step of his approach. As he recollected the terrain, he knew immediately where his exposure lay.

Ussher saw Mingo inhale a breath to steady his nerves as

he cocked the hammer on his Enfield rifle. He felt expectation, apprehension, and total respect bundled into one moment. He knew that this man, this hunter and tracker, now recognized and acknowledged his vulnerability, but was not about to accept fate as inevitable and submit easily. He was not the type to give another man combat quarter, and he did not expect it in return. In that instant, Ussher knew Jack Mingo was about to turn and face in his direction.

Mingo exhaled and cursed his situation. The early half-light fell silent as even frogs and crickets seemed to hold their breath in anticipation. Ussher squeezed the trigger on the Henry. The exploding gunpowder released the malevolent Killing demon. Ussher reflected for a moment on the expression, "All Hell Breaking Loose." While that might be true, he did not hesitate to embrace the maelstrom. Conflict would either kill him and relieve his pain or take him a step closer to the final retribution envisioned in his nightmares.

Mingo's brain acquired complete mental clarity in this moment. He knew that everyone fucks up one time or another and there are always consequences when this happens. He felt completely alert and full of anticipation for the coming fight. He especially looked forward to getting some bounty money from Old Man Harris. Lastly, Mingo knew it was inconceivable he would have missed some amateur farm boy sniper as he reconnoitered his way into position.

There were no obvious signs of ambush. Absolutely nothing appeared disturbed. Mingo had no idea a problem existed until he saw his intended militia targets already in defensive positions. If he missed sensing the danger, it was because his unseen adversary was also a legitimate hunter, the same caliber or better than himself. He heard these Bushwhackers recruited such a man and knew of the deadly results to his Jayhawkers in recent weeks.

A chill spiked through Mingo at the same moment the leading edge of the sun split open the horizon. Though he would never know for sure, Mingo thought for an instant he actually heard the hammer of the rifle strike the primer on the bullet. Doom can play funny tricks on a man.

The round exploded from the Henry's barrel. It carried its earsplitting demise at a low trajectory crashing into Mingo's chest. Ussher saw the shot was true. It entered on an angle in front of Mingo's left armpit and out his right side, spraying blood and rib splinters upon exit. Jack Mingo was horse-kicked backwards in the same instant. Ussher did not know if Mingo was dead, but he saw the heavy way he fell to the ground and his Enfield rifle laying six feet away from his hand.

The seven men with Mingo, as well as Tyler, who was in the rear overseeing the operation, froze in their footsteps. Ussher's men had no idea what exactly was going on. They did not realize Jack Mingo had been watching them and they could not see Ussher. All they heard was that first rifle shot. It sounded like the Henry but in these low hills, you could not be sure. Ussher removed all uncertainty by firing three more times. Two more Kansas Raiders went down. The first one collapsed, as if suddenly cut-down after hanging from some invisible rope. The second fell and then rolled over in apparent agony. When another of the Raiders went to help his wounded comrade, Ussher rewarded him with a .44 caliber round, severing his spine and lacerating his liver. The blood running from the wound was more black than red, as the man died cursing his rotten luck.

Just as the Kansas men located Ussher's position and were about to return fire, they started to receive incoming rounds from the same Missouri boys they earlier sought to ambush. The militiamen were pissed off and jo-fired as hell. They knew that they were lucky to be alive. These Raiders were not the type to take prisoners. If not for Ussher and young Nate, they might be dead already. Each man aimed and fired his rifle and ran to mount his horse for pursuit. Nate held out the reins to each rider. Even though outnumbered, the Missourians charged with confidence. They saw the Raiders were confused and running back toward their own man, who was trying to keep their horses calm. The Raiders mounted quickly and rode full out toward the northwest. Ussher fired three more rounds, causing another raider to slump forward but continue to ride.

As the militiamen neared Ussher's location, he raised both his hands to stop the pursuit.

"Cool your blood boys. You don't know what's out there. If those bastards work for Talbot Harris, there is likely to be a lot more of them looking for us. Right now, we need to get back to Vaughn and let him know all that's going on. Take what you can get from those we shot. Ussher pointed to where Jack Mingo laid motionless, and emphasized, "Be extra careful with that one yonder. I want to be gone from here in five minutes."

As they searched the dead for anything of immediate value, the Missourians were full of energy from adrenaline overload. They awakened, hearing they were about to be ambushed but came through the firefight without suffering casualties. They saw the dead from Ussher's rifle shots and associated his ability with their own perceived prowess. Their blood was up, and their egos were inflated. They were overly confident and loud, some of them even mocking the dead.

"Thought you were going to shoot my ass, didn't you boy?" one of them laughed while kicking a corpse.

Another started pulling the boots off a dead raider, intending to try them on for fit.

Suddenly, Ussher was among them, snarling like a wolf asserting alpha-position. "Why don't you assholes light up a whopping signal fire? Why don't you just shoot your guns a few more times? Maybe a better idea would be to break out some homebrew so you could drink yourself stupid.

Ussher walked among them, man-to-man, grabbing them by the hair or collar and yelling directly into their face. "Y'all should be dead right now. Your dead-ass bodies or your scalps should be hanging on the saddles of those Kansas Raiders right this minute. Those men we killed did their work proper. They put in the time. They tracked you down while you were sleeping. You weren't good this morning; you weren't even close to good. You were lucky. Now, act like men. Act like soldiers. Do your jobs. Collect everything we can use and get your asses back to camp."

The militiamen responded immediately by focusing on the task-at-hand. In less than three minutes, they salvaged anything worthwhile and started their three-hour ride back to the base camp and Vaughn. As everyone else rode out, Nate did not move. He obstinately stood in place with a look of determination.

5

Jimmy, Our Jimmy

"WE NEED TO FIND JIMMY," Nate insisted, "Maybe he's hurt."

Ussher continued to experience distressing feelings about Jimmy's prospects as he watched Hawkins and the others ride off. He always admired that kid and the way he looked after young Nate. Though he was hardly much more than a boy himself, Jimmy did a damn good job setting examples of manhood for Nate. He was honest, hardworking, and learned quickly.

A week earlier, Ussher had trouble suppressing a smile as he saw Nate setting up a rabbit snare and Jimmy stepped up to suggest a better way to rig it. Three days ago, Jimmy told Nate about a river location, which was one of his favorite fishing spots. He promised to take Nate as soon as they could get away.

"Them catfish are large enough to pull your skinny butt upstream and downstream at the same time," he joked. Those two undeniably shared a bond.

Jimmy was also reckless with a brave-to-a-fault characteristic, which worried Ussher the most.

Ussher stated evenly, "Yeah, maybe he's hurt."

He didn't want to set up expectations of any kind for Nate. Whatever was out there, good or bad, was a matter of fact at this point.

"First, we'll find some cover and lay-up for an hour or so to see if those goddamn Raiders come back this way. After that, we will head north/northwest and try to pick up a sign or two as to where Jimmy may be. Likely, we'll find him holed in a cave, a tree, or behind some rocks."

This was Ussher's only comment that made an attempt at optimism.

"Mr. Ussher," asked Nate, "Why are we fighting all the time? For as long as I can remember, we've been fighting. I ain't scared or nothing, but I get tired of always setting up camp and then breaking camp, sometimes the very same day.

"Some of the men say that it's all about the Blacks, the Negros. I've seen a few of them folks. They work on some of the large farms, but I've never talked to any of them, and I don't know what they're all about. I asked Jimmy awhile back, but he said he didn't honestly know either. Ain't neither of us ever had anything to do with them. Jimmy said he heard that some Northerners were trying to take over in this here part of the country and change the way we live our lives. He insisted we've got to stop them any way we can. I asked him where he heard that stuff and all he said was, "Around."

"Why would anyone want to change the way we live? What other way is there to live? Farming and hunting are all my family has ever done. My granddaddy once told me that our family's been dirt-farmers for as long as there's been dirt."

Ussher allowed himself a moment of amusement at Nate's dirt comment.

"I don't know much about Negros either," said Ussher. All I know is that some of the real large farms around these parts and plantations in the Deep South have a lot of them doing all sorts of work."

"How long do they have to work on those farms?"

"My guess... it's maybe forever."

"Don't the Negros get tired of working for someone else? Don't they want to get a farm of their own?"

Ussher said, "I don't know for sure, but I think that would likely be the case. Every family I know in these parts works for itself, by itself. My family has been here three generations. We've never asked anyone for anything other than to stay out of our way. We don't judge other people and we don't give a damn what other people think about us. So when outsiders come in, and try to force us to do something, then that's worth fighting about.

"Most of those Jayhawkers have moved in over the last few years. They weren't invited. They don't know our ways and further don't give a lick about our values. Now, enough questions. It's been a damn rough night, and I'm dog-tired. We have to figure out Jimmy's situation. I need quiet so I can do some thinking."

Nate pushed a little more. "So, do you think we're fighting because of the Negros or because the Northerners are trying to change the way we live?"

No reply came from Ussher. Then Nate asked, "Why are you in this fight, Mr. Ussher?"

Bitter recollection caused Ussher to take a long pause. This question just had too many facets. If he lived another ten years, the question was still likely to go unanswered. He knew why he stayed in this fight, but he also knew that his reasons might not bring him peace. It came down to the conflict between what he needed and what he wanted. What he needed was closure and healing. What he wanted was the opportunity for unmitigated reprisal. Those two concepts are in unavoidable conflict.

Ussher never answered Nate. He had no idea of what to say or how to say it. His feelings, regarding the matter, were greater than his ability for verbal expression. Seething is just too visceral an emotion to define when you are limited to only using words.

Nate pondered if he should venture further and ask another question. He always loved it when anyone took time to speak with him. Sometimes, it didn't even matter when some of the men in the camp were abusive and yelled at him. It just felt good to receive notice by other people on occasion. He could see that Ussher was tired and worried he might become agitated.

Nate believed him when Ussher stated that he was tired from the fight. Nate felt conflicted over the situation. He wondered whether he should risk possible disapproval from Ussher or yield to his desire for more attention. Asking the wrong question might invite discipline, like a quick slap to the ear. Although Ussher never struck him, Nate almost became accustomed to abuse from others in the camp. He assumed Ussher might also resort to this type of reaction. Suddenly, a soft rustling sound became apparent from a shallow wash on their right.

In the confusion of the fight, Jimmy's horse escaped from the Jayhawker Raiders. It was making its way back to the last place it remembered someone offering it feed. Both Ussher and Nate recognized the animal straight off as it browsed leaves from some low hanging branches. They approached the horse slowly, and with calm voices, talked to it in a soothing manner. The horse was skittish but allowed Ussher and Nate to approach and secure the rein.

Nate immediately became upset and told Ussher he wanted to move in the direction he thought Jimmy might be. Nate pointed west. "Let's backtrack this way," Nate urged. This horse would never stray too far from Jimmy.

"We are not riding anywhere," said Ussher. "We're gonna' look for Jimmy all right, but we'll do it on foot. Fact is, I think you should ride back toward Vaughn's camp and take Jimmy's horse with you. I'll stay and check the area until I find Jimmy or figure out what happened to him. He is my friend too."

Nate's anxiety level amplified, and he made it clear that he was not going back to the camp until he knew Jimmy was safe.

Nate combined courtesy with noncompliance, "No thank you, sir. I just have to know where our Jimmy is holed-up. I'm bettin' we'll all get us a good laugh once we find him."

Nate's facial expression betrayed the lack of optimism in his words. He witnessed his share of sorrow and was fully aware of this afternoon's ominous possibilities. Although Ussher dreaded what they might discover, he made the decision that, even at only 14 years of age it might be time for Nate to learn a lesson in life. They secured their horses behind cover. Ussher told Nate that they would search together for an hour or so. If they did not find anything in that time, then Nate would have to return to camp on his own. Ussher would continue the search. He said, "No more arguments Nate, that's the way it's going to be."

Just 20 minutes later, they found the remains of Jimmy's battered young body. Ussher would have settled for revulsion. He would have preferred abhorrence or repugnance, all those things that contribute to the horror of a tragic event. That, which now lay in his full view, transported him back to the brink of the pit he endured over a year ago. What he witnessed in front of him at this moment, was abomination. Self-rebuke washed over Ussher. He knew there was a chance he and Nate would find Jimmy's dead body. He just had not envisioned a situation this extreme and lamented that Nate had to endure this experience.

Ussher stood silently, but Nate was staggered with disbelief. This was the worst thing he had ever confronted. Although he had never been in a battle, Nate had seen men die from wounds and the infections caused by negligence or medical incompetence. Many nights, the agonized groans and feverish hallucinations of the dying left him unnerved and demoralized. Those experiences were what led him to ask Ussher if he could volunteer to join him on nighttime watch. For Nate, sentry duty was the lesser of the two evils.

This experience was horrifically different. Carnage such as this had never shown itself so absolutely without subtleties or mitigations. The indignities gave witness to the frailty of this young body. This victim was virtually unrecognizable. It couldn't possibly be his friend, Jimmy.

"Mr. Ussher," yelled Nate, "What is this?" Then again, "What is this?"

What aberration dared to wear Jimmy's clothing and boots? He was young and robust. He possessed strength and confidence. Jimmy radiated energy and always maintained a good-natured demeanor. He loved to joke and tease around the campfire. Everyone loved him.

"That's not Jimmy, that's not our Jimmy." Nate invoked a tone of certainty as if he could somehow change the reality of what confronted him. As he spoke, he pointed at the remains and backed away. He was unable to avert his eyes from the horror in front of him. Ussher looked at the boy and waited for the reality of the moment to become undeniable.

Nate repeated his question. "Mr. Ussher, "What is all this?"

Ussher answered succinctly, "pure butchery."

Ussher knew this guerrilla warfare was going to leave festering wounds for a generation or more. After cease-fire proclamations decree that fighting as officially concluded, memories of personal loss continue to incite traditional enemies and residual, obligatory vendettas continue. Old scores are the most difficult to put away. Most times compensation in blood is the only acceptable currency. Resolving one man's grudge only serves to generate another. Few men have the courage to stand up and try to stop the cycle of violence. If they do, they are as likely to become the victims of their perceived friends as easily as they were the target of their former adversaries.

If he survived, Ussher intended to leave behind the hate and the scourge of hurtful memories this war produced. In the end, a conclusion of some kind was coming and it would be all about the fire and sulfur of retribution from lost causes. Anyone remaining this area, around these people and their enduring hatred, would become wholly dissolute.

A week or so earlier, Ussher confided to Nate that they were in a precarious situation. He concluded they needed to move out of the area as soon as the opportunity arose. The atrocities happened too fast and escalated too far. The question was, "Who was to be the most feared, their Jayhawker enemies or their Bushwhacker comrades?"

Nate agreed. He longed for a safer life and was thrilled when he heard Ussher use the word We. It brought life to his dream that he'd continue with Ussher and regain a semblance of family. Nate decided to take a chance and express another aspiration.

"And will it be okay for our Jimmy to come along, Mr. Ussher?"

Ussher considered the question for a moment and said, "Jimmy is old enough to make up his own mind, but yes, he's welcome to come along with us."

All that seemed like a long time ago. Now an essential part, the Jimmy part, was gone. Nate came closer to the corpse. He knelt down, waiving his hands over Jimmy, to scatter the flies swarming over the bloody remains.

Finally, the irrefutable truth became undeniable. Jimmy, our Jimmy, the beloved, adopted big brother, was dead and gone forever. Nate looked to the sky, clenched his fists, and let go a cry of incalculable anguish. In addition to pain, it revealed the convoluted internalized hate and disgorged promises of revenge.

"Goddamn you bastards," Nate screamed at the top of his lungs, "Damn you, damn you, goddamn all of you. I'll kill all you cussed 'Hawkers. I'll kill every one of you."

Nate's shrieks assumed demonic portrayal. It was apparent that a full transformative maturity had just inflicted itself into his heart. The wound was deep, and the scar permanent. Nate's tears streamed freely. A distinct wheezing punctuated his exhales. His words became indiscernible as he descended into the depths of inconsolable torment.

Nate stared at the mutilation. Ussher knew Nate wanted to kneel down and embrace the remains to offer his dead friend some measure of consolation and comfort, but felt repulsed by the gore and horror.

As a compromise, Nate began a maniacal assault on the flies swarming around Jimmy. He flayed both arms wildly. He took off his hat and swung it with one hand and then the other. He cursed the swarm and ordered it to leave. He entreated God to make the flies disappear and shrieked in desperation for Ussher to help him.

Ussher responded by wrapping his arms around Nate and holding him tightly. Nate fought the embrace and screamed as loud as his voice would allow and the air from his lungs would tolerate. The scream was long and despondent and fully defined the misery of this moment.

Finally, Nate fell limp with exhaustion. His sobs turned subdued and personal. Ussher sat Nate on the grass against an ancient walnut tree. He placed a canteen of water next to Nate and told him to stay put. He ran back to retrieve their horses. Ussher accomplished the entire round trip in under 20 minutes. When he returned, it did not appear that Nate had moved.

Ussher removed his own blanket from the back of his saddle and walked over to where Jimmy lay. He carefully wrapped the boy in the blanket and carried him behind a small isolated rock outcropping. There was a depression near the edge of the rocks where the earth was soft and moist. He surveyed the horizon for the possibility of returning Raiders but saw nothing. He retrieved a small miner's shovel from his gear. The tool proved useful, both for digging and as a superb hand-to-hand weapon.

Ussher used the shovel to dig a grave of suitable depth and carefully placed Jimmy's body to rest. He recited as much of Psalm 23 as he could remember before placing dirt into the grave opening. As he did so, Nate came over and knelt down. He began to help Ussher by pushing in earth, using only his hands.

"This grave has to stay hidden," instructed Ussher. "We can't take a chance that those boot licking Raiders might try to dig him up to collect some damn bounty."

Nate didn't answer. He was totally exhausted and docile. Ussher brushed over the grave using a tree branch to conceal all signs of digging. He placed that same tree branch over the area and scattered some small stones around the plot. It sure wasn't perfect, but it would have to do.

Ussher said to Nate, "Can you take care of Jimmy's horse for me?"

Silently, Nate took the reins. Once again, Ussher checked the area for signs of the enemy. After reassurance they were reasonably safe, he and Nate started their journey back to the militia camp. Ussher guessed correctly that the ride would be a quiet one. Nate appeared settled, perhaps even defeated. Ussher knew this young boy was in shock and needed time to sort out today's pain. Ussher wondered if the war would give Nate, or him, the time to sort out anything.

6
The Jayhawkers Regroup

EVERY TIME TYLER peered backwards, he pondered how deadly that Bushwhacker was with that Henry rifle. As he and his men stampeded toward home, they frequently looked over their shoulders for danger. The Jayhawkers knew Ussher often followed fleeing enemies and continued the killing. It did not matter to him if they were attempting to break off the fight. The Jayhawkers knew the key component to their safety was maximizing the distance between themselves and the Missouri killer. Tyler kept wondering what measures it was going to take to bring that son-of-a-bitch down.

Then Tyler began to consider what would happen at the Harris ranch. He dreaded the necessity of facing the inevitable wrath of Talbot Harris and trying to explain his latest failure.

Harris always got his own way. His temper was legendary for both its intensity and suddenness. Any man falling into his displeasure might find himself disenfranchised or disemboweled. Anytime the big man was temporarily unable to impose his will in a situation, he simply hired additional help to get the job done. He had more than enough money to employ the minions necessary to see his wishes forcibly imposed. Tyler was supposed to be his key security acquisition. Now he returned with only one Missouri scalp, at the cost of four of his own men, including Jack Mingo. There was still uncertainty if his wounded man would survive or ever be capable of hard trail work again.

Such poor outcomes had a negative impact on recruitment. Union soldiers earned $13 per month. Many were quick to desert and sell their loyalty if they could shoot as good as Tyler required. No one paid better for services rendered or offered higher bounty incentives than Talbot Harris. He got all the men he needed by paying the highest wages in a seven-county area. He posted $30 bounties for any raggedy-ass Bushwhacker they could take, no questions asked. At first, this made recruitment of additional men easy. However, once word got out about these recent setbacks and associated combat casualties, it was going to take additional money and credible strategic assurances to keep men on the job. Even simple country boys understood that wages and bounties served no purpose if they ended up dead, and that crazy Missouri Bushwhacker with that Henry rifle was leaving dead men everywhere.

Suddenly, the seed of a plan began to take shape in Tyler's scheming brain. He desperately wanted another chance to prove himself. He knew current events had damaged his reputation as a tracker and security man. That was an especially worrisome problem since a good part of his reputation was the product of self-promotion more than the reality of his own actions.

Tyler developed the capability to restructure stories of accomplishment achieved by others, and then substitute his own name to claim credit. Using a first-person twist, the descriptions of actions stating, "They did this" or "he did that," turned into, "I did it all." Although the story convolutions worked well enough to this point, it was a persona becoming increasingly more complicated to maintain. Nonetheless, as soon as he felt it was safe to slow down, Tyler huddled up with his riders to dictate the story they would use as an alternative for the truth.

* * * *

Talbot Harris heard the notification shot from one of the perimeter patrols. He kept twenty men around the grounds of the big house at all times. He watched the returning riders coming back in from the east. Using an extendable telescope, he saw the news was bad long before it ever became a report. The horses appeared labored, as if they had been running for a long time.

Tyler had been so goddamned confident. Harris should have known that nothing good was going to come from this ride. Tyler was supposed to be this notorious bounty hunter and security man. What bullshit! He and his men had barely taken enough rations for two days. That meant they would be hunting and gathering for their supper. They would spend too much time thinking about filling their stomachs rather than protecting their backs. With hunting, they revealed their position with every rifle shot. It was unlikely those actions would go unnoticed.

Harris already envisioned what must have occurred because it happened before. These men were on patrol to secure the outer perimeter around his ranch. After midday, Tyler probably split off a man or two to put the campsite together and shoot a deer or other small game for the cook-pot. That Missouri bastard, Ussher, likely shadowed them throughout the day. As soon as he isolated the Harris men setting up camp, he ambushed them. He had a knack for a clean kill. It did not matter if it was one man or two. One man was easy. Ussher's wilderness skills allowed him to get close before he sighted-in the rifle. As soon as the man was motionless, like leaning over to start the fire, there would be one fatal shot. The kill was most always a headshot, quick and painless.

If two Raiders set up the camp, the scenario would be similar. The first man suffered a head shot from the Henry. The second man, startled by the report, would either jump up or turn quickly around, depending on the circumstance. He would look in every likely direction and try to figure out his situation. He would see the fate of his fallen comrade with a hole through his head or a portion of the skull torn away. Such a sight is always compelling. Blood and gore consistently make the average person stop and stare for a moment. In that moment, Ussher chambered the next cartridge, and within two heartbeats, another round would strike its mark and prove fatal. He quickly checked the fallen men for anything worthwhile and took their guns and ammunition.

Ussher left behind his distinctive signature. He turned the dead men over on their backs and crisscrossed their arms over their chests. If they wore hats, he would lay them over their folded arms. Ussher then mounted his horse and gave a light kick, causing it to run away quickly. This action left heavy hoof prints, easy to see and follow. Such posing of their comrades infuriated the Kansas Raiders.

They cursed Ussher and swore revenge. Beginning their pursuit, they might say, "The son-of-a-bitch shot young Josh. I've known that boy's family my whole life. When we catch up to that prick, I'm gonna' rip his balls off."

Seeing the hoof prints, they added, "Look yonder! He's heading out northeast. I want to get my hands on that bastard right now, for Josh. Are you men with me?"

Their anger prevented the Raiders from understanding the consequences awaiting them. When they tried to track Ussher, he led them through narrow gaps in the low hills. At these choke points, he could shoot five quick rounds from the Henry. The Raiders would stop and turn their horses for protection or dismount and take cover. In the meantime, Ussher remounted his horse and was once again on the run.

Tyler kept several groups of riders on patrol around the clock. It took the Raiders a number of fatal experiences to exchange enough information and figure out what Ussher was doing. His tactics often created a breach in the perimeter security of the Harris ranch. At the first opportunity, the Missouri boys moved in to rustle cattle. If the Kansas men detected rustling, they often abandoned their pursuit of Ussher to chase after the stolen cattle. Ussher would then reverse his direction and start shooting at the Raiders from behind as they chased after his Missouri men. The Harris security team lost from either of their choices. Furious could not begin to describe Talbot Harris's anger over the incompetence.

Tyler was not the only man leading raider groups, but he was in charge of the entire security operation and the one answering directly to Talbot Harris. The situation burned his stomach when he thought about Tyler promising, no, more like bragging, that he would solve this problem and bring back the lost Henry rifle.

Tyler had been especially confident before this last outing. He boasted that he hired the best tracker in the entire territory and told Harris, "This time out, we'll bag that fucker for sure." It did not appear, from this distance, his prediction was working. Fear is an easy emotion to read, and Talbot Harris was a man quite literate in its understanding and application. These returning riders epitomized anxiety and loss.

Harris harbored a wretched temperament about the Missouri hunter, Ussher. When the trouble with him started, he had first been dismissive. How much harm can one man do? He seemed to be unusually lucky a few times. As the problems continued and the losses began to mount, Harris found himself increasingly preoccupied with the need to devote more resources to the predicament. No Bushwhacker could be that damn lucky. There had to be elements of competence and expertise to his skill set. This brought Harris to the level of genuine distress.

As he watched yet another posse of his riders returning with diminished numbers, his alarm quickly elevated to dread. He could not remember when a single man caused him so much trouble. Worse, Ussher had become a serious threat to a member of his family, his youngest son, Vince.

* * * *

A year or so before, Harris knew his son lied to him about those strange wounds he sustained. There was an irregular gash on his cheek and an injured right hand. The whole situation had the smell of trouble. He had come home late into the night without his friend, Andy Hester. Captain Metzger awakened Harris to tell him that Vince had returned and that there was a situation. At first, Harris did not challenge Vince over the perceived lie because his son always lied to him about everything. The boy was a bad seed for certain, but that did not matter to Harris. Blood is blood. You take care of your own. It might be a matter of love, loyalty, obligation or a combination of all. The one thing it always proved to be was good business. If people thought you did not care for your own kin, they would presume you didn't care about anyone. In his business, with his responsibilities, he had to personify the belief that he protects everything and everyone related to him, or working for him.

When Vince finally told his father his version of the truth, the old man slapped him in the face twice in rapid succession, forehand and backhand. Harris's anger did not stem from the actions of his defiant son. His anger stemmed from the fact that Vince left behind loose ends that might come back as a pain in the ass for him and a direct threat to Vince personally. That concern had now turned into harsh reality.

Once the senior Harris had most of the facts, he understood the motive for all the recent actions and attacks on his interests. He understood that this adversary was truly dangerous. He knew from experience this type of fighter did several things simultaneously: First, he probed for weaknesses in their defenses knowing he was outmanned and outgunned. Second, he took his time and planned his actions,

Third—and most important—he sent a message. I'm here, I'm focused, I'm determined. Be afraid.

Harris added his own description about this man. He's effective, he's skilled, he's smart, he's deadly, and because of the chances he has taken, he just might be crazy.

After Harris made all the necessary inquiries, he put together a profile of Ussher in his head. Harris was a thinker and a planner. Preparation was the essential characteristic that made him successful. The other elements of his success were fortitude and energy. Harris had always believed in security, but now he hired every man he could find that knew how to shoot and was willing to risk his life for $25 per month. If a guard proved to be a first-rate sharpshooter, he earned a prized posting near the big house. These men earned an additional $10 a month over other sentries. Many nights, Harris walked the property and made a point of reminding each of them that the person they were guarding against was the fighter named, "Ussher." Harris also reminded them that Ussher was worth $500, dead or alive, dead preferred.

"That would be a mighty good cash return on a two cent bullet," Harris often quipped whenever he spoke with any of his men.

"Yes, sir," was a common reply. "I'll be more than happy to take that $500 from you, sir. You just go back in the house and rest secure. I've got everything out here covered."

* * * *

The returning riders slowed their horses from a fast trot as they approached the porch where Harris stood. Harris said nothing as he looked down and across the disheveled group of men. He noticed that only Tyler attempted eye contact.

Tyler cleared his throat and spoke up directly, "Mr. Harris, I'm sorry to tell you, but it was that asshole, Jack Mingo, who buggered the whole operation. Yes sir, it was Mingo, straight up, got himself all liquored up, and took us right into a damn ambush. We were outnumbered two to one, sir, maybe more than that."

* * * *

Back on the trail, Tyler laid out the facts to his Raiders in the form of two choices. The first is that they simply tell the truth. The truth meant their certain return to cowhand duty at $14 a month, living in stink and enduring fly bites day and night. The alternative was to blame the entire fiasco on Mingo. In that case, they would have a chance to stay with the Raiders and make $25 a month plus bounties.

"Why not just blame Mingo?" stated Tyler, as both a question and provocative comment.

"Right now, Mingo's biggest value was that he was dead. Dead is good. There's no way he can call us liars. Just keep things simple. Don't waiver. Stick to what I tell you to say. Repeat the story enough times and think about how you will explain the events. Pretty soon, the story actually starts to feel as real as if it were true."

They decided to practice their story several times during the ride back. Tyler said he would take the lead reporting to Harris. All they had to do was to look positive and nod affirmatively when prompted. By the time they were back, everyone would accept that this night's contrived events had actually occurred.

* * * *

Tyler continued speaking to Harris, but the sight of the man caused his voice to pitch slightly and he displayed nervous shifting in his saddle.

"Each man here is damn lucky just to be alive. I've never been through such a damn fool thing. You can ask any of my boys here, they'll back me up, sure enough. They'll tell you exactly what happened, no problem at all and…"

Harris pushed the palms of both his hands outward in Tyler's direction and retorted with some disdain, "Please, settle yourself, Mr. Tyler."

He looked over at the rider, slumped in his saddle, and remarked, "It appears like you've got yourself a wounded man to look after. Bring him around back to the kitchen, and I'll have one of Abigail's girls look to his wounds. The rest of you, go get some hot food as soon as you look after your horses.

"Mr. Tyler, come back up to the house in an hour or so. That will give you enough time to get your story better concocted with your men. If I'm going to hear a lie, I like it to be a good one. I prefer that a man put some real effort forth when he tries to insult my intelligence."

Tyler was only unnerved for a moment.

"Mr. Harris," he went on, "Sir, I don't quite understand what you're saying. Like I said, it was Mingo. Ask anyone. It was Mingo. We were all so mad that, if he hadn't gotten himself shot dead, we would have lynched him for being so crazy-stupid."

The scowl Harris turned upon Tyler could have pulverized stone. His face reddened as he gestured his right index finger in Tyler's direction.

"Be extremely careful, Mr. Tyler," Harris said in a guttural growl. "Fucking up an assignment like this is cause enough for me to have you whipped. Fact is, I still have not decided against that option. However, if you persist with this bullshit, I'll consider it a personal insult. Is that what you are trying to do? Is that what the man who's supposed to be in charge of the security of this ranch should be doing?"

Tyler answered hurriedly, "No, sir, I understand, sir."

Harris withdrew the finger from its pointed position. Tyler and his men picked-up on this gesture as a dismissal queue and started walking away toward the bunkhouse.

Harris called after Tyler, "I spotted a scalp hanging from

your saddle horn."

Tyler brightened for a moment. "Yes sir. I did that one myself. A right clean cut I'd say. It came off one mean Bushwhacker scout. That son-of-a-bitch was real hard to bring down"

Tyler's men said nothing. They saw what was coming. Tyler was going to take all the credit for the kill, and most likely keep all the bounty money. Being the boss does have its privileges. It actually did not matter much at this point. What they wanted most was some hot food and rest.

"Well," remarked Harris, "then I guess a $30 payout has been earned. I always pay on a promise."

"I appreciate that, sir," said Tyler.

He thought the bounty money would get him a couple days in town and maybe a whore if any were available.

Harris continued, "After supper, each of you can come by and see Abigail, to get your $6 "split."

Tyler's men could not help but smile. Tyler stood bewildered for a moment. Splitting the reward was something he had not intended. As leader, he always received all the bounty money. Afterwards, he split it with the men, using his discretion regarding how much each earned based on their performance.

"Something wrong, Mr. Tyler?" Harris inquired with a glare.

"No sir, everything's fine, just fine, thank you, sir."

Suddenly, Tyler realized the benefit of simply ending the conversation with Harris. Anyway, he'd recover half of the money before tomorrow morning if he could get these assholes into a poker game tonight.

* * * *

On the Missouri side of the ledger, Ussher moved himself and Nate skillfully through the backcountry. Nate remained quiet and sedate. Ussher did not push for interaction, but he came up with an idea he thought might help Nate to deal with his grief. The first evening of this return journey, they did not light a campfire. They ate a couple of pieces of jerky. It was good enough for Ussher, and Nate still had no appetite. These past days had been grueling for everyone. They never intended to stay out for so long a time.

Just before they retired for the night, Ussher confided, "I need you to do something for me, son."

Nate did not respond. He sat on the grass, his knees pulled-in with his arms wrapped around them and his fingers interlocked. His head tilted slightly down as he gazed outward into the night. Ussher thought that this was a good sign. His experience told him that men who stare at the ground are indicating defeat, but men who stare out and away tend to be thinking about future actions and solutions. Ussher saw Nate's eyes shift and then lock their attention onto him.

"Jimmy's horse is a fine animal. One with that kind of speed has real value. He's long-legged and strong, a downright genuine scouting horse," Ussher emphasized. "I need you to make sure that he's cared for proper. Make sure you check his leg joints regular for swelling and keep those hooves clean and shoes tight. He's unique, and it's damn important to me that he's looked after rightly. What do you think?"

Nate listened quietly as he considered the request. Ussher knew Nate cared for everything relating to Jimmy, and this horse was always a source of great pride for his good friend.

Finally, Nate exhaled with a tone of acceptance and said,

"Bolt."

"What was that?" asked Ussher, puzzled for a moment by his response?

"Bolt," Nate repeated louder. "Jimmy's horse, his name is Bolt. Jimmy always claimed he was fast as lightning".

Ussher nodded with understanding. "Okay, that's a good name, I like it. You'll help me out then?"

Nate responded with an affirmative nod. Then he yawned, stretched out on the grass, turned over and pulled his blanket around his shoulders.

7

The Harris Ranch - Instructions

BEFORE REPORTING to the big house, Tyler cleaned himself up and downed a double shot of malt whiskey. Once up on the large porch, he knocked twice on the doorframe. Muslin cloth cloaked the window, allowing some air movement inside the room while deflecting the majority of the insects. Abigail, the French Creole housekeeper, answered. "Good evening, Mr. Tyler," she said with utmost courtesy. "Mr. Harris is expecting you. You will find him at the top of the stairs, second door on the right. I believe it is open, but if not, please knock and await his response. I hope you have a lovely visit."

Tyler watched her dignified walk as she moved away to resume her household administrative duties. She was maybe 40 years old and looked sensational. Her dark hair was long with a soft wave. Her facial features were refined and flawlessly balanced. Abigail's blue-gray eyes may have seemed larger than they actually were because of the way they contrasted against her light brown skin. Her wide hips and ample bosom would be a compelling invitation to any man's caress. Tyler suddenly caught himself staring at Abigail for too long a time. The last thing he needed was for Harris to have yet another reason to shower punishment or retribution onto him. He knew that, with this meeting, his future, and very likely his survival, would be set out in graphic detail. He never envisioned events would lead to this situation, and yet here he was.

* * * *

When Tyler first hired Mingo, he thought his problems would wrap up quickly. Mingo carried the reputation of being the meanest son-of-a-bitch on the entire Kansas-Missouri border. Tyler remembered meeting him for the first time. It was in a small, no-name roadhouse, four months earlier. Tyler sent word out that he was looking for him and Mingo sent word back where the meeting would take place. Tyler arrived half an hour early and placed himself at a table in a darkened corner, to the right side of the entrance. He wanted to get the first look at Mingo as he entered the door.

To Tyler's shock, Mingo walked inside, immediately turned to the right, and looked him directly in the eyes. He was at the table before Tyler could suck in a startled breath. Mingo was all business, placing his Enfield rifle noisily on the table between them. He sat down and looked squarely at Tyler. "Get to the point. Make it good, and don't waste my time."

Tyler swallowed hard and composed himself. He stipulated his terms, "$100 a month, $30 bounty money for any Bushwhacker you bag, and I'm in charge of the outfit."

Mingo stared icily at Tyler and countered, "$150 a month, 25 percent of every man's bounty, and you're in charge, unless we have a disagreement."

As Mingo emphasized the word disagreement, Tyler immediately realized there were many things he did not like about Mingo, but at the same time, he knew Mingo would be the perfect addition to his Raiders.

* * * *

None of that mattered anymore, Tyler thought, as he headed up the stairs. Mingo was dead, and the Missouri Bushwhacker with Harris' Henry rifle, still required killing.

Old Man Harris was Tyler's immediate challenge. It was critical to convince his boss he had learned valuable lessons from the recent setbacks and had devised an updated plan for capturing or killing Ussher.

Suddenly, unexplained energy shot through the base of Tyler's spine. It was simultaneously cavalier and fatalistic. "Fuck it," he whispered under his breath. "I always figure this shit out in the end."

Tyler straightened his shirt and tucked it neatly inside his waistband. He ran his hand across the sides of his head to flatten any stray hairs. He shut his eyes for a moment of composure before stepping to the door.

He knocked firmly on the frame and said, "Mr. Harris, sir. It's me, Tyler."

8

Darby

SPRING, 1859

DARBY'S FAMILY and Ussher's family lived only two miles apart. She was the fourth of five Pritchard children. Her two brothers were five and seven years older. She was the middle sister, with one, three years older and the other, two years younger.

From her first memories, Darby was always aware of Ussher, but he did not begin to notice her until she was about six years old. She was this mildly bothersome, skinny kid, with a crooked smile and quirky sense of humor, but she always looked folks square in the eye and did her best to understand what they were saying.

Most times, you could recognize whenever something impressed or surprised her in a conversation. In those moments, she would arch her left eyebrow and purse her lips slightly. As she grew older, that same expression could also signify that you were about to receive a piece of her mind, or signal she had payback plans, later, at a time of her own choosing. That look could be an enigma unto itself. At times, Darby was unaware it was occurring. At other times, she used it as a signal or warning that someone or something was about to receive the benefit of her input, good or bad, like it or not.

Most folks thought of her as a tomboy up until she reached the age of 15 in the spring of 1856. The waning winter had been one of the worst in memory. Farmers had remained close to their homesteads. Many were almost out of food. Darby's family was no exception. She was bone-thin from just one meal a day for a two-week period prior to the spring melt. After the snow receded to walking depth, her father was able to track the area and bagged a doe behind their barn. The yearling came too close to their empty corncrib, lured by the dormant scent of grain that no longer existed.

In spite of the hardship, something delightful seemed to have happened over the winter. When Darby reappeared outdoors that spring, she had blossomed physically and mentally into early womanhood. She felt emotionally charged from reading *Letters of Two Brides, Jack Sheppard* and *The Tower of London*. She spoke with an enlightened intelligence about her dreams and ideas. Her maturity bypassed boys as much as three years her senior. She certainly did not appreciate the way some of those boys spoke, in her presence, about her body's new form. When she complained to her brothers, they teased her even more.

* * * *

Darby could be fierce. Having to deal with two older brothers had given her the resolve of tempered steel. By the time she was eight years old, they had learned that she could wreak havoc with her punching, kicking, and biting as she retaliated against their sibling torments. She was also willing to bide her time and settle the score at a moment most favorable to her, like when they were asleep. One of her favorite tricks was to catch a bull snake and put it into the sleeping blanket of whomever she targeted. Even though she thought it unfair, her Mama put an end to that tactic after the second time.

"I'll not be having any more of those snakes in my house," Mama scolded.

Darby hesitated. Her mother saw her anger and resolve and knew this incident was not over, so she raised her voice for emphasis.

"Eugenia Darlene Prichard, do you hear me? I need you to answer me, girl."

Darby looked at her mother, allowing the fire in her eyes to simmer respectfully. "Yes ma'am," she said.

She glared at her brothers who enjoyed hearing Mama rebuke her actions. You might be able to face off against mere brothers, but not against Mama, whom many folks said Darby took after in character.

"Darby, get yourself into the house now, and help Maggie make dinner," Mama instructed.

Before leaving, Darby shot a look in the boy's direction and arched that left eyebrow, as a nonverbal signal. This incident was not near settled to her satisfaction, just yet.

The brothers busied themselves by throwing stones at a crow sitting on the split rail when Mama called to them. "I can smell that mule shed from my kitchen. You two get yourselves over there and clean it good. Be sure to bury the manure in the cornfield and lay down fresh straw. Don't just stand there lookin' at me. Get your butts goin' right now, hear?"

The brothers trudged off as instructed to do the one farm chore they hated most.

* * * *

Ussher always took time for Darby, listening to her ideas, as she chattered about the books she read. He grew to appreciate her insight and unique sense of humor. He also could not help but notice that her crooked smile had changed into a beautiful and, yes, compelling feature. Darby liked the fact that Ussher treated her with kindness and even more, she liked that he showed her genuine respect.

By age 17, Darby was fully aware that her body attracted the attention of both men and boys. They would stop and gawk as they passed by her or she walked by them. At first, she was not sure how to interpret this attraction, but she sensed that it gave her a certain control. She found it to be interesting, and upon reflection, pleasing.

She soon discovered that a smile, a glance, or an expression of happiness or dissatisfaction usually fostered some sort of reaction. Men looked for reasons or excuses to engage her in conversation. Darby would be polite and proper when she responded. She would often follow-up with a question or a comment to let them know that she was paying attention. She would give them a sense of worth by responding positively to whatever they were saying.

Ussher seemed to be the exception. Darby's charms usually enabled her to be in control of almost every situation involving men. It irked her that this was not the case with him. For some reason, Ussher was the one from whom she wanted the most interest. She tried setting her own rules of engagement with him. Such actions and tactics came naturally to her.

In order to elicit his response and draw his attention, Darby liked to make statements or ask him questions.

"I think this sunset means we're going to have a splendid day tomorrow. What do you think, Ussher?"

"The Reverend raised a good point in his sermon on Matthew this morning, don't you agree?"

"I like sweet cornbread, the sweeter the better, how about you, Ussher?"

"I think this old dress is a bit too tight. How does it look to you?" While asking the question, she ran her hands, in a smoothing motion, down her ribcage and over her hips.

* * * *

One day, Darby stopped by Ussher's home with some fresh eggs. "Why does everybody call you by just your last name?" she asked.

"I don't know, that's just the way it's always been since the time I was a boy"

What is your first name?"

"Joseph," he replied quietly.

She thought about that for a while. "Joe is a likeable enough name," she said.

"It's not Joe," replied Ussher, "its Joseph."

Darby's left eyebrow arched for a moment at the correction.

"Are you named after someone"?

"I guess so," said Ussher.

"Anybody noteworthy?" asked Darby.

"Don't think so."

After receiving his thank you for the eggs, Darby started her ride back toward home. He watched her for a while and then saw her stop. She turned around in the saddle and hollered back.

"Hey! I think I'm gonna' keep on calling you Ussher."

He smiled and shrugged. "Suits me fine, thanks again for the eggs, Darby."

It was on that day Darby decided her future. Ussher was going to be her man. He would make a fine husband. She would work by his side and give birth to his babies. They would bond together, and die in old age surrounded by their children and grandchildren. She smiled and congratulated herself on such an excellent decision. She would bide her time and figure it out. Yes, sir, Eugenia Darleen Prichard, known to the entire world as Darby, had made up her mind, and that was that.

* * * *

Over the next two years, their friendship grew stronger. Ussher looked forward to Darby's visits. At times, she brought him grits, cornbread, or a small pot of slow-cooked beans with bacon. She always fussed over the food a little, as she removed it from her horse's saddlebag.

At times, she appeared self-conscious when presenting him with these gifts. "I made this for you, hope you like it," she often said. "I remember you saying that this was one of your favorites."

* * * *

Ussher could not help thinking about Darby. Although he was fascinated with this young woman, it bothered him that she was so much younger. Fourteen years was a great deal in age difference. Truth be told, he felt he was too old, too gruff, too poor, and too homely for someone so beautiful and intelligent. When it came to Darby, Ussher found himself to be more timid than he cared to admit.

In spite of his insecurity, inspiration overwhelmed him one

Sunday afternoon. He decided it was his turn to visit her, at the Pritchard home. He picked wildflowers and tied them with an old ribbon he used as a Bible bookmark. He cleaned himself up proper, thoroughly brushed his clothes, wiped off his shoes and headed out. As he thought about Darby during the ride, he found himself smiling and feeling positive about his decision.

Darby's younger sister was the first to see his horse as Ussher drew near the Prichard Homestead. She ran breathlessly into the house, grinning ear-to-ear. There was exhilaration in her voice as she excitedly announced Ussher's approach to both Darby and Mama. The surprise and delight of the moment was electric between the three. Time was short. A good impression was necessary but Darby wanted to appear as natural as possible since he was visiting unannounced. Her younger sister looked out the window and gave them good news; Ussher had stopped to speak with Pa. He dismounted his horse in order to shake the hand of Mr. Prichard and was likely asking permission to proceed with the visit.

Although they never discussed or practiced the routine, the Pritchard women instinctively knew how to react to Ussher's arrival. Darby, her mother, and her younger sister each took charge of different tasks. These chores needed accomplishment with utmost efficiency.

Darby removed her dress and gave it to her sister, who took the garment and ran out the back door. She gave it several hard shakes to remove dust and then began looking it over to see where improvements might be attempted. Simultaneously, Mama went for the comb while Darby picked up a washcloth and confiscated clean water from the pitcher on the table. She poured the water into a wash bucket, stepped in, sat down on a small stool and proceeded to rinse the dust from her legs and feet.

"Ouch Mama," Darby complained as her mother swiftly and vigorously combed the tangles from her thick hair. There was no sympathy from her mother.

"Hush now," said Mama unapologetically, as her sister returned with the freshened homespun dress.

When Ussher knocked at the open doorway, Mrs. Prichard answered with pitch-perfect feigned astonishment and pleasure.

"Why, Mr. Ussher, what a pleasant surprise. We had no idea you were even on the property."

"Thank you ma'am," said Ussher. "I hope I haven't come at an inconvenient time".

Mama replied, "Not at all. What can I do for you this fine afternoon?"

A glimmer flickered in her eyes and a knowing smile revealed itself as she glanced at the flowers in his hand.

"Ma'am" Ussher said politely, "If Miss Darby is available; I'd like your permission to speak with her."

Mama called out to sister, "Mary Elizabeth, do you have a notion where Darby might be?"

Her sister twirled a strand of her hair and feigned a vacant reply, "I don't know Mama. Could be she's out back working in the garden."

"Well," Mrs. Prichard said to Ussher, "I guess you could go out back and see for yourself."

The patch of green beans was only about 20 feet from the back doorway. Ussher did not like green beans, but he let that fact slide by.

"Hey Darby," Ussher said cautiously, as she raised her head after sensing his presence.

"Hey Ussher," Darby smiled back, "You been here very long?"

Ussher smiled and allowed her question to evaporate into the moment, as her beauty washed over him.

Finally, he said. "Darby Pritchard, you have got to be the prettiest bean picker I have ever seen."

"Well, aren't you being polite, for a change. Of course, you must be kidding, 'cause I know I'm an awful mess. I've been out here picking these beans all afternoon. I just started this here third batch," she said while pointing at the four beans sitting on the bottom of her bucket.

Her eyes then went to his left hand, "what you doin' with those wildflowers?"

* * * *

Ussher brought along fresh churned butter, which he gave to Mrs. Prichard. He presented Darby's father with a fine antique hand-axe. He reworked the tool to perfection, allowing the stone-ground edge to carve as easy as a knife. The afternoon went extremely well. After supper, Mr. Prichard took Ussher out to the family barn for farmer-talk, as they called it.

The Pritchard women straightened the table and washed the dishes as background activity for the romantic banter regarding Ussher as a potential husband for Darby. Mary Elizabeth was excited, but older sister, Maggie, said it was unfair that Darby had a man in her life before she did. Mama admonished her by reminding everyone that "Everything is in God's hands" and that she should be happy for Darby. As usual, Mama was right. All the Prichard women knew how Darby felt about Ussher long before he ever had a clue.

Half an hour before sunset, Ussher announced he would be heading back to his home. He thanked Mr. and Mrs. Prichard for their hospitality. He nodded and waved to Darby's sisters. They both responded with shy, self-conscious grins. He smiled back and bid the family a good evening. Darby said she would walk him to the barn-rail where his horse was waiting. They walked slowly as they exchanged bantering small talk.

Darby made sure that she walked close enough to Ussher so that she would inevitably bump into him from time to time. She placed one of the wildflowers into her hair. While she absentmindedly played with a strand of hair, the flower fell to the ground. She stopped, picked it up, and placed it into her pocket with the ceremony of something having exceptional value. As they arrived at the barn rail, the horse snorted with anticipation. He was happy to see Ussher and anxious to get back to his own stable for the evening's oats.

Ussher took Darby's hand in his to wish her good night. He tried to think of something to say that would express his feelings for her without being too forward. He wanted to do well, but that wish left him uncertain. It had been an exceptionally good day. There was friendly conversation and a fair share of laughter. Now would not be a good time to say something stupid. It was probably better to say nothing at all.

Darby sensed that this moment was the one she imagined in her dreams. She knew Ussher loved her, and she recognized that for reasons known only to him he did not feel worthy to pursue her. He stood there awkwardly, just holding her hand and appreciating her beauty. She saw his lips part and could see the sincerity in his eyes, but the words simply could not find a way to tumble forward.

Darby spontaneously took the initiative. She grasped Ussher's extended hand and wrapped it around her waist. Darby then wrapped her arms around his neck and pressed her body hard into his. She looked up and gave him a reassuring smile. He read the meaning instantly and smiled back. In a continuing motion, she brought her lips up to his and kissed him lightly. She pulled back, those mischievous dark eyes flashing, and then kissed him lightly on one side of his chin and then the other. Ussher went silent and still. Once more, Darby kissed him on the lips. This time, the kiss was long and deep and filled with passion. Once their lips parted, they both let go a satisfied exhale.

Darby intoned, "Ussher, look at me. Look at me as a woman, your woman." I've loved you my entire life. I've prayed to God I would grow up in time to tell you that before you found someone else."

Ussher looked at Darby with an expression of awe and happiness. She saw the look of joy and disbelief on his face and recognized it symbolized the thrill he was experiencing. It made her smile even more. She realized in that moment, though he had loved her all along, he never expected that he would be fortunate enough to have her share his life. They held each other through long moments of complete happiness.

Then, for the first time in his life, Ussher confessed to a woman. "I'm totally in love with you."

Ussher's words spilled forth effortlessly because their expression and clarification originated in his heart. Darby felt completely immersed in the moment as she folded herself into his embrace. She was confident that together anything was possible and life would be good for them from this day forward.

They married one month later.

9
The Ussher Homestead

USSHER AND DARBY were in love and delighted with their recent good fortune. They completed the final touches on their new cabin the same week their neighbor, Lewis Randall, agreed to sell them five adjoining acres, featuring a sweet-water artesian spring. This purchase would significantly increase the size of their farm.

"Twelve acres," Ussher exclaimed, smiling broadly and looking into Darby's beautiful eyes. In his excitement, there was a combined note of amazement and enthusiasm. "Think about what we can do with twelve acres."

Darby radiated with pride as she looked at her husband's elated behavior.

"You are quite the man, aren't you Mister Ussher?" she quipped, revealing her widest smile. "I hope that new five acres won't keep you so busy that you forget you have a wife who needs some attention on occasion."

He walked over to Darby and wrapped his arms around her waist. He lifted her up and whirled her around. "Girl, you're the reason I get up every morning. You never have to worry yourself on the whereabouts of my attention."

She laughed spontaneously with a lovely voice and its melodic earthy tone, although it sounded a little strained from Ussher nearly squeezing the life out of her.

Randall also agreed to let Ussher and Darby work out the payback through sharecropping. It was perfect. Time they had, but money they had none.

The negotiations with Randall were difficult at first. He was a fourth generation Missouri man. His property and his soul were as one to him. His family had fought Indians, poachers, and scalawags of all sorts to maintain control of this land. Randall family blood, bravery, and backbone ran deep into this soil. It was the only home he and his wife, Emily, had shared for the 51 years of their marriage.

Emily was a sage 66 years old. Everyone deemed her the finest midwife in the county. Those duties gave her a place of importance and respect throughout the farming community. Emily supervised hundreds of births over the past 35 years. She was especially good at detecting and repositioning babies to avoid breech births. The midwife calling was part of her heritage, going back two generations to her grandmother. There was always great relief, in any farm family, when Emily arrived prior to a birth. Everyone, especially the mother, felt more comfortable once her capable presence entered the room.

Randall did not need the money from the sale, but he appreciated the kinship Ussher and Darby had always shown to him. They were honest and friendly. Besides working their own land, they found time to help him with his 80 acres. He paid them a modest amount for their labors as well as allowing Darby to take what they needed from his garden and orchard, most of which she put-up in jars for the winter.

At 72 years old, Randall was undeniably beginning to slow down, and his younger neighbors were extraordinarily helpful. Although the negotiations seemed thorny at times, he always intended to help the young couple as much as possible. There was never a real doubt about the outcome. Randall knew he would eventually let Ussher and Darby acquire that perfect 5 acres. He understood they needed the added property to make their homestead truly self-sufficient.

Randall particularly liked Ussher. He was a competent, knowledgeable neighbor who always demonstrated common sense. His opinions were thoughtful and he was slow to anger. Ussher knew how to display respect without ever kissing anyone's ass. The world had gone mad because such men were in short supply. It felt good to share a cup of homebrew, from time-to- time, and discuss matters of all sort with such a man.

He knew the couple came from good stock. Randall had known the Prichard and Ussher families as good Christians and hard-working farmers. Sadly, both families were now gone. In a two-year period, death from hardship had taken Ussher's parents. Years before, his oldest brother Benjamin, went to St. Louis to live with an uncle. The Prichard family left Missouri as the troubles in the area escalated and became increasingly intolerable.

Tenaciously, Ussher stayed on his farm. Much like Randall, this was his land and country. He was not sure where else he could go. The war was all over the region and he was no city boy. He remained determined to keep to himself, work his land, and not be political. He led his life, staying within self-imposed boundaries while retaining unpretentious beliefs.

Ussher's reputation all the way back to childhood commanded respect. In his teens and 20s, he proved himself an excellent tracker and single-shot hunter. There was no area in Jackson, Cass, Bates, and Vernon counties he had not explored. He knew the switchbacks, caves, sinkholes, and game trails. He would make the ultimate scout, and Missouri militia commanders unsuccessfully tried to recruit him. Although they criticized his decision to stay out of the conflict, they were careful not to force the issue and risk animosity. The men who grew up in these parts respected Ussher's decisions and understood his resolve. They knew him to be a man who minded his own business and kept matters confidential.

Ussher's position on most subjects was simple. Situations are what they are. Everything happens for a reason, and he was not required to stand in judgment with regard to another man's circumstance. On the other hand, if you posed a question or sought him out for advice, he responded thoughtfully, based on fact or experience, never on speculation. He had no problem saying, "I just don't know." He was not one to speak simply to hear himself talk.

Ussher's kitchen was modest, but he always kept enough food for a rider who might pass his farm. The only charge was the common token of courtesy and respect. A man could come in quietly and sleep securely under his watch. When it was time to leave, he was to do so with a handshake and his word not to refer to Ussher's assistance when speaking with others. Ussher made that condition clear to everyone whom he offered an evening's shelter.

Darby loved Joseph Ussher with all her heart. A little thing like a Civil War was not going to separate her from this man. She heard the stories that he could be stubborn and single-minded. She knew he had a reputation that men both respected and feared, but they still sought his advice and fellowship at every opportunity. She understood, he wasn't much of a talker but when he gave an explanation or offered an assessment, it was an honest account of his thoughts and opinions.

When neighbor women warned her of Ussher's faults, Darby noted that it was often after their failure to attract his attention for themselves.

She heard many comments such as, "I'm sorry to say, the man just cannot make up his mind" and "He has no idea what he wants" or "He doesn't know how to treat a woman." One particularly embittered acquaintance stated, "All he ever thinks about is urging two additional potatoes out of the ground. How does he ever expect to raise a decent family on that pitiful little farm of his?"

Darby read the tea leaves of each woman's comments when they criticized Ussher. The negativity of their message often lacked conviction and their concentration seemed to drift toward moods of personal disappointment. Darby sensed that, at some level, a few of them were still assessing how they might have manipulated things differently so their outcome with Ussher would have turned more favorable.

When these negative conversations occurred, Darby would thoughtfully reinterpret them as she thought their meanings actually to be.

The man just cannot make up his mind; really meant that Ussher did not think the way she wanted him to think.

He has no idea what he wants; turned out to be that the woman wanted him, but he did not have mutual feelings.

"All he thinks about is getting additional potatoes out of the ground" came from an acquaintance Darby understood all too well. She reflected that her companion was likely fantasizing about Ussher's muscular body against hers. The woman would have preferred his masculine energies expended in her bed than into the land he cultivated.

In the end, each made some negative comment about his farm. Women intuitively know that when men do not respond to derision, criticizing the way they earn their living is usually an effective means to cause hurt. With Ussher, their best efforts to feign scorn were always ineffective. He stayed so busy working his farm that he never took the time to note their disapproval or care about their commentary.

10
Clarity

PRESENT DAY

ABIGAIL'S WORDS ECHOED through Tyler's mind as he climbed to the second floor of the ranch house. "Mr. Harris is expecting you."

Tyler swallowed the excess saliva inside his mouth, knocked twice in rapid succession on the door, and called out to Harris.

"I hear you, Mr. Tyler," Harris responded, "Please step inside."

Tyler was surprised at the size of the room. It was much larger than he anticipated. The first door on the right, which he spotted in the hallway, was also part of this room. What initially gave the impression of two rooms was actually an impressively large antechamber, where you entered from one door and exited the other. Animal trophy heads adorned the walls, some so exotic that Tyler did not recognize the species. As he perused the collection, he half-expected to see human skulls in the compilation. None was visible, but then again, there were many more rooms inside the Harris house.

Tyler suddenly understood why there were rumors of broken bodies after an unsuccessful get-together with the big man.

Unproductive meetings could have abortive endings. In such an occurrence, the guest found himself immediately ejected out the door closest to the staircase. Depending on Harris' intended emphasis; the expulsion might be followed by a push and fatal fall down those very stairs.

Men who met their demise on the Harris ranch had their remains deposited at The Meadow. Contrary to the image that such a pastoral sounding name invoked, the Meadow was the last place on earth you wanted to visit. It was a swamp with several sinkholes. Rumor was that these sinkholes led to submerged chambers in an ancient cave system. A body could be lying in a sinkhole one day and then disappear after the next rainfall. If the area went through a dry spell, you could depend on coyotes or wolves to handle the disposal chores. Both of these predatory groups became accustomed to investigating the area for dead bodies as they patrolled their territories. The worry for anyone condemned to this place was the application of some final sadistic castigation prior to execution and disposal.

The unlucky deceased, who resided there, reportedly suffered from "eye" problems. At first, this metaphor required clarification for Tyler. The explanation was simple. Harris did not speak about anatomical eyes. His reference was about alphabetical I's. Harris thought he was incredibly clever with the allusion. The I's represented the incompetent, the inquisitive, the inquiring, the irresponsible, and the irritating. With any or all of these personality defects, the offender would soon find himself in the company of Captain Metzger and a member or two of his staff, meaning doom was a certainty.

"Pour a drink for yourself," Harris instructed.

Tyler thanked him as he walked over to the ornate stand holding the Kentucky single malt whiskey. He poured himself a double and took a seat in the straight-backed chair. Harris noted, with some satisfaction, Tyler's choice of the straight chair. He had full confidence that Tyler was on edge and completely alert. Attentiveness was a good thing. Harris intended to use it to his advantage.

"Mr. Tyler," Harris began, "Afford me your undivided attention. When I am finished speaking, there will be no questions. If you cannot understand what I'm saying, then I have chosen the wrong man for the job. Once you leave this room, the only thing I want to see from you is results."

This man sure wasn't one to stand on formalities, thought Tyler.

Harris continued, "Since your progress to date has been unsatisfactory, allow me to restate your mission one final time. I hope you heard that last emphasis, Mr. Tyler, one final time."

As he was speaking, Harris walked over to Tyler. He stopped in front of and towered over the sitting man. He leaned downward, nearly placing his mustached mouth against Tyler's face. His intimidating words crackled through the air.

"I want this man, Ussher, dead. Once again, for clarity Mr. Tyler, I want this man, Ussher, delivered to me dead. He is a threat to my son and to my home."

As Harris spoke, Tyler smelled the cigar smoke and alcohol on his breath. Some spit drops hit Tyler's forehead as Harris emphasized the double S in Ussher's name.

Harris concluded, "Do you fully understand what I require of you?"

The tension in the pause was palpable. Tyler nodded in the affirmative, while only making momentary eye contact with Harris. "Yes, sir, I understand completely."

"Well then, Mr. Tyler, you're excused. Thank you for your

visit. Let's not waste precious time by sleeping in a warm bed tonight or waiting around for a hot breakfast in the morning. There are plenty of fresh horses in the barn. Abigail is already putting together saddle rations for you and your men. Hardtack and beans do not require a fire, and I told Abigail that tobacco and papers wouldn't be necessary either. Fact is I would be profoundly disappointed if your men carried any matches at all. Campfires and tobacco smoke would certainly draw Ussher's attention and could put you at a fatal disadvantage.

"In addition, I'm sure you already understand that failure to bring me Ussher, or his scalp, along with my Henry rifle, will most unquestionably ensure you will encounter another kind of fatal disadvantage.

"Put together as many men as you need. The property superintendent, Captain Metzger, already knows you will be leaving tonight. You're familiar with Captain Metzger, am I correct?"

Tyler returned an incredulous stare, which was longer than it should have been. It was a needless question.

Everyone was familiar with Otto Metzger, who had been with Harris even longer than Abigail and was every bit as loyal. Where Abigail attended to Harris personally, Metzger attended to his business interests. He was especially adept with the task of employee discipline. At 6'4" and 250 pounds, he was an imposing presence and, for a big man, surprisingly agile. He employed various options when meting out punishment.

From years of experience, he knew exactly what to do when Harris issued his characteristic, understated, and arcane instructions like, "make things clearer to him" or "no more than a limp" or "we need to make an example here."

One summary order was always extremely clear. When

Harris said, "eviscerate the fucker," his voice sounded like a gunshot, with its tenor focused and targeted. Metzger interpreted this instruction literally. At first, few of the other ranch employees understood the meaning of the word "eviscerate". Then one day several riders came across the disemboweled remains of a known offender. They were in a remote ravine just outside the property line bordering the Meadow. Within a day, every man on the ranch knew the meaning and significance of the word.

* * * *

A slight movement in the background caught Tyler's eye. He focused on the spot approximately 20 feet to the back of the room. It was Vince Harris, standing there listening to his father order and berate him. He seemed to be judging or assessing Tyler's ability to protect them from Ussher.

"Mr. Tyler," thundered Mr. Harris, "Would it be too much to ask that you focus on me? You did come here tonight to discuss your future, did you not?"

"Yes sir, Mr. Harris," Tyler quickly replied.

He returned his attention to his employer, the man who could snuff out his life at any moment.

"I'll be pulling out right quick. I'll get this job done right this time, sir."

As Tyler left the house, it occurred to him that the poker game for which he hoped was not going to happen. Ussher was such a pain in the ass. Tyler would thoroughly enjoy the moment when he shot-gunned that dirt bag through the gut or slit his throat ear-to-ear.

11
An Unexpected Consequence

MINGO'S PAIN ELEVATED from perceptible to dreadful and then accelerated to excruciating. Unconsciousness only helped temporarily because it didn't allow his voice to intone and acknowledge the palpable misery of his situation.

Where was Hell when you needed to escape into it? No nightmare in his experience had ever been this extreme. As the pain raged through his body, the taste of blood, marrow, and vomit heaved from his gut and expelled from his mouth. He had no idea as to his current location, and it didn't matter since he was unable to move.

"Do you think he's still alive?" a voice asked.

The question confused Mingo as he asked himself, were these angels, or worse, were they demons? Were they talking about him? Could they even see him? Could they hear the screaming inside his mind that was trying to deal with this incredible pain?"

"Maybe so, maybe not," a second voice joined in.

"You want me to check?"

"Suit yourself," the second voice replied.

"What do we do if he's alive?"

"I guess we could harness something behind your horse and drag him back to camp. He'll most likely be dead long before we get back."

"It looks like he might have a little color in his face," observed the first voice. "Hey Mister, can you hear me? Mister, do you need some help? You got a name?"

The only indicator of life was a slight movement of the man's right hand, trying slowly to close into a half-fist.

Jack Mingo defiantly signaled the world. That gesture announced he was far from ready to surrender his life. He had clung to bare existence minute-by-minute, throughout a day and night. The pain, although awful to endure, reinforced the reality that he was still alive. That fact alone was enough to make him hold on and see if destiny would eventually give him his chance for payback.

12

Conception of the Bad Seed

VINCE HARRIS was the youngest son of Talbot Harris, the highly successful East Kansas cattleman. Talbot's accomplishments stemmed from his unadulterated determination to persevere in all endeavors, whether it was business or personal.

Vince's attitude was also one of determination, but it was rooted in narcissism. His every action or response found basis in the question, "What's in it for me?" Vince's self-absorption found reinforcement under the protective umbrella his indulgent father provided. He constantly found ways to rendezvous with trouble, and Talbot always provided a secure exit and cover up from every potential consequence.

There was some disagreement as to whether Vince was a full-blood son of the Harris lineage, given Talbot's penchant for extramarital liaisons. Mrs. Harris abetted these trysts through her decades-long practice of extended absences, traveling the Eastern

United States and occasionally Europe. For reasons never officially known or reasonably explained to her friends, Evelyn Harris always left Vince with his father whenever she traveled.

Both Talbot and Evelyn Harris were fair skinned with light brown and blonde hair, as were their two older sons. Vince had a decidedly darker complexion. Some suggested it was halfway between that of Talbot and Abigail.

Those who rumored this speculation never did so too loudly. If discovered and reported, it would likely result in a calamitous outcome for them, their family and their property. Talbot Harris never did anything halfway, including reprisal.

It really did not matter anymore. Whatever happened 22 years earlier was all ancient history. Talbot Harris claimed the young man as his own and that fact alone made his heritage golden and his legitimacy unimpeachable.

Regardless of the circumstances surrounding Vince's conception and the whispered inquiries as to whether he was a bastard by birth, there was no disagreement to the fact that he was a bastard by nature. The spoiled child grew to a vile adolescent. Teenage depravity developed into adult degeneracy.

13
Abigail

MOST ACQUAINTANCES and associates were aware Evelyn Harris suffered from bouts of melancholia. She often spent months with relatives and medical experts, convalescing in comfortable St. Louis or Chicago society parlors. In reality, she was more of a visitor to the Harris ranch than mistress of the household. Abigail tirelessly and capably fulfilled that position for two decades. Along with her workforce, she maintained an impeccable house and tended enviable gardens, while trying to raise and nurture Vince.

At any time, there could be ten or more women working on Abigail's staff. About half of them were long-term employees with established and responsible duties in the household hierarchy. They were cooks, bakers, launderers and storekeepers. The remainder of the workers were decidedly younger and their tenure was noticeably transient. These young women found employment by assisting the senior staff with their duties as well as performing the majority of the cleaning.

Holding any position in the Harris household was a prized opportunity for many women. Most were refugees, widowed and orphaned by the civil warfare. The position gave them a small income, sleeping cot, good food, and reasonable amount of personal security.

Abigail resided in a well-appointed, two-room apartment next to the main kitchen. A small, discrete staircase rose from the kitchen to the second floor. It exited next to the door of Talbot's master bedroom.

Some nights Harris would smartly tap his walking cane three times, followed by two taps, on the floor of his room. The sound transferred into the ceiling of the apartment below, indicating to Abigail that he desired her presence. Most of the time, it was only her company Harris craved. Abigail was intelligent and thoughtful. It was common for Harris to be satisfied just to have her sit quietly next to him. They both studied books or manuscripts and afterwards enjoyed discussing the topics of their readings. She attended to Talbot's needs throughout those evenings, bringing him brandy or whiskey and cigars.

Abigail never resisted if Harris wanted intimacy. She always made certain she bathed prior to ascending to his bedroom. At the end of the evening, she would ask him if she should stay or leave. She was never sure which answer she would receive or ever seemed disappointed with his decision.

Abigail's relationship with Talbot Harris had been a poorly kept secret for more than 20 years. She truly loved the old man and never spoke negatively or exhibited displeasure when he occasionally forayed with younger women in town. Abigail accepted her situation for the practical reality it was, a well-compensated, domestic substitute for an absentee wife. She was never foolish enough to think that one day she might carry the Harris family name.

14
Spawning Wickedness

WHEN HE WAS 11 years old, Vince began capturing King snakes. He was particularly fond of this snake because of its large size and vitality. He enjoyed nailing them to the back of the barn door and whipping them with strips of rawhide until they split in two pieces. Over time, a similar gruesome fate befell frogs, rodents, and rabbits. Observers often heard his gleeful cackling laugh as he inflicted torture on these peaceful creatures. Afterwards, his mood was elevated and he appeared energized and cheerful.

His father was determined to change this unhinged behavior. Talbot Harris understood that people would likely view his son as a deviant. Normally Harris did not care what anyone else thought, but Vince's behavior actually left him deeply troubled.

Maturing into manhood did not alter Vince's depraved activities. Talking did not work. Yelling did not work. Pleading with him did not work. Eventually, Harris decided that the only way to prevent Vince from torturing animals was to have him beaten to illustrate the counterpoint. The beatings did not succeed. When Harris forcibly confined Vince to his room, he screamed obscenities and challenged his father to beat him further.

For reasons unknown, Harris could not sustain these attempts at discipline. He had personally killed five men in his life. He ordered the killing of 22 more and paid bounties for Missouri Bushwhackers on a regular basis. This situation was different. This was his son, and he possessed an inexhaustible supply of forgiveness and sympathy for the young man.

Finally, Talbot Harris did what only Talbot Harris could do. He accepted the deviance and made a decision to ignore the inevitable results as long as possible. He even provided Vince with his own venue, a barn, where he could torture animals in his self-created world with the privacy and comfort he desired. Vince found exploring his dark side brought heightened levels of satisfaction and validation. Soon thereafter, the father-son relationship noticeably improved.

Andy Hester worked on the Harris ranch, and like everyone else, knew of Vince's penchant for brutality. Andy shared this interest in abuse, although for him it was more from a voyeuristic standpoint than sadistic application. Where Vince enjoyed the tactile feedback of contact, tearing and reactive writhing from the torment, Andy liked to watch. He was actually mesmerized with the talent Vince demonstrated for inflicting pain.

Andy made certain that the instruments of corruption and torture were properly maintained and in good supply. He provided water, whiskey and food so Vince could stave off the exhaustion that sadism exacts from its disciples. Most importantly for Vince, Andy supplied vitally needed feedback and critique, which assisted him in elevating the mastery of his skill set. Together, they possessed an innovative energy, dedicated to the infliction of pain, capable of making the Grim Reaper flinch.

Andy became a devotee to the service of Vince's every need. He captured the animals for him. He prepared them in ritualistic detail for their coming ordeal. He could not reason why, but he especially enjoyed the snake whipping. The large ones were remarkably capable of absorbing long periods of extended abuse.

One warm afternoon, Andy spotted what looked to be an exceptionally large King snake. In his enthusiasm, he ran the creature down and stepped on its tail. Andy failed to notice that the markings on its back were not the King's characteristic round spots. Instead, the markings bore the shape of an hourglass. The toe of Andy's boot caused the snake to coil in retaliation. The powerful Copperhead viper struck his left hand before he was able to draw in a startled breath. The pain of the bite was agonizing, but the justice of the incident was conspicuous. His hand never recovered its full strength and functionality.

Circumstances on the ranch worsened over the following year. Two of the youngest female household staffers disappeared without taking any of their belongings. Anything could happen one time, but after the second incident, everyone on the Harris ranch came to the same conclusion; Vince and Andy were somehow responsible for the ultimate fate of the young women.

Unnerved by the disappearances, Abigail assigned two women to every chore requiring them to venture outside of the big house. She performed bed checks as a nightly routine. She was doting and caring for all the women who worked on the staff and dedicated herself to their protection at all costs.

Abigail despised the rumor speculating Vince was the offspring of a liaison between Talbot and herself. The fact was, nature made the fertility decision for her shortly after her introduction to puberty. Abigail accepted the fact childbirth and biological motherhood would not be part of the joys in her life experience. This truth was part of the reason she took such good care of all the women and girls in her charge.

With tighter security for the women, Vince and Andy took to disappearing off the property more frequently. They would sometimes be gone two days or three days at a time on what they joked to be their excursions. These forays were outings to exploit needy or helpless women created by the war. Vince calculated that his money, family name, and situational charm would give him better than a 50/50 chance to use their desperation to his deviant advantage. His calculation was tragically accurate.

Irresistibly, Vince's fantasies became full-blown obsessions. His urges fixated on achieving a distinctive flawless experience in domination through the infliction of suffering. He was unable to describe the perfection for which he was searching, but he was certain that he would know when it occurred. He was always looking for the ultimate female and the ideal opportunity. When that day came, Vince was confident that he would enter into a rarefied standing known only to men of his unique enlightened status. Vince was convinced that he was part of a socially elite cabal that warranted privileges far beyond those available to ordinary men.

Everyone knew Vince was the son of Talbot Harris, and Vince used his status whenever it served his purpose. He and Andy would ride up to a farm and act as if they were travelers, passing through on a day's journey. If men were present, they would ask for a drink of water and move on.

If men were not around the property, Vince used his notoriety to get close to the women and girls living on the farm. He was quick with a smile and kept his voice soft and friendly until the very last second. When close enough, he enjoyed punching a woman in the face. He liked hearing the involuntary combination of moans and sobs created by the trauma. Andy immediately moved in to hold the woman down or pin her arms behind her back.

The battering was often incessant and lengthy. Their technique became more efficient through practice and repetition. Their goal was always the same, humiliation through pain. The longer the woman could sustain the punishment, the more exciting it became for Vince.

Once a victim fell incapacitated, Vince occasionally instructed Andy to finish the kill by strangling her with a piece of rope. Although he savored bloodshed, Vince sometimes enjoyed forcing Andy to perform tasks he knew caused his assistant discomfort.

Every successful assault ultimately proved deadly. Providence sometimes allowed grieving relatives to discover the bodies of these lonely victims but, more often than not, their abandoned remains simply dispersed organically into the wilderness void.

The war was exceptionally helpful with supplying numerous victims. Many of these women were already on the edge of survival. Both enemy and friendly militias commandeered their mules or draft horses. Without these animals to pull a plow, raising a garden of any size became nearly impossible. If anything actually grew in their small, hand-dug plots, it was subject to confiscation from the warring militias. It was no wonder that when Vince offered a dollar to fill his canteen, the desperate women were often quick to accept the deadly temptation.

Many of the women heard the rumors that Vince was a dangerous man. Several prepared to defend their family and household when they recognized the two men approaching. Mothers and daughters might stand shoulder-to-shoulder with a shovel or pickaxe while defiantly holding their ground. Ever on the defensive against receiving a severe cut or bruise, Vince would smile and attempt to turn on his disarming charm. If the women appeared steadfast and ordered them to leave the property, Vince acted insulted. As he departed, he promised that they would regret their lack of courtesy sometime in the near future.

15

Resurrection on the Third Day

AGAIN, THE FIRST VOICE spoke to Mingo and repeated the same question.

"Hey Mister, can you hear me? Mister, you got a name? What happened here?

The younger man turned to his father, "What do you think we should do?"

The older man was disciplined and deliberate as he answered thoughtfully. "Let's set up our camp for the night. After that, we'll take us another look and decide how to attend to him. If the good Lord wills it, he'll keep him alive until we're ready to look after his injuries proper. Everything is in His Almighty hands, praise God."

"Yes, indeed. Praise God," said the younger man.

With their location settled, they secured their horses and removed the saddles. The older man designated the site for the fire and proceeded to surround that area with their saddlebags, foodstuffs, and blankets. The younger man went to gather kindling and firewood. He filled the canteens and a small camp pot with water from a nearby creek. When he returned to the campsite, the older man already started the fire and had the area settled for the night.

Both glanced at Mingo and then each other. The older man said with tired acceptance, "I guess it's time to take a look."

Together, they dragged Jack Mingo close to the fire and laid him on his back. They heard shallow moans as they picked him up and rolled him over onto his back. They cut away his shirt as best they could except for the portion that was stuck to his chest with dried blood.

The older man sighed as he began to pull forcibly on the fabric and dried blood combination to reveal the full extent of the wound. "There's no point in delaying the unavoidable."

Mingo's chest lay bare and began to bleed freely.

"Any man who bleeds like that has a heart with a good beat," remarked the older man. Then he looked at his son with an educational admonishment, "Always remember, a heart with a good beat does not mean there is goodness in the heart, until the Lord provides the light to be followed."

The younger man nodded in affirmation as he used a stick to remove cloth from the boiling water. He waved the fabric in the air to speed the cooling process, rang out the excess water and placed the hot compresses over the gash in Mingo's chest.

The riders stayed up all night with Mingo. They kept the water boiling and continually changed hot bandages throughout the night. In the morning light, the older man picked out the remaining rib splinters with the tip of his knife, and prepared to cauterize the full length of the wound.

* * * *

At the last minute of the dawn battle, Providence outbid Doom and spared Jack Mingo's life. After Ussher fired the Henry, the bullet struck Mingo, but did not penetrate his rib cage to savage his internal organs. Instead, the round cut a broad, inch-deep crease across the entire width of his chest. It was a gaping, bleeding, and excruciating painful wound. It would leave a lifetime scar, but it was not fatal.

Then Fate stepped in and played her part. When Ussher ordered the Missourians to scavenge the dead Jayhawkers for guns and ammunition, they simply neglected to check Jack Mingo at all. Instead of enjoying the scarce opportunity to slit the throat of an exceptionally dangerous enemy, they foolishly allowed him to live. Such extreme carelessness seldom results in positive outcomes.

* * * *

Halfway through the process of cauterizing the wound, with a knife blade heated in the campfire, Mingo regained consciousness. He screamed with the pain from the wound. He screamed with the pain of the cauterization. He screamed with the pain his body generated from the very act of screaming.

Mingo's first conscious thought was that he was in Hell and receiving torture from demons. He felt the pain, saw the fire and smoke, and smelled his own burning flesh from the cauterization.

"Calm yourself, my son. You are safe."

The voice was deep and authoritative. "You are in the care of Aaron and Micah Russell. We are disciples from the Meeting House of the Holy Ghost. Be still now. Be brave. Allow us to complete our work."

Mingo looked into the eyes of Aaron Russell. In those eyes, he saw the reflection of the campfire and another fire coming from deep inside the man.

Aaron went on, "My son, Micah, will continue to hold your arms, so I can properly treat your wounds with the heat from this blade." Aaron held the blade in front of Mingo to demonstrate his actions.

"Will you allow us to proceed with your healing without a struggle? If we do not finish our work, an infection will be likely and you will most assuredly die. I do not believe that is God's will. If he wanted you to die, he would never have sent us in the direction that crossed your path.

Mingo did not answer but his stress melted into acceptance. Aaron Russell turned to Micah and said to the younger man. "This exorcism will be a tribulation for us all. Bring the elixir."

* * * *

At sunrise, Nate was still quiet, but Ussher noticed that his energy level appeared to be up. He quickly put together the few things that he owned and was ready to go before Ussher. Nate went over to Bolt. Ussher could hear him talking quietly and sincerely to the horse as he checked his teeth, ears, and hooves. He examined every inch of the animal, caressing his hands across the horse's body in the process.

Ussher moved a little slower that morning. The action of the previous day, and the unforgiving ground on which he slept, had left him with body aches.

Nate remained patient for a while and then announced, "Bolt's ready to go."

Ussher pinched out a half-smile and said, "Well I guess if Bolt is ready, we better get our asses moving."

16
The Cauldron Simmers

USSHER AND NATE passed the outpost guards as they returned to the Bushwhacker camp around mid-afternoon. Almost everyone was happy to see them. Their reports from the area had supplied the militia with credible intelligence on the Jayhawkers. That information also helped the Missourians rustle cattle from the Harris ranch, which supplemented the scarce venison in the area. With around 150 men in camp, keeping them out of sight, with adequate food, were major challenges.

Vaughn walked over to Ussher and extended a welcoming

hand. "There's a lot going on," he said. "Get settled so that we can have a talk. We are holding a senior council meeting after supper. I know that you like to avoid these things, but both Quantrill and Anderson want you there."

Ussher nodded understanding and then reaffirmed his position. "Just because I'm there, don't mean I've got anything to say. How many times do I have to tell these people? I will help this militia and its cause, as long as I get the chance to kill and walk over that piss-proud, sodomite, Vince Harris. Once that asshole is dead, the way I want him dead, I'm gone from these parts forever."

Ussher had participated in these meetings before. First, there was excessive drinking, followed by loud talk, bragging and threats of impending reprisal. The problem with this group was they always tried to carry out that which they threatened to do. There was an element of competition when they discussed the retribution they would bring on the Jayhawkers. Sometimes there were fights between the militiamen disputing which among them had brought more destruction to the Kansas Raiders. There could be no doubt evil men populated portions of this assembly, but their iniquities went unnoticed or ignored.

Hatred was a useful tool to nourish motivation and employed frequently to bolster courage. At this point, fighting was no longer about anyone's beliefs. Having a cause or purpose was only a label a few men, like Vaughn, clung to in order to sleep better at night. Few men had broad-based, higher objectives or moral grounds with a defined goal. The Bushwhackers killed because they considered taking enemy lives as a worthwhile accomplishment. They believed they needed to eliminate Jayhawkers before the Jayhawkers killed them first.

Tonight, the hostility was all about Nevada City, over in Vernon County. The Kansas Colonel, Andrew Morton, conducted a surprise raid on the town and disarmed all the residents.

"Disarmed, my ass," George Todd yelled. He was another of Quantrill's commanders. "They executed eight men like they were worthless dogs." Todd headed a group of his own fighters. They hooked up with Quantrill from time-to-time, whenever it suited their interests.

"We heard those boot-lickers went to every home and told the folks they only had 20 minutes to carry away their belongings. After that, they burned every goddamned house to the ground. Our Missouri brothers and sisters had to watch their homes and everything else they owned go up in smoke. Those raider twats took all the good horses, all the livestock and anything else they wanted from our people. May every one of those bastards burn in Hell for all eternity."

It troubled Ussher, as much as the next man, when he heard about atrocities. If the stories of destruction were only half-true, the outrage would still be justified, although he reflected that the residents of Nevada City should have been more vigilant with their own security. He could not understand why everyone was so surprised the Jayhawkers targeted the town in the first place. Nevada City was widely known to be sympathetic to all the Missouri militias. Hell, folks often referred to it as the Bushwhacker Capital. Everyone should have known the town was going to be marked for attack when it carried such a provocative moniker.

After the strategy meeting, Ussher ran into an old adversary, Archie Clement. Ussher was not happy with the circumstance, but he kept that fact to himself.

Archie Clement was described by many as "the crazy, son-of-a-bitch runt, who butchers and scalps for Bloody Bill Anderson." When Archie first heard that description, he decided he liked the fearsome image it engendered. His personality was chameleon-like. He could be cordial, and even likable in one moment, and then abruptly turn on a man with deadly ferocity.

Archie was only 5'6" tall and weighed maybe 135 pounds. Depending on the time of day, the cast between Clement's light grey eyes and their whites made the contrast virtually undetectable. He enjoyed staring hard at men to see their reaction. Finally, there was the continual presence of that self-assured grin. Its insidious quality communicated that Clement feared nothing in this life or the next. This combination of features and personality, along with his killer reputation, unnerved almost everyone who knew him.

* * * *

Ussher recalled his last encounter with Clement, which was a bitter memory for both men. In early April of '62, Archie Clement and Bill Anderson, along with three other riders, stopped at the Ussher homestead. He was not pleased to see them because he did not like either Anderson or Clement. On the other hand, neither had done him harm and they only asked permission to sleep under a lean-to-shed next to the house garden. Ussher and Darby lived just within what most considered Bushwhacker Militia territory. The location offered some protection from raids by Jayhawkers.

As luck would have it, the day before their arrival Darby made a thick potato, carrot, and onion broth along with fresh baked bread. Ussher recently reworked the brick oven, and the bread came out with a darn nice yeast-rise and almost no burn marks. They had also churned butter and cooked preserves from Mr. Randall's orchard.

The men were downright celebratory when Darby brought over the food in a small pull-cart that she used around her house and garden. The evening was crisp so she wore a bonnet and modest shawl over her homespun housedress. Anderson and the three were courteous but Clement said nothing as he immodestly surveyed Darby's form up and down. While doing so, he took a bite of the bread, continued his stare, and uttered a not so subtle, "Umm, Umm, I sure like things that are warm and tasty."

The double meaning was obvious to both the men and to Darby. She held her ground and looked directly at Clement, slightly arching her left eyebrow.

"My husband sure did a good job fixing my oven to make that there bread come out so fine. I'll be sure to tell him how much you appreciated his work." Darby then bid them all a good night, turned on her heel, and walked away.

Clement just smirked. It was clear to everyone that he was about to say something inappropriate. A moment before he could make another comment, Anderson placed the tip of his riding switch against Clement's shoulder. Clement snapped a stare in Anderson's direction. Anderson did not flinch, stared straight back at Clement and shook his head slowly in the negative.

"You do not want to screw around in any way with that," he nodded toward the departing Darby. "In case you've forgotten, her husband is one of the best bare-knuckle fighters and most effective killers in these parts. Don't let the fact that he's one of those quiet types fool you."

Clement responded defiantly, "Are you telling me this dirt

farmer asshole has killed more men than me?"

Anderson countered, "No, Arch, I'm convinced that you have killed more men than Ussher, but there's something about him that's kind of unexplainable. You and me, we choose the fight and we want the excitement that comes with it."

Archie responded with an energetic positive nod.

Anderson continued, "The fact of the matter is, we look for reasons to stir up shit."

Archie laughed with self-assured bravado. "You're damn right on that account." The three companions also laughed and nodded their agreement.

Anderson continued, "Archie, listen to me, we are guests here. If you insult this man or his wife, on his property, you are heading for more trouble than you need."

One of the companions chimed in, "Bill's right, Archie. Ussher and me have never been friends, but I've known him for 20 years, and I've seen what he can do if his blood is up."

The locals knew Ussher rarely got angry, but if he did, an offender was destined for serious injury or worse. You could criticize Ussher, even be bad mannered, and he might not be fazed. However, if you insulted someone he loved or respected, Hell was coming your way. Over the years, at least seven men shared this experience. Two of them were dead, another nearly died, one gained a lifelong limp, two carried permanent scars, and another ran for his life, abandoning all his possessions.

When necessary, Ussher fought and killed with methodical efficiency. There was no hesitation and no remorse. Once he made the decision to stand and fight, it was like every other judgment he concluded. He thought it through, warned the offender of the pending consequences one time, and then acted decisively.

* * *

Ussher raised-up about an acre and a half of his own fire-cured, dark leaf tobacco. Tutored by Lewis Randall, he was well versed in both the raising and curing of the blend. This year's crop was rich and these sacks had turned out especially aromatic. After he and Darby had finished their supper, Ussher brought over extra pipes, a small tobacco pouch, and sour cherry homebrew to share around Anderson's fire. As was appropriate, Darby stayed back at the house. Again, the men were exceptionally pleased to receive these unexpected indulgences. When they attempted to offer Ussher some of their own homebrew, they discovered it was nearly gone. Clement had started drinking early and sharing or considering others were not one of his attributes. His early intoxication was evident in his speech and belligerence.

Archie felt vexed over Anderson's earlier warning about the danger Ussher presented. Ussher didn't look like much, just an average, everyday dirt farmer. It might be entertaining to determine how much of his tough reputation was justified. The effect of the alcohol had kicked in hard on Clement's brain, and his already low inhibition levels disappeared altogether. He could not understand what such a good-looking young woman saw in a shit-kicking sodbuster like Ussher. It was obvious that he was much older than that fine-assed female of his. Archie noted that Ussher's beard already had some grey in it. Maybe, once Darby knew that he was the better man, she'd think about spreading those long legs for him.

As the evening progressed, Clement decided to stare Ussher down and take his measure. He started to spew offensive, alcohol-induced remarks regarding how he might service Darby if she were his woman. He stated he could recognize her type a mile away, and that type always liked it fast and hard, and best of all, often.

Anderson's response was pointed, "Arch, shut your mouth. You're drunk. Don't make things worse by being stupid."

Clement did not miss a beat and followed up with another rude comment regarding Darby's bosom. The three companions exchanged anxious glances. Anderson looked down at his feet with a perplexed exhale. To this point, Ussher remained calm, but now he locked his own deadly stare back on to Clement.

"That's the last time you'll ever make mention of my wife."

Clement, feeling comfortable in the company of Anderson and the others, continued with another comment. He negatively compared Darby to a roadhouse whore with whom he spent the previous night. As he started to detail his technique for dominance over a woman, he suddenly felt overwhelmed by unanticipated vertigo.

Clement realized his feet were unexpectedly dangling, as Ussher lifted him abruptly by the neck with his left hand and pushed him against an oak tree. Ussher's face pushed nose-to-nose against Clement's face. Archie choked against the inexorable force that Ussher applied.

The pressure was so intense that he immediately started to blackout. His arms fell heavily against his side. In less than a heartbeat, Ussher's right-hand had loosed his Bowie knife and was about to deliver a strike to Clement's throat.

"No," Anderson thundered in Ussher's direction. "Don't do it. I'm asking you not to do it. He's drunk, and he's an asshole, but he's useful to the Cause and me. Ussher, we're not looking for trouble with you, and you don't want trouble from us. Let him go! I need you to let him go."

Ussher pressed with emphasis for another moment and then lowered Clement down. He allowed Archie no air until his feet returned to the ground. For Ussher, the matter was over. He, along with Anderson and the other men, felt convinced Clement now fully appreciated the civility limits allowed on Ussher's property and in the proximity of Ussher's wife.

After Clement caught his breath and regained some composure, he swore an oath to himself that Ussher would pay for this embarrassment. He was Archie Clement, for Christ-sake. If he did not gain some payback in the future, others might fail to recognize the amount of fear he required of his companions.

* * * *

The memory of that previous encounter, on Ussher's farm remained with both men. For Ussher, it was simply a recollection, and there was no value in resurrecting it beyond that fact. For Clement, it was festering, unfinished business, searching for a retaliatory conclusion, but for the next day or two, the Jayhawker problems would keep Archie busy. There were already three reprisal attacks planned to avenge Nevada City, and right now Ussher was everyone's Man of the Moment.

Clement knew he made the mistake of underestimating Ussher once before. He would not make that same blunder this time around. Ussher has to have enemies, thought Archie. These high-moral types always pissed someone off. Now that he knew Ussher was back in camp, he would ask around to get more background. He felt confident he would find someone to give him additional insight into Ussher's weak side. Bide your time, Archie thought.

"Hey Ussher," said Clement, as they passed shoulder-to-shoulder. His voice engendered a tone of reckless abandon.

"Archie," Ussher intoned, returning a slight nod. Each man walked on.

Just before he turned in for the night, Ussher noticed Archie Clement and Charlie Hawkins drinking together around a campfire. Charlie talked while Archie listened intently and nodded in the affirmative. They occasionally burst into laughter, while giving each other a reinforcing poke or elbow nudge. The activity confirmed Ussher's distrust of both and warnings went off inside his head.

"The Demons abound," Ussher whispered aloud into the night.

* * * *

Bear grease salve eased Mingo's pain from the pull and pinch of the cauterization scar and the elixir allowed him to sleep through the night. Now, just three days after Reverend Russell discovered his abandoned vestige and battled death for his mortal existence, Mingo was walking unassisted. His movements were slow and painful, but yes, by God, he was moving once again. In another week, he might even be able to ride.

Mingo's mind was active and the activity it generated had the singular focus of planning revenge. That was good news for him and a deadly foreshadowing for his enemy. Settlement of this grievance was not a vague, random, conceptual aspiration. It was a core necessity required to offset the injustice he suffered. This act of reprisal needed consideration in its planning, premeditation in its scope, and ritualistic symbolism in its execution.

Every time Aaron Russell knelt by his side to pray for the recovery of his body and salvation of his soul, Mingo invoked his ancestors to curse the man responsible for leaving him sprawled helplessly in the dirt. They had never failed him in the past, and he was confident of their assistance as he planned the desolation of his enemy.

17

Saving Nate

ALTHOUGH HE RESISTED the impulse, Ussher developed a strong attachment and fondness for young Nate. Whenever Ussher felt dispirited over losses he suffered in the war, the youngster came to mind. Any fool would realize Nate had endured extreme hardship at an amazingly young age. Ussher did not know if his family was dead or if Nate was somehow separated from them, but he guessed the former. Ussher figured the kid would tell his story when he felt ready. He was exceptionally smart and retained a positive nature, proving himself adaptive across diverse situations. This was obvious from the fact he had been on his own for a year and a half. So far, he had not given up hope or lost his mind, although Jimmy's death brought him close to both.

A plan to rescue Nate from the fates of this war soon germinated in Ussher's brain. He was somewhat pessimistic Nate would like the idea at first. That problem would settle itself in the future. In the meantime, he intended to teach Nate everything possible about wilderness life. He knew the youngster would be a good student.

"Nate boy, come on over here and talk with me." Nate brightened immediately and hurried to where Ussher stood. "Yes sir," he said. Ussher looked thoughtfully at him for a moment and asked, "Did I ever tell you about my upbringing?" With that invitation, Ussher gave young Nate a detailed and intimate account of his early life.

Ussher's only sibling was a brother, Benjamin, a boy six years his senior. Everyone considered Benjamin gifted with an impressive intelligence but plagued by a frail constitution. For Benjamin, life on the prairie brought about recurring bouts with asthma and bronchitis, causing some to speculate he suffered from consumption. From his earliest memories, Ussher worked hard to compensate for his older brother's physical limitations.

Finally, at age 12, the family sent Benjamin to St. Louis to become a legal understudy to his uncle, Samuel Trenton, his mother's brother. The move proved a good one for Benjamin and Uncle Samuel. The nephew found a useful, constructive niche in life, and his uncle established the blood legacy he always wanted but his marriage failed to create.

Over the years, Ussher exchanged letters with Benjamin. As anticipated, Benjamin achieved the success expected of him and would assume leadership of the law firm whenever Uncle Samuel decided to step aside. Their correspondence was always cordial and genuine. Because of differences in age and circumstance, the brothers sometimes struggled to find subjects of common interest, but there were always the ties of blood, and family news of any import was appealing to both.

Ussher's parents had died much too early. His father contracted pneumonia when Ussher was 15 and his mother, who refused to leave the land, died of heat exhaustion, two years later, in a damn bean field. She collapsed while harvesting a row not ten feet away from Ussher. Unfortunately, Benjamin never made it home for either funeral.

Ussher was only 17 when he inherited the farm. Because of his youth, few people expected him to succeed. Lewis Randall generously offered to buy the homestead and then give Ussher a job working on his larger farm. The young man demonstrated both courtesy and stubbornness when he turned down both offers.

* * * *

Ussher stood a solid 5'10" tall. He was somewhere in between muscular and wiry. He shaved frequently and maintained a moustache trimmed closely to the corners of his mouth. Women did not necessarily consider him handsome but found his features to have a pleasing symmetry and deemed him easy to look at.

He had the eyesight, focus, and visual acuity of a Red Tail Hawk. It was rumored he could spot a flea jumping off the back of a field mouse from 50 yards.

Ussher was a fast runner and fearsome hand-to-hand fighter, with efficient movements best described as quick. He had the ability to change directions effortlessly while running a crisscross pattern cover-to-cover. His natural balance and speed enabled his feet to make minimal impact with the ground, and he moved as silently as any Indian native who had ever passed through this land.

The quickness was not only evident in his legs and hands;

it was most noticeable in his intelligence. His movements were competent and seamless whether farming or hunting. Because of his mobile efficiencies, every action accomplished a task. As a result, he would complete jobs and assignments twice as fast as average men, without expending extra energy.

* * * *

The two most influential people in Ussher's life were his father and his father's best friend, an old hunter/scout named Sam Kensington. The senior Ussher and Kensington served together in the Mexican War. After the conflict, his father returned to Missouri to work the homestead and raise his family. Both his father and mother instilled the values of God, family, hard work and minding one's own business into Ussher's core.

While growing up, Kensington periodically drifted in and out of Ussher's life. It was always exciting when the somewhat eccentric wanderer came to visit. His belt pouch was always well- supplied with gold or silver nuggets and he told remarkable stories of interesting people, exciting locations, and a life full of possibilities.

Kensington never sent word he was coming or announced when he was departing to chase another adventure. After he was gone, someone in the family would inevitably find the payment he faithfully left, always amounting to double the value of anything he consumed while visiting. He also possessed an ability to show up when needed most. He inexplicably appeared the day of the funeral for Ussher's mother and stayed on for nearly a year. From Kensington, Ussher acquired similar and yet different values from those of his parents.

Ussher's father showed him how to farm and harvest. Kensington taught him how to gather and stash. From his father, Ussher learned how to track and trap. Kensington taught him how to stalk and ensnare. Through his father, he learned how to shoot and kill. Kensington taught him how to slaughter and eradicate. Ussher internalized the lessons from both men.

From his father, Ussher "learned." His father was an instructor who presented knowledge from a diligent, intellectual standpoint. He was persistent and urged Ussher to do his best. Ussher reciprocated and became a good student. His father always acknowledged the limits of men and acquiesced to the common view that life would enlighten his son in those areas where he could not adequately educate him.

From Kensington, Ussher was "taught." Kensington believed that Ussher had exceptional intelligence and ability. He maintained it was Ussher's responsibility to use these gifts every minute of every day, in all endeavors, both simple and complex. There was never compromise with him. He believed peace and harmony were possible only after all enemies lay vanquished. Enemies came in all forms. An enemy could be a man or a summer drought. An enemy could be Satan himself. They were any obstruction that prevented you from reaching your goal. Having such obstructions was never an excuse for failure.

With Kensington, there was never acceptance of second best. He constantly drove Ussher to excel. It did not bother him if Ussher only owned a small, seven-acre farm as long as it was the best seven-acre farm possible. Success did not require grand displays. It could come in small portions of exceedingly high quality.

Ussher valued his father's memory and the lessons he offered, but it was Kensington after whom he styled his life. He realized that planning meant doing what you want on your own terms and that was his essential nature. He liked the idea of self-sufficiency. It made a man strong, and in the end, strength of body, mind and purpose was all that mattered in life.

Ussher awoke early one morning to see Kensington had already saddled his horse. As Ussher approached, Kensington smiled widely, shook his hand and then gave him a bear hug. "If you were my own son, I couldn't be prouder." Ussher said nothing. Words were unnecessary. Before mounting his horse, Kensington handed him a folded piece of coyote hide. It was cured and soft. He gave Ussher a casual salute, then tugged on the rein, gave his mount a light kick, and rode away.

On the inside of the coyote hide, there was a simple map with arcane scribbling and a dozen or so instructions. It did not disclose a rationale for the markings but did indicate a Colorado location. There was also a name affixed, Carlos Rocha. He wondered if that name would have any meaning in his life. Ussher refolded the map and secured it for future reference. Colorado was far away, and he had a farm to tend.

That was Kensington's last visit. Ussher never saw or heard from him again.

* * * *

Ussher only thought about two objectives. One was positive and named Nate. For the next five weeks, he would listen and learn lessons from Ussher's father, Sam Kensington, and Ussher himself. Nate was a good student, and Ussher hoped he would become a devotee of the Sam Kensington philosophy of life. After that, Ussher felt he could reveal the plan he had for Nate's future.

The other objective for Ussher was Vince Harris. "Tonight,

sleep-well Vince boy," Ussher often whispered aloud.

"I haven't found the path to you just yet. Your Daddy has got his legions all around, thinking that will keep you protected from me. He is wrong. You are far from safe. Soon enough you and I will meet. Before long, we will settle the grievance between us. Won't that be one good time?"

18
A Force of One

As Mingo convalesced from his wounds, he conjured the details of his intended retribution. He was confident he could kill this man and desired the satisfaction of seeing the surprise on the bastard's face. The man's reaction would be one of disbelief with his eyes opening wide and his mouth going agape. His confusion would create a profound disconnect between the last time he saw Mingo and the current reality.

Mingo thought about a scenario where he might taunt the man with a question or two, indicating he was rethinking his intention to kill him, then wait to see the spark of hope reignite in his eyes. In that moment, Mingo would reveal the totality of his target's desolation. He could watch the fear return just before pulling the trigger for a gut shot. The wound is disabling and lethal, but the dying is measured and painful. As the light in the man's eyes extinguished, Mingo would tell the bastard he enjoyed watching him wither and writhe before his descent into Hell.

Joseph F. Dwyer

* * *

It was good to be healing so quickly. Mingo received excellent medical care, food, and a bushel of prayers from the Russell men. He genuinely appreciated the care, but the continual prayers were almost intolerable. He would have preferred being left alone, rather than feeling compelled to act interested. Because of his situation, Mingo listened patiently and respectfully to the Reverend Aaron Russell talking about the benefits and requirements of salvation. He watched his son, Micah, constantly nodding in the affirmative throughout the lessons, to reinforce the scriptural authenticity of his father's wisdom. Enduring this process and pretending he was open to salvation was a small price to pay for the conscientious care these men extended on his behalf.

The good Reverend and his son mistakenly assumed they held the authority to save Mingo's soul, simply because they interrupted their crusade to salvage his body.

When it was obvious Mingo would survive and recover his former strength, the two men announced they would continue on their evangelical mission. They gave him several days' supply of food and water as well as one of their pack mules. It was a good animal with a homely face, strong back and calm disposition. Micah gave Mingo a piece of paper with the names of towns they were planning to visit and deliver the Word, God willing. They both expressed hope he would join them at a prayer meeting if he traveled near one of their revivals. Aaron blessed Mingo and shook his hand before they separated onto divergent paths.

19
The Bad Seed in Manhood

IN ADDITION TO HIS larger Kansas properties, Talbot Harris owned 1,500 acres in West Missouri. He enjoyed beneficial political connections in both states. Along with his mining and timber interests, he managed a sweetheart deal with the Union Army. He sold virtually all of his livestock to the federal government. The deal allowed him to get top dollar for any steer, alive, lame, dying, or dead.

His oldest son, Morgan, was a commissioned lieutenant adjutant back East, but young Vince wasn't much for military life. Talbot Harris paid three times the required $300 draft-obligation deferment fee to keep him a civilian. That amount was more than most farmers could earn and call spending money in an entire year. Harris voluntarily paid the excess in the attempt to demonstrate support for the Union cause as well as keeping his unruly son out of harm's way.

The Union Army enlistment Major made note of Harris' contribution and commented positively regarding his patriotism. With thoughtful recollection, the officer made the decision that these excess funds might not have any real strategic impact on the war effort. Until he determined how best to use the money, he placed it amongst his personal possessions. It joined a sizable amount of other skimmed military funds, also awaiting his discretion.

In spite of his deferment, Vince savored the adrenaline rush that came from shooting and killing. He thoroughly enjoyed taking an occasional ride with large bands of Kansas Raiders when they conducted forays to punish alleged Bushwhacker sympathizers. Most of these targeted men were small-time farmers working isolated acreage. If they helped one side or the other, from time to time, it was because they had little choice. When armed hungry men ask for a meal, your best response is to comply, even if it means going hungry yourself.

Riding with the Jayhawkers meant Vince had a good chance to pursue one of his favorite pastimes, beating defenseless victims. For him, the transference of abuse from a blunt instrument into a writhing helpless victim produced visceral sensations as satisfying as drunken sex. The Jayhawkers hated the times when Vince joined them. His actions were often irrational and frequently put them at unnecessary risk, but no one had the courage to say, "No" to the son of Talbot Harris

Vince always brought Andy Hester along. Vince did not consider him a friend but Andy was useful. He was more of a collaborator and personal assistant and knew all about his past transgressions without the burden of moral judgments.

The excitement from raiding was oft-times the perfect way to compensate for the long hours his father required him to work with those goddamned steers. Shooting a cussed, redneck farmer, followed by raping his woman was one damn good time. Another plus of being a favored son was that Vince enjoyed first honors with these lowlife farmwomen.

Ever concerned with his personal safety, Vince held back from participating in the chase until the farmer was subdued. When he did take part, he and Andy worked out an almost perfect system to protect themselves. They positioned their horses behind and in the middle of the other riders. This maneuver provided maximum safety in case there was return gunfire from the intended victim. The idea was to find an isolated farmer suspected of being a Bushwhacker, or of helping them out. They ran the farmer down in the attack, then killed him and hung his body from a tree. This action signaled a warning to others about the consequences for helping Bushwhackers.

When executed correctly the attack prevented the farmer from getting off the first shot. If they did, their panic would usually make the round go high or wide. Vince always sought to get a view of the farmer in his moment of terrified indecision. The man would look to the left and then to the right, searching for a path of escape. Sometimes he would turn a complete 360°, only to return to the view of the raiders continuing to close the gap.

When the farmer tried to flee on foot, the Jayhawkers whooped, hollered and ran him down with their horses. Victims often lived but sustained severe injuries.

Then the real fun began. That was when the Demon whispered to Vince, "This is your time, enjoy." The Raiders always deferred to the son of the Big Man. No longer in the back of the group, Vince was out front and the center of everyone's attention, especially the wounded man lying on the ground. If the victim displayed impudence enough to lay unconscious from the trauma, Vince poured water on his face from his canteen. This was an especially gratifying moment. The suspected Bushwhacker was startled back to consciousness, reintroduced to the pain from his wounds, and confronted with the sadistic figure of Vince Harris standing over him.

The most common injury to a man trampled by horses was a broken collarbone. This made it impossible for him to raise his arms in defense. Vince would almost be emotional with gratitude to the Demon for these gifts of helplessness. He often stomped and kicked his victim for a moment or two before bringing out the whip.

Bullwhips come in lengths that vary from six to nine feet. During his formative years of self-apprenticeship, Vince became an expert with all of them. For this application, he enjoyed the six-foot version. The shorter length stiffened the leather twists and caused the whip to become a decidedly blunt weapon.

Vince's frenzied attack did not desist until exhaustion forced him to stop. For refreshment, Andy brought him water, whiskey, or both. They liked leering at the dead man, and often exchanged congratulatory smiles of satisfaction from a job well done.

The other riders exchanged glances of their own. It was obvious that being rich did not exempt you from being crazy. If he had not been the son of Talbot Harris, many of the Jayhawkers would have put a bullet through Vince's skull. It was the only known cure for being rabid.

20

The Reconnoiter

PREVIOUS APRIL 1862

TWO HARRIS SUPPLY WAGONS successfully returned to the ranch with prized cargo. It was two Henry repeating rifles, 1000 rounds of ammunition, and five cases of Old Crow whiskey. Old Crow was reputed to be the favorite of General Ulysses S. Grant.

Talbot Harris ordered ten of the Henrys, which were difficult to obtain even if you paid twice the price. He paid the double premium but only found two of the weapons available. In a world of single-shot rifles, the Henry's capability was astounding. The magazine held thirteen .44 caliber bullets, which loaded into a spring-tube below the barrel. After firing, a quick push/pull of the receiver's lever ejected the spent cartridge and chambered a new one.

Harris' intention was to arm the guards closest to the big house with the lethal Henrys. He reasoned that since they had proven themselves the best shots, giving them repeating rifles would increase the security exponentially.

A small band of Missouri militia tried an unsuccessful raid on the wagons, which resulted in the killing of the lead shotgun guard and wounding of an out-rider. Vince did not personally know either man and he was not particularly grieved over the casualties. What he thought about was he now had the perfect excuse to ride over to that little farm by the artesian spring. He and some of his boys should question that couple who worked that land. The man, he remembered the name as Ussher, was just too quiet for Vince's liking. He kept to himself and always worked that miserable piece of farmland. Therefore, he was suspect. No man Vince knew was so dedicated to working that much, and Vince decided everyone had to choose sides. A man was either with the Jayhawkers or not with them. Neutrality was unacceptable.

That woman of Ussher's, now she was a subject for some very close consideration. She was likely to need some focused attention to find out what she knew about Bushwhacker activity in the territory. It might even become necessary for her to yield the information in the form of a confession. Vince genuinely liked confessions. It did not matter if a crime or transgression had actually occurred. He would make up his own scenario as an excuse to apply necessary interrogation techniques. She would soon confess to whatever crimes she might know about, as well as those that Vince intended to invent. Vince had his ideas on the kind of attention that would work best. The more he thought of her, the more excited he became. The more Old Crow he and Andy Hester drank, the higher their bravado level ascended. The excitement and the bravado led to a decision on their course of action.

Vince removed one of the new Henry rifles from the wall rack along with four, 50-round boxes of ammunition. He and Andy enlisted Little Bill Hooker, who was more experienced with the terrain than either Vince or Andy.

Although both men had lived in the area for years, they did not possess a good working knowledge of the backcountry landscape. Since Vince was the son of the most influential cattle baron in the territory, his father provided for his every need. Likewise, Andy was never the type to go into the wilderness. He had always made his living by working in some sort of service capacity. He had been a store clerk and a bartender in town before landing his job as a stable hand at the ranch and finally his big move to Vince's helper and collaborator. Whenever either man traveled, they stuck to the roads or established trails. If they did venture into rough country, it was always part of a larger group of riders.

Little Bill was a country boy who frequently hunted squirrel and raccoon. Vince and Andy figured that it was going to be dark by the time they returned. Little Bill's backwoods experience would be useful. The three men rode toward the artesian spring, stopping about 300 yards out.

Little Bill commented that they should walk the rest of the way. "Go quiet-like," Hooker whispered. Everyone knew this rich boy as well as his friend had no wilderness skills. This part of the country was not welcoming. There were Bushwhackers everywhere.

Vince laughed at Little Bill. "This is going to be easy. Billy-boy, if you're worried, just stay back and play things safe. Me and Andy can take it from here."

After thinking about the situation, Hooker decided to go along. If something happened to the son of Talbot Harris, and he received blame, his life would be worthless. He had seen the things his angry employer could do. More worrisome would be that his death would occur only after Harris instructed Otto Metzger to administer some unthinkable, merciless punishment. For better or worse, just because Vince Harris had decided to choose him this afternoon, he was in for whatever was going to happen. Life can be a bitch.

* * * *

A few weeks earlier, Vince was riding past the Ussher farm with five companions. He noticed the man and woman fetching water from around the rocks where a spring bubbled through. They did not look his way until his horse snorted displeasure over the delay in returning to the barn for the evening oats. Vince pulled up on the reins to take a longer gaze at the woman. He liked everything about her. She was shapely and appeared full of vitality, a perfect candidate for a perfect experience.

The man noticed the riders and turned to face in their direction. He and Vince stared at each other across split-rail fence line. He looked to be average height with a solid build. He did not appear particularly threatening but neither did he seem to be a soft target. Vince was an expert at soft targets. One of his accompanying riders circled back and pulled up next to him.

The man cautioned, "Mr. Vince, you don't want to hang around here too long. That man over there has earned himself a rough reputation. He can shoot a rabbit between the eyes from this distance."

Vince moved on, making special note that the woman would be worth a second, much closer look. She was much too beautiful to have her body wasted on some low-life, sod-busting farmer. Vince determined that he would claim those tender female curves for himself, down the road, at a more opportune time, after her man lay stone cold dead.

21

Bittersweet Memories

CURRENT DAY 1863

Whenever Ussher experienced a quiet moment, his mind flashed involuntarily to that early springtime evening over a year ago. Because of his love for Darby, everything in his perception assumed a context relating to her approach of living an exceptional life. He recalled every detail about her, her beautiful face and her strength of character, the fullness of her figure and the sharp analytics of her mind, the taste of her lips and the fierceness in her nature. Nothing in Ussher's experience was more rewarding than simply standing by her side as her husband and partner. For that reason, the extremes of that day's experience were indelible, and haunted him without mercy. The recollection was always the same and the reality as absolute as the grave.

* * * *

That early evening day was warm and clear with the musky sweet scent of springtime promise. For several hours, Ussher walked behind their draft mule, navigating the plow through the moist earth. It would be two more weeks before the planting started, but unusually temperate weather presented a good time to loosen the soil from the grip of winter freeze.

Darby occupied her time shaking out linens and curtains and hanging them on the line for the sun to freshen. They discussed the layout of their crops, the repairs needed around the homestead and the priority of getting everything accomplished. Ussher loved it when Darby shared her ideas. Her enthusiasm was infectious, her eyes flashed, and her voice was always smooth and confident. He often found himself forced to ask her to repeat what she said. He became so entranced with the way she spoke that he sometimes did not hear the core message she was conveying. He often broke into a smile as he listened to her bright conversation. She immediately picked-up on the fact he had lost focus and was aware that his love for her was the cause. These times were also special for Darby and she knew how to turn them into playful moments.

Darby might stop and say, "Ussher, are you listening to me?"

"Yes ma'am," he'd say while looking sheepish.

"Well sir, then please tell me what it was that I just said to you."

Ussher would hesitate and say whatever came into his head. It was always an incorrect guess.

She would look directly at him and declare, "Ussher, you listen careful now, 'cause I'm not going to say this again and you do not want to get on my bad side. Am I wrong?"

While scolding him, Darby generated playful, mock anger, placing her hand on her hips and shaking her finger in front of his face. She did her best to appear suitably exasperated and thoroughly provoked, always raising that eyebrow for added emphasis. Life with Darby was an amazingly good life indeed.

She was most always in a good mood, but today Darby seemed especially spirited. She sang her gospel and country songs all afternoon. Ussher saw her stop once or twice and face into the wind to take in its freshness and vitality. Using both hands, she ran her fingers through her hair, pushing the thick black waves away from her forehead, absorbing every ray of sunshine. She picked early blooming wildflowers, arranged them perfectly in her hand, and held them close to enjoy their fragrance. He heard her break out into impulsive laughter and observed her whirl entirely around as she walked the bouquet into their house. As Ussher smiled widely, he felt grateful for the joy this woman continually brought into his life and treasured the spontaneity Darby expressed in both word and action.

It occurred to Ussher that Darby might have something on her mind. He knew the signs, and from the way she was behaving, he anticipated that her news was going to be special or unique, maybe both, time would tell.

* * * *

These days, the memory of the horror putrefied all recollections of happiness. The optimism of those earlier times was now abhorrence and the effect was visceral and mean spirited. The aching image was always vividly the same. It stalked him like his own shadow. He was hostage to the way it deconstructed a moment to propel him to that place where there was never sanctuary from torment.

From that day to this, Ussher pledged his life to a righteous, final reckoning and invoked curses through his misery. In the bowels of consuming emptiness, he dedicated himself to avenging the injustices inflicted on his wife and the intolerable violation of the bond he shared with Darby.

22
The Bitter Root

PREVIOUS APRIL 1862

VINCE, ANDY, AND LITTLE BILL lay on their bellies, looking over the crest of a small knoll. They watched Ussher and Darby as the couple worked around their property. Andy and Little Bill mostly watched Ussher and assessed the potential danger he represented. Vince watched Darby, growing increasingly excited with anticipation as he evaluated every aspect of her.

* * * *

Just before sunset, Ussher finished plowing. He walked over to the garden to see if Darby needed help. After separating bulbs, she intended to plant, she might sort through sprouted potatoes and decide which ones to cut into pieces for planting. Ussher said he would take care of the potatoes. To that, Darby informed him she was going into the house to cook dinner. Ussher told her not to bother. There was apple pie that Darby baked the previous day. He suggested they boil eggs and make a pot of coffee. The combination would be a fun and easy meal to prepare. Darby laughed and agreed.

They needed fresh water for making coffee and boiling eggs. Ussher said he would fetch the water from the spring. Darby hollered for him to wait so she could join him. She even offered to carry the water. Her lowered voice volunteered that Ussher needed to conserve his energy, for later. As she made this remark, her eyes flashed and the tip of her tongue spontaneously moved from the corner of her mouth and then arched over her upper lip. As the tip finished the vaulted movement, her face brightened into an enormous grin accompanied by a squeal of happiness. Darby grabbed Ussher's hand and the two of them began their journey to the artesian spring.

* * * *

Vince stared as the couple walked together and held hands. In this moment, Vince made several crucial decisions. First, he decided the Henry rifle needed testing for accuracy, and second, Ussher would be the ideal target to confirm its capability. The third decision, and for Vince the most important, was Darby needed to be his, this night, for that special but elusive experience that evaded him to this point.

Tonight, that farmwoman would be on her back and helpless, with her face bruised and bleeding. He imagined her terrified, crying, and pleading for her life. At that moment, he intended to fall onto her and spread her legs. His plan was to rape and choke her until she passed out. Vince would take his time. The torment for her, and enjoyment for him, would extend for as long as her strength permitted. Each time she lapsed near unconsciousness, he would relent and allow her to catch her breath, so once again she could plead with him for the suffering to stop.

For Vince, the pleading was the best part. When he used to torture the animals, he often mimicked voices and pretended they were begging for mercy. After Andy Hester joined him, he assumed the imitation of the suffering voices. This change improved the experience allowing Vince to concentrate on the application of torture. He never admitted the fact, but Andy actually performed the voices better than he did.

Vince employed the technique of choking and reviving his victims until they finally died of trauma or he tired from exertion. On the last cycle, he continued the pressure until asphyxiation was complete. Vince enjoyed feeling the last shutter of life escape from a woman's body. At these times, he might speak softly to her or he might be verbally abusive. It depended on his mood, and his mood depended on the satisfaction he derived from his victim's responsiveness and vitality.

Vince used this method with Abigail's two missing girls. He learned from those experiences and now he was ready to elevate his technique. Those girls had not been the right type to contribute to his satisfaction. They gave up without resistance because they knew him. He was the son of their employer.

They submitted, with the mistaken belief that their torment would end after the conclusion of the rape.

* * * *

There was something about Darby, which caused Vince to anticipate she would not surrender easily. Farmwomen, by the nature of their lifestyle, are stronger than domestic servants. He knew something about the reputation of her husband and guessed she possessed an assertive and energetic temperament. Vince acquired the feeling that today was going to be the most memorable experience in his uncontrolled, indulgent life. As that thought energized his brain, he spontaneously released his signature cackle. The demented sound startled both Andy and Little Bill.

The knoll was only 60 yards away from where the water bubbled through from the artesian spring. Vince figured he would wait until Ussher and Darby started their return to the cabin before firing at Ussher. In his opinion, next to a tormented woman, there was no better site than that of a man's exposed and unprotected back. This shot was going to be easy.

As Ussher and Darby began walking back to their home, Vince sighted in the rifle on the base of Ussher's spine. Andy watched with anticipation. He glanced over to Little Bill as if to share the experience. He was surprised and disappointed when he saw the look on Bill's face. Bill seemed disconcerted and displayed no enjoyment of the moment. In fact, he looked repulsed. Andy shook off the thought and returned to watch Vince with eagerness over the action about to take place.

Vince drew in a ragged, hasty breath and pulled the trigger. The hammer struck the primer, and the primer combusted the powder. Fire and gas exerted inexorable pressure on the .44 caliber bullet. The round spun through the barrel, discharged with a loud report, and streaked toward its target to draw its first blood.

Ussher simultaneously felt the pain in the back of his leg as he heard the gunshot. The impact threw him to the ground and a throbbing ache pulsed through his body. Darby was terrified and shocked in one collective response. Vince anticipated that she would have such a reaction. He hungered to see her bathed in dread. After he pulled the trigger, he forgot all about Ussher and immediately looked in her direction. Because he did not follow through with his concentration, the bullet went off target. Although Vince enjoyed watching Darby's distress, Ussher survived the attack.

Ussher's legs were heavily muscled. The shot lodged in his thigh but did not break the bone. The transfer of energy from the bullet entering into his body spun him around. When he tumbled to the ground, Darby looked back. She could see three men behind the knoll. Two of the men jumped up and started running toward them. Darby could tell from the way they moved, the attackers were not used to navigating over rough terrain. After stumbling a time or two, they slowed their pace to manage their balance.

Darby reacted in seconds to their situation. She instinctively went to Ussher to determine the extent of his injury. He was already attempting to stand up. Although bleeding, they judged that he would be able to make a run toward the cabin with her help. The pursuing men began yelling for them to stop. One of the men fired a warning shot over their heads. Ussher and Darby continued running as fast as possible toward their cabin.

At that time, Ussher owned a Sharps model 1851, single-shot carbine. He always kept it close-at-hand in these dangerous times. Darby had shown interest in learning to fire the weapon and became a good student regarding its use. On the run to the cabin, she grabbed the Sharps, which was lying against a nearby tree.

As Little Bill watched the scene unfold, he became more and more anxious. Vince's half-assed plan was turning into a nightmare. If the couple made it back to the relative safety of their cabin, Vince might have a real fight on his hands. What Vince and Andy first thought to be an easy ambush, now turned into an entirely unpredictable situation. Bill had to deal with this dilemma. Vince might be injured or even get himself killed. Even though none of this was his idea, he would likely be held accountable, especially if he came away unscathed.

Instinctively Bill knew it was time to commit to the action. He got up and started running after Vince and Andy. Since he was used to rough terrain, Bill quickly caught up and took the lead. As he passed, he heard Vince's order through labored breathing,

"Don't shoot, you might hit the woman."

The three men began to close the gap between themselves and the fleeing couple. Blood loss and shock were setting in on Ussher, and he struggled to maintain consciousness. Darby urged him on and supported his weight to the best of her ability as they approached their cabin.

At this point, the three men were only 30 feet behind them. As Darby and Ussher reached their doorway, Darby yelled for Ussher to grab the doorframe. Then she released him to turn on their pursuers. The leading man was almost on top of them. Ussher did exactly as instructed, although vertigo overtook him.

A surge of protective adrenaline electrified Darby in that moment. The man she loved was injured and helpless. It was up to her to deal with the situation. In less than a second, Darby wheeled around and leveled the Sharps rifle at point blank range toward Little Bill Hooker. He was only five feet away when the .52 caliber round exploded from the rifle. It struck him in the sternum and lifted him off his feet. He flew backwards, between Vince and Andy, as they ran up to the doorway.

Andy hit Ussher on the back of the head with the butt of his rifle. Ussher stumbled forward into the cabin. As he fell, he struck his forehead against the edge of their table and went unconscious. Darby swung her empty rifle like a club, aiming for Andy's head. Andy ducked backwards. The barrel caught him hard on his right shoulder and he yelped with pain. At the same moment, Vince followed through with a hard punch to Darby's left cheek. The blow sent her reeling onto the cabin floor, face-to-face next to Ussher.

When Darby saw the man she loved, bleeding from the wound on his forehead, fury raged through her and she instantly started to get up and continue the fight. Her own safety did not matter. Darby's only thought was to protect her injured husband. Vince punched her again, and she collapsed heavily to the floor. This time she fell back, dazed and temporarily helpless. Vince felt a sharp throb in his hand as he looked around to find Andy. He decided he needed help with this strong and obstinate woman.

After Andy determined that Ussher was no longer a threat, he went back to the doorway to double check Little Bill's condition. Bill lay stone still on the ground, spread-eagled, with a look of disbelieving surprise frozen onto his dead face. There was a large wound in his chest and blood pooled under him.

Vince screamed at Andy, "Get your ass in here and help me with this bitch."

As Andy returned to the room, he saw Vince kick Darby twice in the ribs. Vince dropped down to the floor on one knee and put his face next to Darby's ear.

"Your man is dead," he sneered. "You're all alone little girl, and right now, you're all mine. We're gonna' take our time and have us some fun. It ain't gonna' do you no good, but I sure do hope you got plenty of fight left in you, 'cause I like it when we play rough."

Vince grabbed Darby's hair and brought her to a sitting position. Her bruised face throbbed as she tried to clear her mind. Darby did not believe Ussher was dead, but she knew she had to figure out a way to distract these bastards in order to save his life.

Andy interrupted, "What are we gonna' do with Little Bill? Everyone knows he works at the ranch."

Vince responded with sarcastic irritation, "Who gives a shit about Little Bill?"

Andy was troubled and distraught over Vince's self-absorbed reply. It gave him sudden insight about the value of his own life to this rich boy.

"Pick her up and hold her arms back," ordered Vince. He was immensely gratified to see tears streaming down Darby's cheeks. Vince misinterpreted the meaning of those tears. Darby was not emotional because of fear. It was because she felt despondent over her inability to protect Ussher. This was the man she had loved her entire life. Ussher had always been her singular focus. Darby was certain God created her so she could become his wife. She committed herself to his protection using every resource she possessed.

Darby struggled with all her might against the grip on her arms. Vince was thrilled as he saw her thrash about. He laughed and encouraged Andy, whose eyes widened from the effort required to control this woman.

Vince laughed as he yelled out, "Hold onto that wildcat, boy."

Darby let go a shriek that was a combination of a growl and scream, emitting elements of threat and reprisal. Vince was barely able to contain his excitement. He decided it was time to strip off her dress, molest that succulent body and kiss those perfect lips.

As Vince approached, Darby kicked hard and caught him above the knee. Vince yelled in pain, cursed Darby, and backed away for a moment. Andy tried to wrap one of his legs around the leg that Darby had just used to kick Vince. As Darby's focus centered on the struggle with Andy, Vince stepped in and slapped her. The slap was painful but not disabling. It snapped Darby's head backwards and into the bridge of Andy's nose.

Andy's left hand, permanently weakened from the copperhead snakebite, caused him to struggle to maintain his grip on this farm-strong woman. Now the pain from the blow to his face distracted him significantly and his grasp loosened further.

Vince grabbed both sides of Darby's face with a vise-like hold. He kissed her hard on the lips. He used his tongue. Darby gagged, as she smelled his whiskey soaked breath. She pulled away and spit back in revulsion. Vince literally shrieked with exhilaration and delight. He had been right. This woman was going to be perfect in every way. Vince stepped back with gratification. He decided to remove his pants before advancing once again to continue the assault.

With all the strength she could muster, Darby used this

moment to break from Andy's grasp. She stomped down hard on the end of his boot. The blow landed on target. Andy felt his middle toe crack as pain shot across his foot. Darby thrust her shoulders forward and away from Andy's hold. His fingernails raked across her skin, as she broke free. As Andy lunged forward, Darby swung her elbow backwards to deflect his attempt to grasp her once again. The blow landed against the right side of Andy's chin, knocking him sideways. As Andy and Darby involuntarily stopped to inhale a resuscitating breath, they heard Vince screaming at them. "Don't stop. Keep fighting… keep fighting." Vince stood mesmerized with euphoric delight watching Andy struggle against this woman / she-wolf combination. The experience congealed toward perfection. The only addition the scene still required was for Vince to assert personal mastery and discipline this bitch for her insolence.

Darby found herself between both men as Vince balanced on one leg, trying to undress, and Andy stood, bent over, holding his knees and fighting exhaustion. This was the opportunity Darby needed. She lunged toward Andy and pushed him hard with both hands. As Andy stumbled backwards, Darby whirled around and grabbed Vince by the hair. Surprised by this move, Vince pulled away and turned his head to one side, still trying desperately to kick off the remaining pant leg and maintain his balance. Andy rejoined the fray by hooking his arm under Darby's chin to gain advantage and control.

Darby pulled Vince's face violently towards her own. For a critical moment, she persevered long enough to control momentum. Holding Vince by the hair with both hands, she bit the side of his cheek and jaw as hard as she was able. Her teeth connected top and bottom. Darby held on.

Andy saw her bite down and yelled, "No!"

Vince pushed on Darby's face with both hands. Darby held on and bit down even harder. The panicked brute shoved Darby backwards and pulled away from the pain. There was a tearing sensation and sound. While blood spilled down his chin, Vince stood in disbelief as pain crashed into his jawline.

Darby looked Vince in the eye. She waited for a long moment, allowing his shock to settle in and for him to look back in her direction. Vince moved his hand from his torn cheek and stared at the blood on his fingers. The moment he looked back at Darby, she spit out the chunk of flesh. It landed on the floor by the toe of his boot.

Vince screamed as loud as his voice would allow and put his hand against his bleeding wound. The expression on his face turned demonic. Darby was defiant. Andy grabbed her once more. She desperately sought to strike again at Andy's face with the back of her head. Twice she made contact with his nose and mouth. Andy not only tried to restrain Darby, but he swung her left and right. He attempted to reduce her ability to do further damage to his already bleeding nose.

As Andy swung Darby one way, Vince delivered a vicious punch from the opposite direction. The blow landed hard on the left side of Darby's face. She immediately collapsed into semi-consciousness. Again, Vince screamed at the top of his voice and grabbed his right hand. The results of the blow fractured Darby's cheekbone, but it also dislocated two of Vince's fingers.

Darby was not finished. She moaned as she struggled to get up. She turned over on her back and then pushed herself into a sitting position, against the hope chest she had received from her mother. Darby inhaled deeply and screamed at both men.

"Damn you both to Hell. Damn your wormy souls into

salt and sulfur."

Before Andy could think of anything to say, Vince picked up the Henry rifle with deliberation. He levered a round into the chamber and aimed the front sight at Darby. She looked fiercely back at him and screamed, "Do it, you coward. You don't scare me one bit. You've been measured as a man and there ain't much there."

Vince bellowed out disgruntled and frustrated anger, "You ruined everything, you bitch. This wasn't supposed to happen like this. Who in Hell are you? No woman fights like that."

Vince lowered the rifle for an instant and then once again aimed it at Darby. For him, this was the worst experience he ever remembered. He thought about the unfairness of it all. What was supposed to be his perfect moment had backfired at every turn.

Darby again spat blood and saliva in his direction. "Ha! How hard is your pecker now, you little shit?" she taunted. "You'll never have this woman. You ain't anything more than a worthless ass-licker and there ain't no reward for your type, other than some sorry corner in Hell."

Darby indicated toward Andy. "The only tail you've got a chance of getting is off your Mary-boy over there. Only a real man can ever have me, and that's not you, not today, not ever. This is my house…My House. Now, get out!"

Vince looked over at Andy, who stared back blankly with his mouth agape and chest heaving from fatigue, waiting for instructions. Flushing color suddenly rose from Vince's collarbone and into his face as another wave of pain circulated through his body. His rising anger matched the recurring pain.

Vince's focus again centered on Darby, although he found some difficulty maintaining eye contact against her fierce glare.

He was accustomed to his victims cowering and pleading but this woman ignored her injuries, held her ground, and dared to challenge him.

"You spoiled everything," he complained with guttural frustration. "This was supposed to be my perfect goddamn day. How does some stinking little farm bitch dare to think she has the right to ruin something that belongs to me? I'm Vince Harris, for Christ sake."

Vince wasn't sure what to do at that moment. He had planned and simulated this event for days but instead of experiencing fulfillment, he felt overwhelmed with stress and emotional disappointment. There was intense pain in his face and hand. He needed to react to feel back in control. There had to be an outlet for this rage he was experiencing. Vince made up his mind and released all his anger in a single summary action. He pulled the trigger.

Inside the little cabin, the rifle's report was deafening. The ballistic energy was devastating as the Henry recorded its inaugural kill. Darby died almost instantly as her body convulsed from the bullet's impact. Her startled eyes never closed. The force of the bullet reoriented her body against the hope chest. In her last moment of this life, the trauma left her looking, for the final time, directly at the place where Ussher lay unconscious.

Darby's spirit floated free on her final breath and cloaked her love around Ussher, veiling his wounded vulnerability against further notice from Vince or Andy.

23

Aftermath

When Ussher awoke, the first face he saw was Emily Randall. He was lying on a bed in one of the rooms of the Randall house with his leg bound and elevated. Bandages circled his temples and his head ached like a son-of-a-bitch.

"Where's Darby?" asked Ussher.

Emily did not answer, but Lewis Randall stepped into the room when he heard Ussher's voice.

"It's good to see you back with us, my friend," smiled Randall. "You sure had us worried for the past two days."

"Where's Darby," Ussher asked again, this time with urgency contributing its own punctuation.

Randall knew he had no chance delaying the dreadful news. Ussher's anxiety level was increasing by the moment, and there were no words for Randall to use which might mitigate the coming pain.

The memories flooded back to Ussher, but he could only remember half the story.

Ussher pressed, "What happened to my wife? Where is Darby?"

Randall exhaled the words slowly and with regret. "Darby died two days ago."

Emily reached out and took Ussher's hand. Ussher politely but firmly pulled away.

Randall said quietly to Emily, "Bring the jug and two cups."

He then turned to Ussher and said, "I'll do my best to explain everything."

Randall pulled up a straight chair. "From what I can figure, this is what happened. It was the damnedest thing. Day before yesterday, Emily and me went to your place early because Darby said we should stop by for coffee with sweet cornbread."

"We could see straight off that something terrible had happened. Your door was open wide, and then we saw him, the dead man. He was just outside your entrance. We took a quick look and knew right away that he was gone. Had a hole in his chest large enough to put two fingers through and was staring straight into the morning sunlight.

"I told my Emily to remain in the wagon while I had a look around. That is when I found you and Darby. You were barely breathing, and Darby, well sir, that girl had gone on to Jesus. I don't know what to say Ussher, Emily and me are just sad beyond words. What a sweet girl and a wonderful friend. I know how much you loved her."

Ussher inhaled a deep breath, "I appreciate the fact that you and Emily most likely saved my life, but it's important for me that you tell me everything. Don't sugarcoat anything. Tell me what you know and tell me now, please."

Randall continued, "Well, sir, I think I got it pretty well worked out. You and Darby were ambushed by Vince Harris, Talbot Harris' youngest son."

Ussher snapped, "I know who he is, but how do you know it was him who came after us?"

"Several things," stated Randall. First off, I saw Vince, along with two other riders, pass my place late in the afternoon, but I never saw them return. Next, we heard some gunshots coming from the direction of your homestead. Once here, we found saddlebags and a blanket left behind. The saddlebags have initials burned inside on the cover flap. The initials are VH. The leather looks to be quite expensive. It is high-class and hand-tooled. However, the fact that cinches it, as far as I'm concerned, is this."

Lewis Randall stood up and walked over to a corner of the room. He returned holding a brand new Henry repeating rifle.

"We found this on the floor of your cabin. In those saddle-bags I mentioned, we found the ammunition for this rifle. I'm sure Vince used this weapon to murder Darby. I know it in my bones. If I would have dug that round out of your leg, I'll bet it would also be from this Henry."

Ussher's hand involuntarily passed over the bandage on the leg wound. Randall said, "The bullet went deep but the wound was clean, and it didn't break the bone. Emily and me figured trying to find and cut it out would cause more damage than leaving it alone. It should heal just fine, although it will probably give you some aches from time to time."

Ussher did not respond.

Randall continued, "Afterwards, I found out that the dead man works at the Harris ranch. You put all this together, with what everyone knows about that crazy Vince Harris, and it's not too hard to figure out what happened. To my thinking, it is further confirmed with the fact that you were shot from behind and poor Darby, I'm sorry to tell you this, was beaten pretty badly."

Ussher was stone still. Randall could see a change overtake him. Ussher stared out into the void in the middle of the room and asked quietly, "Is there anything else?"

Randall looked over to Emily, who was standing in the doorway. As his eyes returned to Ussher, he took in a breath and said, "Yes, I'm afraid there is more." Ussher looked up and waited for him to go on with his explanation.

"I think that Darby put up one hell of a fight," said Randall. "There were blood drops all around the inside perimeter of the cabin, as well as at the entrance by the dead man. There was splatter everywhere, like someone who had been shaking an injured hand, or a hand used to stop blood, and then shaken to remove that blood.

"The fact that impressed me most was this." Randall turned around and reached into a cup currently filled with homebrew. He used the alcohol to preserve a piece of prized evidence. It took Ussher a moment to focus and confirm its identity. Randall verbalized what Ussher saw. It was a chunk of human skin.

"I found it on the floor." Randall said, "I checked you and Darby, as well as that dead Harris ranch hand. No one was missing a piece of flesh. Someone is out there walking around with a permanent scar that is probably quite evident. If I were a betting man, my money would be on Vince Harris having that injury."

Ussher listened. He did his best to assimilate the information, looked away for a moment and then back to Randall.

"I just realized," he said as an afterthought, "Darby never told me anything about you and Emily coming for breakfast. That's not like her, to say nothing about company coming to the house. What was that all about?"

Randall and his wife exchanged glances. In that moment, they both realized that there was more grim news coming Ussher's way.

Randall cautiously replied, "You are aware that my Emily is the finest midwife in the county, aren't you?"

The coming revelation started to throttle Ussher's soul. The reality numbed him completely. Darby had been pregnant and now Ussher understood her high spirits that day. His intuition had been correct. She did have something to tell him. She was simply biding her time and waiting for the right moment. With Darby, it was always about making a situation or event as perfect as possible, especially if it was for Ussher.

Continuing the analysis, Randall said, "Emily and I were talking matters over the last couple of days. As bad as this situation is, you have to admire how hard Darby must have fought. There can only be one answer. She was fighting for you. My guess is that the girl never stopped thinking things through as she was kicking, scratching, and biting those bastards. We found blood on the back of Darby's head, but there was no injury there. The way I see things, it looks like someone might have been trying to hold her arms from behind. As she fought, she probably gave that particular bastard a backwards head-butt or two into the nose.

"Knowing how smart she was, I'm sure she read the situation perfectly. You picked one great girl. She would never be one to panic, no matter how grim the circumstances. She knew these assholes were there to rape her and kill you both. Your leg was gunshot and your head split open, front and back. She knew that if she did nothing, both of you would die. She made the decision that if she fought hard enough, Vince and his boys might get distracted from cutting your throat. She probably figured that the best way out was to induce them to use the gun one more time. Further shooting, on top of the shots already fired, might finally draw enough attention from neighbors like us. She saw her opening in the fight. Somehow, she was strong enough and smart enough to get close and bite the dog shit out of someone's face. That must have been a sight. Losing a chunk of meat that large, had to hurt like hell.

Ussher did not speak for hours. He cared about nothing, other than exacting revenge at that moment. Vince Harris had to die immediately. He tried unsuccessfully to get out of bed. The pain was excruciating and he fell down straightaway. This caused the wound to start bleeding again. With some effort, Randall and Emily got him back into bed. Tears of rage forced their way onto Ussher's face and his body shook from fury.

"You need to settle back, my friend," Randall said firmly. "If you rip those wounds too severely, you'll be dead by tomorrow. If that happens, Darby's death will go unavenged. Since I know you so well, I understand what the next step in this affair will be. What's more, other women will die if someone doesn't stop that crazy asshole. As much as I hate to say it, you may be the only one strong enough and smart enough to get it done."

Although still trembling from anger, Ussher nodded affirmatively toward Randall. "You're right. I know exactly what I have to do, and I intend to get it done, by God."

Ussher rested by himself for an hour to absorb everything Randall told him, before asking his friend to join him again. When Randall appeared, Ussher came right to the point. "I'll be needing that Henry rifle for myself. I've got work to do."

Vince Harris had ripped Darby from him. The Henry rifle now belonged to Ussher. It would become his full-time companion. They would eat together, sleep together, and kill together. Revenge would replace love as Ussher's dominate emotion as long as Vince Harris kept breathing.

Randall said nothing but nodded affirmatively. Shit was going to happen. Nothing, short of death itself, was going to stop Ussher. It just made sense that he should be thoroughly prepared and armed well for the task.

Three days later, Ussher summoned all his available energy.

With help, he made his way to Darby's gravesite. During the ride in the back of the wagon, he barely had enough strength to raise his head.

Randall chose the ideal place for Darby's rest. It was on an incline, about 25 feet above the point where the artesian spring waters bubbled through the earth. Sunrise washed the area in dazzling light. The hill face enjoyed a continuous freshening breeze. Wildflowers grew everywhere. With sunset, the light gave way to long shadows, which blended softly down the curve of the mound running back toward the stream. Ussher was pleased with the location and thanked Randall for his thoughtfulness.

One week later, Ussher commissioned a headstone for the grave. The simple inscription read, "Darby Prichard Ussher, Beloved Wife." It was a statement of fact and absolute as Scripture.

24

Friends No More

WHEN VINCE MURDERED Darby, the recoil of the Henry rifle caused intense pain to pulse through Vince's hand. He cursed and let the weapon drop to the floor. Andy truthfully thought that Vince had gone insane. As the adrenaline in Vince's body diminished, the agony in his face and hand amplified. He ran, forgetting all about Little Bill's body lying just outside. He tripped over it and fell onto his already injured hand.

Vince yelled to Andy, "Get out here and help me, you asshole".

Andy hesitated. Again, Vince yelled, "Get your ass out here." This time his voice cracked from the effort of the volume. Andy appeared at the door, cautiously peering outward.

Vince said loudly, "This is your fault. What kind of man can't control a woman? Look at me. How am I going to explain this? This is not finished between you and me."

Vince ordered Andy to bring their horses. When he returned, Vince needed Andy to assist him getting into the saddle. To make it easier for Vince to mount up, Andy removed the blanket and the saddlebags, tossing both to the ground, where they remained abandoned and forgotten. The saddlebags contained 195 rounds of rifle ammunition.

Andy never went back inside the cabin. The Henry lay on the cabin floor in the exact location where Vince dropped it. As the barrel heat cooled, the rifle waited patiently for its new master and next assignment.

Vince instructed Andy to stay behind, bury Little Bill and hide the gravesite. "You come and see me as soon as you get back to the ranch, understand?"

Andy nodded and answered, "Yes sir boss."

As soon as Vince was out of sight, Andy rode away in the other direction. Little Bill's funeral arrangements would have to wait. It was obvious to Andy that his employment prospects at the Harris ranch had turned unfavorable.

Andy experienced a restless night on the trail. He finally fell asleep just before sunrise, and then awoke one hour later, finding himself surrounded by four riders from the Harris security detail. Their assignment was to escort him back to the ranch, and they did so without explaining their purpose. At first, Andy experienced extreme dread but eventually began to calm down when he thought of an alibi to excuse his actions.

He decided to explain to Vince that he became disoriented in the dark, and inadvertently rode off in the wrong direction. After all, the whole idea about including Little Bill stemmed from the fact that neither he nor Vince had exceptionally strong backwoods skills.

It seemed reasonable to Andy that he could sell this story, and he was actually sorry about riding off. After a night sleeping outside, Andy changed his mind about leaving behind the good life he enjoyed on the Harris ranch. Andy knew Vince was pissed off with him, and he was most likely going to receive a beating, but then things would return to normal. He figured he could live with that situation. Halfway back on the return ride, Andy started feeling confident enough to engage his bodyguards in small talk conversation.

Once back in front of the big house, there was no sign of Vince. From the porch, he received a stone cold greeting from both Talbot Harris and Otto Metzger. Andy did his best to look upbeat.

"Hey, Mr. Harris, Captain Metzger," he said cautiously. "I sure do appreciate you sending these boys out to find me. I got myself turned around and lost, sure enough."

Andy looked back and forth between Harris and Metzger in anticipation of their response. There was an icy, distressing silence from the two men as he awaited their reply. Anxiety caused beads of perspiration to creep onto Andy's forehead.

Finally, Harris turned to Metzger and barked, "Eviscerate the Fucker."

25
Back in Camp

PRESENT DAY

USSHER AND NATE sat together after their beans and bacon supper. The first of the three planned Bushwhacker reprisal raids occurred earlier in the afternoon. The sought-after revenge for the attack on Nevada City was not achieved to anyone's satisfaction. Three Missouri men were shot dead in the action and another four wounded. One of the wounded would likely die before sunrise. Tension in the camp was high and allegations of stupidity and cowardice flew between the militia commanders. Even Quantrill and Anderson were at odds.

Ussher and Nate had not participated in the fight, Ussher by choice, Nate because Ussher had forbidden it. Nate shared his displeasure and irritation with Ussher that he had not been part of the raid.

Ussher explained, "Fighting this kind of conflict takes experience that needs to start on a smaller scale. There had to be 150 or more men out there today. You are riding an old plowhorse that is not familiar with all the shit that goes on in a fight. He would likely panic while trying to avoid other horses in the charge. You could get your ass trampled, and I am not of a mind to see that happen".

"I'm not afraid," stated Nate with determination in his voice.

Ussher told him straight up, "I understand, but you're not

ready yet. There is no doubting your bravery, I see that and I respect it, but I'm going to tell you again, you are not ready. Damn you boy, do not mess with me over this. If you go out, then you and I will have a problem. You follow me?"

Ussher tried to make the point most experienced fighters understand. Individual bravery is celebrated only when luck favors the foolhardy and not too many fighters get hurt. They also know that bravery without good reason is grossly overrated. If there is no strategic value or rescue incentive to take the risk, those acting on their own usually place everyone around them in danger.

An impulsive fighter rarely takes into account the wider picture of the battle. Anyone who decides it is time to prove his manhood is likely to attract the attention of the enemy and draw concentrated gunfire in his direction. When this happens, his fellow fighters are likely to respond and come to his side. Their motivation may be momentary inspiration or desire to protect the reckless fighter. Either way, the actions of the one attempting bravery usually brings as much risk to his comrades as it does to himself.

Nate refused to back down, "And I'm telling you again, I am not afraid."

Ussher stood up, grabbed Nate by the arm, and pulled him to a quiet area.

"Boy, for someone with a smart head on his shoulders, you can sure act stupid at times. Don't you remember Jimmy, our Jimmy? Have you forgotten what happened and what he looked like? What do I have to do to make you realize that the conflict here has a particular kind of deadly? Everyone out here has gone crazy with killing."

Nate yelled back, "Jimmy is the reason I want to fight. I

miss him. It's not fair that those bastards took him the way they did. I want them to die. I want to be the one to kill them. I think about it all the time and I want to go out there and do it myself. You can't stop me. No one can stop me."

Nate's agitation and anger fed his determination and defiance. Ussher ordered, "First thing in the morning, go get some firewood and bring enough for two days. When you get back, start up a good fire, and make me some coffee. I've security watch all night, so I'll be looking for something warm when I come back in. You understand me, boy?"

Although angry, Nate gave an affirmative nod. Ussher hoped the passing of time and exertion from the work would help to level out Nate's emotions so he might settle down and maybe listen to reason. There would be more discussion in the morning. Ussher pondered how much detail he should try to explain to Nate. He was probably too young to understand who these men actually were and what motivated them. Ussher made the decision to do his best and explain their situation to Nate in the clearest terms possible. He would start with an explanation of the two men in the most prominent leadership positions, Quantrill and Anderson. The way things shaped up, Anderson looked to be the one who might take over the decision making for the Missouri militiamen. Although Quantrill was more dangerous and deadly than any of the Kansas Jayhawker leaders, Anderson was far worse.

There was nothing in Quantrill's personality that would ever call his bravery into question. With a schoolteacher background, he was a planner and a plotter and liked everything laid out in logical order. He calculated the odds for success based on accumulated information about the Jayhawker's location, strength, and preparedness.

The one thing that bothered Ussher about Quantrill was his focus on stripping the dead of all their valuables. It also seemed that many of the militia targets were not strategic or military. He started to believe that Quantrill was more of an opportunist than a patriot. Where Ussher had no clear expectation of survival or future prospects, it looked like Quantrill undoubtedly had a plan for his future and was using his position to finance its implementation.

Anderson was a completely different leader. There was a good reason why everyone called him Bloody Bill.

"That son-of-a-bitch is fearless beyond belief," Ussher explained of Anderson one evening in his discussions with Nate. "The problem is that he will sacrifice as many of his own men as needed to keep proving that point. But when he and that crazy-ass-runt, Archie Clement get together, it's worse than Hell on Earth."

Ussher understood that leaders like Quantrill needed brave men, but he knew Anderson wasn't the right fit for any group of fighters because he was self-absorbed and mean. He exhibited both stamina and imagination with his battle tactics and could fight for hours. Conflict invigorated him. In spite of his selfish nature, he possessed the ability to inspire his followers because he was the first to attack the enemy. Anderson would be the focus of defensive fire from every rifle in the opposition and would continually come away virtually unscathed.

Many of his followers would not be as lucky as scores of rounds missed Anderson or grazed his ear or arm and then lodged into the chest or forehead of his comrades. He often came away from a fight with several holes in his clothing. He never seemed truly concerned about the danger and never showed emotion over the deaths and injuries to his companions. He handled their misfortune business-like, ordering the camp cooks to treat the injured and the stock handlers to bury the dead. After that, he never spoke of them again. Trouble was, Anderson had achieved almost legendary fighter status and Quantrill needed to prove he was Anderson's equal to maintain leadership.

With his thoughts arranged on how he would talk to Nate in the morning, Ussher left the camp to take up his security position for the evening. Several of the militiamen watched him walk through the perimeter and out into the night. A few of them mumbled the polite greeting of "Ussher" with a quick nod of the head.

Ussher did not respond, but no one was offended. They all knew that once he was headed out for the night, he was totally focused and would not be distracted by something as trivial as courtesy. After passing Ussher by five or six paces, one of the men took a quick look back. "Where'd he go?" he asked a companion. The other man looked back and then at his friend; they gave each other a quizzical smile and shook their heads in bewilderment. Ussher had been there one moment and gone the next. He stepped off the path and into the woods without a sound.

26

The Bear Trap

JACK MINGO WAS almost out of food. He had a rifle, powder, ten rounds of ammunition, a knife, and a good length of rope. He almost felt like his old-self as he made his decision to reenter the action. The circumstances appeared skewed in his favor since no one realized he was still alive. He needed a horse, food, and as much ammunition as he could obtain.

Mingo came up with a good plan. He slipped into the Missouri territory unnoticed with the mule he received from Aaron and Micah Russell. He tied the mule to a walnut tree using a long piece of rope. The markings in the surrounding area identified the nearby trail as well traveled. Mingo settled into an ambush location with good cover and quick access.

One hour later, two riders approached and spotted the mule. They stopped for a moment and looked around. They saw nothing suspicious, because they weren't supposed to see anything. This was a Jack Mingo trap, meaning no one ever sensed danger until it was too late. Mingo came into his crouch and prowl stance. He gave his head a sharp left and right stretch and then started a zigzag, cover-to-cover approach. He was about to find out if those prayers of salvation from Aaron Russell had the power to keep him safe as he sought the merciless elimination of these fools while they focused on his mule.

Mingo thought about the day that rifle shot cut the gash across his chest, and the man who left him for dead. These two riders would be good preparation for the sweet revenge he sought from the man he hated most.

Mingo's strategy was to get as close as possible to the riders. He planned to shoot the first one in the head. The sound would spook the horses as he ran toward the second rider. He hoped to drag the man off his horse to cut his throat. Once the action began, Mingo figured that the entire time of the assault would be less than 15 seconds. He liked pondering such details. It gave him confidence. It forced him to look at his actions as tasks requiring completion. Using this elapsed time concept allowed him to appraise the results of his actions. He could then evaluate the improvements he needed to make on subsequent missions. To be a successful wilderness fighter, you had to be dispassionate and resourceful when it came to killing the enemy.

Mingo drew near to his targets. While sighting in his rifle he spotted additional movement. A third mounted man advanced toward the two whom Mingo watched. His two targets saw the approaching rider at the same time as Mingo. He noticed that they did not make any defensive moves. He was close enough to see that the third rider was a young man with a slight build. It would be easy to describe the kid as skinny. There was something familiar about his appearance and Mingo tried to remember where he had seen him in the past.

What captured his attention most was the horse. It was young, lean, and muscular, appearing to be full of spirit and undoubtedly fast. That horse was familiar, but he was not able to connect the horse with that young rider.

Mingo evaluated his tactical situation. Killing one man is easy. Overcoming and killing two men is difficult but doable in the right situation. Surprising, overcoming, and killing three men, without incurring injury, did not favor the attacker unless he was so close that he was virtually in their midst. He spotted a rocky outcropping less than 20 feet from these men. The location would be perfect. Mingo could be there in less than a minute.

Joseph F. Dwyer

27

The Pain Inside Dreams

THE NIGHT WAS QUIET, and the lookout responsibilities uneventful. Ussher grew unexpectedly tired. The problem, as always, was that his mind began to churn out memories when he needed it most to be quiet. There wasn't much he could do about the problem. Whether his conscious mind wandered or his resting mind dreamt, he was likely to imagine or dream about the unthinkable. These times always challenged his sanity.

The dream might be so real that Ussher could actually see Darby's face. He was aware of her scent and could feel the texture of her hair. He was able to taste her lips and sense the intensity of her body. This night, although he struggled to stay awake, he uncharacteristically fell asleep. Although asleep, Ussher was aware he was dreaming. He knew the dream would draw him into a state of unbridled happiness and, if he did not force himself to awaken now, eventual consciousness would make him angry, bitter and vengeful. Ussher's mind inexorably drifted toward Darby's memory, and he knew he would regret the morning.

The combination of passion and pain from loss became compelling and then turned irresistible. Having a moment with his Darby, even if her presence was only an aberration, was just too powerful of an emotion to oppose. As Ussher's fatigue overtook him, Darby's personage gradually materialized into form and accessibility next to him. Once again, her presence became available for as long as the dream might last. Yes, there would be acrimony when he awoke, but he would deal with the inevitable bitterness later. The dream was simply too compelling. Resistance was futile. Ussher relaxed and allowed his mind to drift back to their farm. Softly, as his dream commenced, Darby touched his arm as her vestige appeared at his side.

* * * *

Ussher and Darby cherished their two and a half years together working their land and making it produce. The blood and blisters of hard work blessed and strengthened their relationship. Ussher often stood motionless while gazing at his beautiful wife. The sweat and the dirt never detracted from her charm and appeal. He constantly found himself in a state of love, longing and bewilderment. He was astonished that such a perfect woman had settled for the likes of him. Just the sight of her made him smile. Watching her perform the simplest chores captivated him like a love-struck schoolboy.

Darby frequently noticed him gawking. She enjoyed glancing over her shoulder in his direction. She developed that move until it was elevated to an art form. Darby would turn the long line of her neck and flash those mischievous eyes in his direction. Ussher would be lightening-struck, looking like a youngster caught sampling the frosting from a cake. Darby would then turn fully around and stand straight up, allowing him the full view of her feminine form. She would place both hands on her hips, give him an amused, rebuking smile, and say, "Boy! I ain't about to do all this work by myself. There's lots to get done and you need to get yourself going. You hear me?"

Ussher loved it when Darby emphasized her scolding with

that country-girl drawl. The exaggerated rural accent contradicted her exceptional intelligence. She figured out most problems with ease, and her intuition about people she knew or recently met was far beyond her years. Her family made sure that she received a solid education. They left her with a fine collection of books, each one of which she reread until they were dog-eared. She never hid her education, but neither did she use it to appear better than other folks they knew.

Regardless of her state of exhaustion, Darby bathed almost every evening before retiring to their bed. Just before sunset, she would bring two pails of water up from the artesian spring. She liked carrying the water herself. She knew Ussher would be watching her. He loved the fact that she was both beautiful and strong. The stress of this exertion revived her after a hard day. She poured the water into a large basin, which sat near the foot of their bed. As the water settled, she unfolded a washcloth and dabbed errant droplets from the tabletop. The ritual invigorated her, along with the anticipation of Ussher's coupling embrace.

When ready, Darby would approach Ussher, getting his attention with a simple "hey." She would stand very close to him and brush back an unruly strand of her black hair. As she lightly caressed the side of his face, she would say, "I'm going for my bath now, you better come along, in case I need some help."

She expressed the whole verse with an instructional tone but it always revealed itself for the compelling invitation it was. Darby would arch that left eyebrow and pivot on her heel. There would be a quick glance over her shoulder as she flashed those dark eyes and started walking away. Her pace was fast enough to compel him to follow but slow enough to allow a longing look at the lazy swing of her slender hips. Whether watching her from his chair or sitting on the ground by the spring, Ussher found Darby's grace and sensuality to be extraordinary. She would step out of her homespun and dress, as smoothly as if it were silk, and stand bare-assed naked in front of him. She assessed the wear-and-tear her dress had suffered from the day's labor and fussed over pulls in the stitching or spots where the threadbare was becoming thinner. Darby enjoyed Ussher's appreciative gaze. While conducting the appraisal of her clothing, she turned one way and then the other, allowing him to candidly appraise and appreciate every angle of her form.

On the warmest summer evenings, she often immersed her body into the spring itself. The chilled artesian current was a sublime contrast to the summer heat. The cool ripples caused her to elicit a low feminine groan of appreciation. When she looked Ussher's way, she laughed playfully and tossed a scoop of water in his direction. As Ussher felt the refreshing drop cascade around him, knew he was the luckiest man alive.

While bathing, Darby might touch a location on her body with the circling motion of her finger to draw Ussher's attention to that area. She knew, full well, the intense sensuous response she could evoke through the simplest of actions.

She might remark, "I just can't imagine how this spot could get so dirty." Then Darby would exhale a little, shrug her perfect shoulders, flash an impish smile and ask, "Now, where were we?"

Ussher's breathing would go shallow as Darby teased him. She liked passing the washcloth around and over her breasts, across her stomach and down inside her thighs. Here she would hesitate and make solid, commanding eye contact before continuing. Some nights, she lingered with that washcloth between her legs, caressing back and forth for a minute or more.

"Do you think this part needs a little more attention?" She would inquire. Darby answered her own question by continuing the washing process, slowly and deliberately. Ussher became transfixed as granite. Finally, she would exhale satisfaction, smile and say, "There, that's better."

After her bath, Darby only used the washcloth as she caressed away the droplets lingering on her skin. By the time she finished brushing her hair, the moisture from her bath evaporated, leaving just a thin sheen of her own perspiration. Darby's skin was at first cool to the caress but quickly warmed in carnal response to Ussher's experienced hands.

Darby also enjoyed sensually focusing on Ussher. Often, after she refreshed the washcloth, she assumed a take-charge intonation, "Now, Mr. Ussher, you need to remove that shirt."

As he responded to her bidding, she occasionally mocked impatience by rolling her eyes and pushing her hip to one side. She made certain he knew that she was appraising his body and, grudgingly, giving her approval. Darby began Ussher's bath with his hands and arms. From there, she moved across his chest and down to his belly. She sometimes pushed him back, forcing him to sit on a chair as she washed his neck and face. At this point, she might stand over him, tilt his chin back up, and bring her lips down to his, finishing with a long hard kiss. She would stand close, drawing his face into her cleavage while she washed his back. Darby's scent and softness, along with her love and commitment, propelled Ussher into a rarified state of unbridled happiness.

Moving on, Darby would instruct, "Let's get these old pants off," By this time, Ussher would be completely at her mercy and in her charge. At night and occasionally early morning, he was also hers in the flesh. She wanted it that way. It aroused her to know that she was arousing him. The small bruises and scratches from the farm work became highlighted beauty marks for him to kiss tenderly with acknowledgement and appreciation. Darby's hips would rise and fall slightly as Ussher moved from one small scrape to the next. Darby liked to run her hands through his hair. She enjoyed grabbing two handfuls while guiding his lips to other parts of her body whether they indicated a scratch or not. Her body radiated. Ussher was always cooperative and enthusiastic. Darby was appreciative and reciprocal. This was their world. It was beautiful, seductive, and exclusive.

Darby was entirely comfortable and relaxed with Ussher, whom she trusted totally and claimed in word and deed as her own. They shared every thought, whispered every concern, and celebrated even the smallest success. He was also hers in mind, spirit, and confidentiality. He was her best friend, and she was his. Their bond was absolute and unbreakable. They bantered, they laughed, they moaned, and they surrendered totally to each other. Both Darby and Ussher shared their intimacy to a perfection that only they could ever comprehend.

28
Consciousness and Damnation

WHEN USSHER AWAKENED, he reached out into empty air, grasping toward a memory now materially tangible as smoke. His reality was almost unbearable. Instead of finding himself in the warmth of his home, a hearth, and his loving wife, he found himself in a small, cold, and camouflaged sentry outlook. He had returned to the realism of bitterness and retribution. The ache in his heart for his lost love magnified ten-fold and the scar from his leg wound pulled and throbbed.

God in heaven, how he missed his Darby. Goddamn, how he hated Vince Harris. The intensity of the hate for Vince Harris had grown and mutated to the point where it equaled his love for Darby. The equilibrium of that fact was an appalling and inescapable certainty. Ussher could no longer think of Darby without thinking of Vince. The injustice of the situation was an oppressive tyranny on his existence. Vince Harris had to die. He was a malignancy needing to be excised. Once gone, Ussher would never think of him again.

Ussher shook himself back to consciousness from the daydream. He realized he was squeezing his fist so hard that his fingernails were digging into his palms.

"Damn," he whispered, "It's been more than a year. I need to get this over."

Ussher's pain had been so great that he had even thought about putting the Henry in his mouth, pulling the trigger, and ending it all. If he did that, he might be with Darby in heaven in a few short moments. If there was a heaven, he was confident that Darby was there and waiting for him.

"Enough of this shit," Ussher snapped aloud to no one in particular. "Get yourself together. There's work to do, important work. Get it done!"

When Ussher finally returned to camp, Nate was not there. At first, he wasn't overly concerned because he saw Nate's horse tied as usual. Then he realized that Jimmy's horse, Bolt, was also missing.

Ussher stopped one of the militiamen, closest to the horses. "Where's Nate?"

The man answered him directly, "Away scouting. He's been out all night".

Ussher became visibly distraught. "What son-of-a-bitch was stupid enough to send a boy to do scouting?"

The man replied, "I ain't got a comment on stupidity, but the one who sent him out was Hawkins."

Ussher now remembered the evening that he saw Hawkins and Clement talking. He guessed that the decision to use Nate as a scout had something to do with that conversation. Ussher figured the decision had more to do with payback against him than the need for gathering information on the Jayhawkers.

Suddenly, the energy from a disturbance rippled through the Missouri camp. Most of the men looked in the same direction. Several looked at each other with an apprehensive expectation of bad news, as a frenzied, riderless horse stampeded back into camp.

29

Poor Lonely Rich Boy

VINCE HARRIS WAS experiencing a miserable day, a continuation in a series of miserable days, since murdering Darby Ussher. For over a year, he had remained a virtual prisoner on his father's property, an enterprise overrun with stinking, shitting, boring cattle. If it were not for regular provision deliveries, brought from St. Louis, his existence would be unbearable.

Included in the shipments were magazines and catalogs, many with nude female photographs. The photographs depicted young women performing basic everyday tasks, like caring for a garden, sweeping the kitchen, or watering flowers. They were tasks identified as obedient and submissive. For Vince, obedient and submissive were positive attributes. He liked his women subservient and compliant for starters.

For months now, Vince's existence had become solitary and coarse. He was continuously reminded of being the target of a worthless Bushwhacker pig named Ussher. His father made him sit in on security meetings with Tyler. Vince had to listen to Tyler report on the ongoing ambush killings of Harris riders. He heard that Ussher posed each of these dead men with their arms crossed over their chests. Apparently, this was his signature and it was supposed to inspire fear, dread, or some other sorry-ass emotion.

Vince was not afraid. The fact that some farmer's son was stupid enough to get himself killed did not mean it was going to happen to him. The way he looked at it, Vince remembered shooting Ussher and watching him run to his tiny, worthless cabin. He recalled, with a half-smile, how Ussher was in extreme pain from the leg wound, and his woman was frantic with worry, probably thinking Ussher might bleed to death. That had been a perfect scene for Vince. Too bad, it ended so differently from its initial plan.

Now he was stuck listening to security reports based on the death of men for whom he cared nothing. Additionally, he hated Tyler. He was a kiss-ass. Anyone could see that. Tyler wanted to be someone of importance. He was always hustling some new safety measures that required more funding to implement and from which he was probably skimming a few extra dollars.

Vince could not imagine someone like Tyler being on par with an individual like himself. At the same time, he realized Tyler served a purpose. One day, he actually had the revelation that Tyler was to his father as Andy Hester had once been to him.

Vince finally realized how helpful Andy had always been to him and had never comprehended the importance of his contributions until now in this dreary lonely time. More than a year had passed since his father and Captain Metzger made Andy a permanent resident of The Meadow.

When Andy ran, the senior Harris looked upon that action as disloyalty. Disloyalty was the equivalent of treachery and that was intolerable. It required a decisive response. That response would be a useful example from which others could learn. The lesson had worked well. Anyone who left the Harris compound after Andy's demise made sure that he did so with the knowledge and permission of Captain Metzger.

Nonetheless, Vince sure missed Andy. He regretted his hasty words that convinced Andy to attempt escape. Vince rationalized that he never intended to do real harm to Andy once he returned to the Harris ranch. Maybe, he would have had him whipped but that wouldn't have been too harsh. It would have been ironic for Andy to catch a beating after all the times he assisted Vince in whipping animals and men. Vince wondered if he would have been able to stop punishing Andy once he started. In all the years he indulged in that activity, he could not remember ever stopping until his victim was dead.

He didn't realize his mind had wandered so far off until the senior Harris yelled at him.

"Vincent, you need to pay attention to Mr. Tyler. There is a message here. Do you understand what is happening here? Look at me."

Vince returned to reality and looked at his father.

Harris repeated, "Do you understand the message Tyler is conveying with these reports? Your life is on the line. Since you and that ass bugger, Hester, tried to have your fun with Ussher's wife, 22 of my men have been shot, and 16 of those have died. That Bushwhacker animal is a killing machine, and he's doing his best to figure out a way to come after you. Question is…do you give a goddamn?"

Vince did care, but not just at this moment. He left the meeting with his father and Tyler and retreated to the barn to gaze at the magazine pictures. He used his imagination to recall those times when he and Andy Hester plied their trade with unappreciative local girls. They were weak and common. They always left him wanting more.

The Ussher woman should have been the answer. That experience was supposed to have raised the level of his expertise and enjoyment. Of course, Vince never viewed Darby's death as a murder. In his opinion, it was her own fault, the result of her refusal to cooperate with his needs. The fact that he had always intended to kill her was irrelevant in his perception.

* * * *

In the ensuing months, everyone in the area knew about what happened at the Ussher Homestead. Lewis Randall made certain of that fact. He and Emily had lived in the region their entire lives and enjoyed many friendships. Ussher also lived there since childhood, although not as friendly as Randall, he was well known and respected. The lonely homestead became somewhat of a shrine, symbolizing victims of tyranny and an emblem of bravery because of the way Darby sacrificed for her husband. Even if the roads traveled were not in the immediate area, farmers would stop, point over a hilltop and say, "Over yonder is the Ussher place. That's where it all happened."

Randall's forensic interpretation of Vince's predatory attack and Darby's heroic defense became legend. The fact that so few people had seen Vince since that day reinforced the validity of Randall's story.

Every farmer in the area was aware Ussher had placed his own price on Vince's head. The only legitimate currency for that payment was blood. The whole countryside heard about the way Harris' riders were being ambushed. This was an obvious challenge and affront to the power of Talbot Harris. The bounty on Ussher doubled to $1,000. In rural Missouri, this was a remarkable sum for average folks. The big man was convinced this increased bounty would bring him Ussher's scalp because it was enough incentive to make your best friend turn against you.

30

The Tables Begin to Turn

USSHER CAUGHT up to Vaughn as both men ran toward the crowd who huddled around the returning horse.

"Oh brother," Vaughn remarked," this situation sure don't look good."

Everyone could see that blood covered the entire saddle and the horse was excited, almost to the point of panic.

"Move out of my way," Vaughn ordered. "Unless you men

can help me figure out this situation, clear out and let me work".

He and Ussher pushed their way through and on toward the horse. In that moment, all Ussher saw was the blood. It was everywhere, on the saddle, the saddlebags, and the horse itself. He also saw what appeared to be brain matter. Death had come from a headshot, probably a rifle. It was a gruesome sight, but the end had doubtless been quick for the victim. It didn't much matter to this rider, dead was dead.

Within a minute, Ussher understood part of the circumstance. He had seen this horse many times before. He knew his facts without doubt. This horse was not the one Nate would have been riding. This was not Bolt. It was not "our Jimmy's" horse. There was still no accounting for Nate's whereabouts, but right now, there was hope he was still alive.

Ussher became temporarily overwhelmed with conflicting emotions of relief and anger. He turned and walked decisively through the center of the camp. His fury grew with each step and soon he was storming from one location to another looking for Hawkins. A minute later, he found him by a wagon in the company of none other than Archie Clement.

Both men saw Ussher approaching. Each man read his body language and became defensive. Hawkins started to backpedal when he realized that Ussher's eyes locked directly onto him. Clement stepped back, not thinking he was in immediate danger. His impression changed once he saw Ussher's piercing glance as he swept by toward Hawkins. Archie un-holstered his gun and held it to his side in his right hand. He remembered his previous run in with Ussher and determined he was going to be ready for trouble if necessary.

As Ussher advanced toward Hawkins, he became more menacing. Hawkins held up both arms, palms extended outward.

"Hold on now Ussher, hold on. No reason to get your blood up."

By this time, Vaughn realized there was a problem and ran toward the men followed by six others from the militia.

Hawkins was not sure what he should do. In an instant, he calculated his odds of fighting against Ussher and quickly deduced he was outmatched. He was unable to backpedal faster than the speed of Ussher's advance. When Ussher was almost on top of him, panic convinced Hawkins to turn and attempt to run away. Before he could take his third step, Ussher reached out and grabbed him by the hair. He jerked Hawkins backwards, fast and hard. As Hawkins fell back, Ussher brought his left knee up hard in between Hawkins' shoulder blades. The blow rippled pain waves through his spine in both directions. He was thrown forward and over onto his stomach, knocking the wind out of him.

Hawkins knew Ussher and he realized his situation had turned desperate. He struggled to get to his feet. A kick from Ussher's right foot sent him reeling to the left and tumbling over one and a half times. Before his momentum stopped, Ussher was on him once again. The initial blow from Ussher's knee left Hawkins' head throbbing and his lower back numb.

Hawkins was experiencing the total panic a condemned man might feel the moment an executioner pulls the drop lever on a gallows. Strangely, he noticed the look on Ussher's face no longer appeared to be angry. The look became one of simple determination. There was a job to do. The job was to beat the shit out of Hawkins for the offense of putting Nate's life at risk. At this point, Hawkins figured Ussher intended to do that job thoroughly.

He knew Ussher's opinion toward him would be; if he dies, then he dies. Death would be a consequence of the beating in the same way that the beating was a consequence for Hawkins putting Nate in danger. Hawkins did the only thing he could do under the duress. He screamed loudly, "It was all Archie's idea."

Hawkins stayed on the ground and pulled his body together as tightly as possible to protect himself from Ussher's onslaught.

At that moment, Ussher finally heard the yells of Vaughn to stop the fight. Two of the militiamen grabbed each of Ussher's arms. Ussher instantly broke free and again pursued Hawkins with renewed ferocity.

It was clear to Ussher that their previous confrontation had not educated Hawkins sufficiently. He did not intend to see that mistake repeated. A third militiaman joined the struggle by tackling Ussher at the knees. The first two fell back on top of him. The combined strength of the three men forced Ussher to submit for the moment. As they lay on top of him, the men could feel the intensity in his muscles, accompanied by his labored breathing. All three men did their best to sound as friendly as such a situation allowed. They assured Ussher that they meant no harm. They urged him to give them a promise that the fight was now over. As soon as they had his word, they would be happy to release him and shake his hand.

While the men restrained Ussher, Vaughn got Hawkins to his feet. He could see that Hawkins was not seriously injured.

"Get your ass clear of this camp for a couple of days," he instructed.

Hawkins hesitated, looking around for his lost hat.

Vaughn said to him, "If you're not gone in five seconds, I'll let those boys turn Ussher loose and this time I will help him finish you."

As Hawkins jogged off, Vaughn noted that he carried a decided limp. It would require a few days to allow Ussher time to cool down. Hawkins needed this same time to heal his bruised spine and ribs. Vaughn hoped, in the meantime, young Nate would return safely to camp and the incident would have no further consequence.

The situation seemed downright unfair to Hawkins. It had been Clement's idea to send Nate out on the scouting assignment. Archie thought it would be a damn cunning scheme as a way to get back at Ussher. Everyone knew he liked that worthless kid and was looking after him. It seemed like a perfect plan to Hawkins and Clement, as they drank and schemed the night before. Nate wanted his chance to avenge his friend Jimmy and to show himself to be capable and trustworthy. He mistakenly shared his anger over Ussher's decision to keep him out of the fighting. Hawkins and Clement feigned understanding and friendship.

It was then that Hawkins dangled an irresistible challenge in front of Nate. He told him that he could accomplish two things by completing a successful scouting mission. The first was that he could gather information that might account for a shitload of dead Jayhawkers. The second was that he would be seen as having capabilities greater than Jimmy, who was two years his senior. Nate accepted the challenge and assignment with courage and enthusiasm. Now he was missing and Hawkins had paid a heavy price for that fact.

"Well, ain't you a sight?" Archie Clement commented as Hawkins worked his way past to exit the camp.

"I heard what you said back there to Ussher and Vaughn. It looks to me that you ain't much more than a sorry little cunt. I'd say that me and you ain't best of friends anymore."

Hawkins hesitated because Clement's comment pissed him

off. As he did this, Archie squared up to face him, still holding his revolver. Hawkins decided that he had experienced enough rotten luck for one day and walked away. He would figure out how to deal with Archie Clement another day.

31
The Return of Jack Mingo

As Nate moved down the trail through the Missouri timberland, he saw two riders about 250 yards out. He brought Bolt to a halt and rubbed his neck to keep him calm. He talked to the horse in a low voice while he focused on the riders. Nate recognized them as members of his militia group but approached slowly, not wanting to startle anyone and tempt a rifle shot in his direction.

Ussher taught Nate the difference between using stealth and being quiet. When you are being quiet, you proceed in an easy manner where all the residents of the local environment can easily decipher your non-hostile intent. It is a natural read for both wildlife and people.

When the approach uses stealth, even creatures who recognize they are not the hunted observe the activity carefully. They notice the tension in the stalker's shoulders and see his eyesight focused downrange. They take note that every step is purposeful. The forest population uses the occasion to watch the way the predator is stalking. They learn, and those with the most intelligence, remember. Nature considers the creatures with cognition and recollection to be breeders. Animals that do not take time to watch the drama or learn from the experience often suffer an early demise. Nature deems this second group to be prey. Ussher told Nate these same principles apply to people.

Although animals do not always sound an alarm, they inevitably stop making natural sounds. Squirrels stop running, birds stop singing, and raccoons stop scavenging. They become curious about the focus of the hunter. All are interested in seeing how the drama will begin and end. The very absence of sound from inactivity becomes a warning signal to those trained to listen.

Therefore, the quiet approach was Nate's choice. It was smooth and deliberate. The critters barely took notice and busily continued with their daily routines. As a result, the sounds of forest activity masked Nate's arrival until he was nearly in earshot of the riders and clearly visible. The two militiamen looked his way and immediately recognized him. They waved and signaled for him to continue his approach. Nate recognized the first man as Big John Harper. The second man was familiar, but Nate did not know his name. Big John was his usual friendly self. He was one of the few that knew Nate's name and actually used it when responding to a hello or a good morning whenever they passed one another.

Mingo saw the fellowship between the three riders. He was not quite able to hear their words, but he could hear the friendly inflection of their voices. He knew that this activity would work to his advantage as he continued to move closer. People, who have not seen each other, even for a few hours, have new things to talk about. Talking is an all-encompassing activity. When interacting face-to-face, you are not looking around for signs of danger. When you talk to someone, you are not listening to the environment. Mingo's anticipation for success increased. When he first saw the third rider approaching, he was apprehensive. Once he realized that this rider was a distraction, his confidence fed his aggression and he was ready to act.

Nate and his two Missouri comrades remain mounted. The small talk exchanged was sincere and genial. The men were surprised to see a boy scouting the area and said as much to Nate. He related the information that Hawkins and Clement gave him the assignment. The riders exchanged a look of derision when they heard those names. The look escaped Nate's detection as he continued to speak excitedly about his mission.

An exception to this amiable moment was that Bolt began to act highly agitated. Horses have an acute sense of smell. It helps them identify the presence of predators as well as using it as a socializing mechanism between themselves and other horses. One of the most impressive attributes is that a horse can actually memorize and recall the smells of other animals and humans. It turned out that Jack Mingo had a distinctive scent, and Bolt's sharp nose and excellent memory triggered recollections, which caused him to be skittish.

32
Planning the Big Ride

AFTER USSHER SETTLED down, Vaughn shook his hand to make sure their relationship was still intact. Ussher liked Vaughn. He understood that Vaughn's motivation to stop infighting originated in his responsibility for keeping order and discipline amongst all the men, himself included. Vaughn invited Ussher to his campsite. He had news to share and wanted Ussher's counsel.

Vaughn informed him a new militia plan, cobbled together all too quickly in his opinion. There had been some discussions on the idea three months ago, but Vaughn had always considered the scheme more bravado than reality because of its proposed magnitude. Such a raid would become the largest and most deadly action the militia ever sanctioned. Now, its implementation was becoming a certainty and its execution was accelerating. This was a result of a tragic incident involving the family of Bloody Bill Anderson.

Vaughn told Ussher, "Do your best to stay away from Anderson. I've never seen him crazier than he is right now. Turns out, they placed his sisters in some dilapidated jail over in Kansas City. The only crime they committed was being related to Bill Anderson. We think the 'Hawkers were going to use them as bait, or maybe hostages, to trade for prisoners our side is holding."

Ussher uncharacteristically interrupted, "Holy Jesus, you're talking about them in the past tense. Please tell me that those Kansas assholes were not stupid enough to kill Anderson's sisters."

Ussher knew Anderson and Quantrill were competing for leadership. He also knew that on any particular day, Anderson could devolve rapidly, from amiable to fanatical. Ussher and Vaughn shared the mutual observation that Anderson had been searching for a reason to escalate the violence. Killing by itself was just no longer good enough for him. The obvious question was, what more can you do to someone than kill him? Neither of them knew that answer, but both men knew Anderson would try to discover a way to elevate the violence.

Vaughn exhaled and reported, "Anderson's baby-sister, Josie, is dead, killed. She was only fourteen. General Tom fucking Ewing ordered friends and family of Missouri patriots arrested for any reason and Jim Lane's Jayhawkers carried out the instruction. It looks like they are trying to remove all sources of support from our people. If they are unable to kill enough of us with bullets, they will see if starvation will work just as well. I think this is just the beginning."

Ussher agreed. The militia's most direct point of weakness was their inability to protect family members living on homesteads.

Vaughn continued, "Anderson's other sister, Mary, was hurt real bad. We don't know for sure but have heard she has a broken leg or hip. The 'Hawkers were holding them, and some other women, in a piece-of-shit building. It just has to be the work of Jim Lane, and maybe Doc Jennison. Both those sons-of-bitches use Lawrence City to rest up and re-provision all the time."

Ussher asked, "Who in Hell told them they had the right to arrest women?"

"Like I said, it has to be General Ewing," Vaughn answered. He became more rhetorical as his anger grew.

"What kind of coward does such a thing? Ewing calls himself a fucking general and then acts as if he's God Almighty. He issued an Arrest Order to all the local army commanders as well as Lane and Jennison's raider companies. You give some of these assholes a piece of paper and they think they can do anything they want. Vaughn's voice became louder and angrier. He paced around the fire, gesturing with his arms, as Archie Clement walked into their campsite.

"Looks like you boys are having yourselves quite a conversation," Archie commented.

"Make your point Archie," said Ussher tersely.

Archie gave Ussher a long look.

"Quantrill wants all of you important types over to his campsite right quick. There's serious business coming our way."

Ussher looked toward Vaughn. "You go," he said. "I'm going out after Nate. There might be half a chance that he's still alive."

Clement squared up with Ussher. "Ussher," said Clement, "Quantrill wants you at this meeting. More importantly, Anderson wants you there. That's why he sent me with the message, you understand?"

Vaughn said, "I could use you at this meeting myself."

Ussher looked hard at Clement. Archie's pale eyes did not blink and that weasel smile showed ever so slightly. Ussher thought back to that time at the old homestead when he affixed his left hand securely around Archie's throat. That would be a sweet moment to repeat right now. His left hand flexed involuntarily. Then he heard Vaughn speaking again.

"Ussher, I'd appreciate it if you joined me at this meeting. I could use your support and advice."

Ussher nodded his affirmation.

As he left their campsite, Archie yelled out enthusiastically, "Yes sir, we gonna' have us some fun with those 'Hawkers soon enough."

Joseph F. Dwyer

33
Mingo and Nate

BACK ON THE TRAIL, Bolt continued to act agitated. He did not relate Mingo's scent to Jack Mingo himself but to a previous event, when he and Jimmy had been out riding. They were standing in the woods at the edge of a clearing, watching some men around a campfire. Bolt first picked up this scent, when a man sprung from the bushes and struck Jimmy with a rifle butt. Jimmy's head snapped to one side and his twisting body followed as he fell to the ground. Bolt was frightened but did not run. Jimmy rolled over and attempted to stand up. The man hit Jimmy again and he fell down even harder. Then the attacker tied Jimmy's hands and took him away.

Now, as Bolt once again detected the scent, his excellent recall connected it to the previous dangerous experience. Unfortunately, for Mingo, the price to obtain the ideal location for his ambush placed him upwind from the riders. That would rarely be a problem since the human sense of smell is not exceptional and these farmers were not good woodsmen. Once Bolt identified the direction from which the scent originated, he kept nodding his head and dancing his hooves to indicate his anxiety. The other horses picked-up on Bolt's distress signals and began looking for the cause. The young mount maneuvered Nate and himself so that the other riders and horses were between them and the scent.

Mingo observed all of this activity. He did not immediately relate himself to the problem but he identified the fact that the horses were agitated. Their constant movement would make his first shot difficult. He un-holstered and readied both of his revolvers. He cocked and sighted his Enfield rifle on the back of the head of the closest rider. The first shot had to be accurate and lethal. The rifle's report would startle the other two riders and their horses. After that, he would use the revolvers to fire five shots at each of the riders. That might be enough to knock them off their horses. Once on the ground, he could finish each man with his knife.

* * * *

Mingo touched the heel of his knife. He received the weapon from his Grandfather more than 20 years past. Most elders of his people would never have honored a half-breed with such an exclusive gift but Mingo was unique. He was brave, fearless and most importantly, intelligent. Grandfather recognized and admired these qualities. Only the most deserving of the young men could receive a gift carrying such esteem.

The unique design, crafted from ten inches of Spanish steel, exhibited a sword-like hilt. The tip was honed, top and bottom, with an upswing curve. The base of the blade, nearest the handle, revealed deep serrations. Carved buffalo bone replaced the original handle. For comfort and stability, its finger grips were wrapped with strong rawhide strips and stone-rubbed to a smooth hand-fit. It was the perfect knife to cut, scrape, stab, and scalp.

The most notable attribute about this knife was its history. Originally, it belonged to Grandfather's father. The blade took part in many great hunts. In battle, it defeated all fighters who dared stand against it, including numerous scouts, considered the bravest of warriors. The most honored victory was the death of a war chief from the hated Lakota Sioux tribe. Mingo's father died, still clinching the knife in his fist. Next to him lay a 450-pound black bear, dead from stab wounds inflicted after their chance encounter.

The connection of the knife to Mingo's father meant nothing to the young men of the Pawnee. This was a warrior's weapon of extraordinary value and preeminence. His father was full blood and worthy. Mingo was a half-breed, suckled from an inferior, hostage, white mother, so he was undeserving of such an honor. Mingo's half-brothers and cousins first voiced their anger and disapproval of Grandfather's judgment. Then other warriors joined them in repudiating the decision. They were all insolent, questioning Grandfather's sanity and challenging Mingo's merit.

Grandfather looked toward Mingo and then at the angry eyes of the defiant young men. He considered the repercussions of his choice but recognized that second-guessing was ultimately unproductive. Mingo was his selection. The decision was a good one and he would stay with it. In front of everyone, he ceremoniously handed the knife to Mingo. The effect of the presentation was electric and fury surged through the assembly.

As Mingo's fingers closed around the handle, he felt the power of the blade surge through his arm and into the center of his heart. Pride and appreciation, from this most singular honor, validated his manhood. The weapon instantly became an inseparable part of him and he vowed to add to its legend.

Grandfather exhaled an extended breath and ceded the moment unto destiny. Fate would be the ultimate judge in this process and Grandfather trusted Fate as much as he trusted Mingo. As he turned to leave, he instructed the warriors, "Let any man who decides I am mistaken and believes he is more worthy to carry the blade, simply take it away from Mingo."

By nightfall, the ground was soaked with the blood of two dissenting warriors. The first man suffered wounds to his body and pride, the second was dead. Each of the encounters required less than a minute to conclude, leaving Mingo the undisputed guardian of the knife. The remainder of the warriors reevaluated their opinion of Mingo's worthiness. Whatever the makeup of his heritage, his warrior instinct and his prowess as a fighter were undeniable. From that measure, he was a full-blooded Pawnee. As they carried the dead man away, many warriors acknowledged Mingo with a nod of their head. Others approached Grandfather to apologize and concede to his wisdom.

* * * *

Mingo's assumption was correct. Nate and the rider closest to him were startled when his first shot penetrated the skull of Big John Harper. Mingo's long convalescence had not diminished his marksmanship. He immediately pulled his revolvers and fired at the second man, scoring one hit. The rider stayed in the saddle for a short distance before falling. It was this horse, which eventually made its way back to the camp of the Missouri militia.

Blood and tissue struck Nate from Big John's wound. Bolt did not wait for directions. The instant the horse heard the rifle report; he spun around and streaked down the trail, carrying himself and Nate toward safety.

Nate heard another shot and a bullet whistled past his ear. He looked back to see Jack Mingo mounting Big John's horse to pursue after him. Dread worked its way through Nate's core.

His dread was distinctly different from fear. Fear is all

about retreat and salvation. For Nate, dread stemmed from the fact that he was not sure how to confront this man. He was not afraid of fighting and dying, but he dreaded the thought of dying poorly. The only gun he owned was Ussher's old single shot, Sharps rifle. He needed to put more distance between himself and his pursuer in order to get enough time to stop, dismount, and take proper aim.

Nate leaned forward, pressed his knees into the side of his horse and urged him ahead. The response was magnificent. It seemed as if the horse could read Nate's mind and sense the importance of his urging. His muscular body flattened out, and the strides seemed to double in length. The countryside blurred as they flew past.

At a point where the land turned flat and level, Nate ventured a backwards look toward Mingo and found there was nothing to see. As he thought about it, Nate realized that Big John's horse was old and broken down. It had been a draft animal before the war and its muscles were thick and bulky. Because he was tall and sleek, Bolt had always been a saddle horse. His muscles were long and lean. Nate allowed Bolt to run another mile and then brought him to a walk. There was no need to dismount and prepare for Mingo's approach. He was miles behind. Nate was safe. He rubbed Bolt's neck and praised him for a job well done.

Jack Mingo cursed that damn horse. He could not remember the last time he saw one that fast. That kid was not too bad a rider either. They disappeared down the trail so quickly that Mingo immediately gave up the pursuit. He returned to the site of the ambush. The first rider was dead. That was no surprise. The second rider was badly wounded but still alive. Mingo turned him over. He could see the man's eyes attempting to focus. It appeared he was going to try to speak, but Mingo was not interested in listening. His knife thrust was decisive and quick. The militiaman died as Grandfather's blade feasted on another man's life-blood.

Mingo recovered guns and ammunition, a canteen, hardtack and three dollars in silver coin from the dead men. Although one of the riders escaped, Mingo felt positive about this encounter. He had proved to himself restored as a fighter and ready to pursue the enemy he hated most. The time was getting closer. He could feel power surging through his body as he swiped the knife across the dead man's shirt to clean off the blood. Soon, he thought, very soon, he would settle this matter.

Down the trail, he heard additional riders. In seconds, Mingo, along with this modest pillage and new horse, blended into the surrounding forest. He thought for a moment about attempting another ambush. That thought disappeared when he heard one of the riders call out an alarm after he spotted the first dead Bushwhacker lying alongside the trail. Again, there were three riders, but this time they were fully alert to danger. For Jack Mingo, it was time to go.

34
Movement over the Countryside

TYLER WITH THREE other men returned to the Harris ranch to report and re-provision. The report would have to come first. As soon as Harris heard the notification shot from the ranch's perimeter patrols, he walked out on the porch to see who was coming. Otto Metzger joined him. Harris was immediately angry. Tyler had been out for a mere three days and did not appear to be returning with his Henry rifle. As the men approached the big house and brought their horses to a halt, they could read the displeasure on their boss' face.

"Mr. Tyler," said Harris, "You've got bigger balls than I gave you credit for having. You were ordered to stay out on the hunt until you brought me my rifle along with that son-of-a-bitch who's been using it."

Tyler turned to one of his men and said, "Tell the man what's going on, Davey."

Dave Tesson replaced Mingo as the lead scout for the Harris ranch. He was not Mingo's caliber, but he was capable nonetheless. He had a direct, businesslike demeanor. Almost immediately, Harris decided that he liked this man.

"Mr. Harris, we've got Bushwhacker movement all over the countryside. I've never seen anything like it. Something major has got to be comin'. Three times, we spotted large companies of riders. We were damn lucky to get back alive. Every group we ran into outnumbered us."

Tyler interjected, "We need to consolidate the herd and bring the perimeter patrols back in closer to the big house. We don't know what's going on, but with this many men involved, we have to assume this ranch may be a target."

Harris gave the story credibility. It was remarkable how you could read a man's sincerity, simply by the way he speaks and explains a situation.

"Let them come," Harris said defiantly. "We've got 50 men and enough food and ammunition to last two weeks. Besides, all I need to do is get one rider out with word that I need help, and I'll have another 200 within a day. These Bushwhackers had better think twice before they challenge me."

Standing along the inside edge of a front window, Vince Harris listened to the conversation. It was good to hear his father speaking so confidently because a new plan was taking shape in his perverse mind.

Vince received a revelation from the voice of the Enlightened One; the Demon is called by many names. From the message, he concluded that past failures were not the product of his own doing. It was a result of the inexperience and incompetence of people on whom he had depended. The Voice confided that if he tried the game once again, his desires would find satisfaction and his needs fulfilled. It also assured him that those requisites were valid and worthy, especially for a man of his status.

The bite mark on his face had healed and faded, but it remained a permanent reminder of an experience filled with disappointment. He often rubbed the scar between his cheek and chin with bitter contemplation. That farm bitch should have been more obliging; Andy should have been more capable. The Voice helped Vince understand that his situation was about to improve. All he needed to do was try one more time. He clenched his fist; I can do this thing. After all, I am Vince Harris.

* * * *

As Nate pulled up on Bolt to bring him to a walk, he guessed he was about ten miles away from the Bushwhacker camp. The sun was down, and in these deep woods, it would be dark in half an hour. He had water and hardtack, and Bolt could graze for his supper. Nate felt exhausted as the adrenaline from the day's action subsided. He left the trail and led Bolt through the countryside to hide his tracks. He found shelter under a rock outcropping and settled in without a fire to spend the night.

The moon was in its new phase, and enveloped Nate with total dark. At first, it seemed unsettling, then he took comfort in the fact his position appeared virtually invisible. Bolt was calm but alert. Nate noticed this slight contradiction in the horse's behavior. Things were not quite right. He tried to think about Ussher and guess what he would do on such a night. As his eyes adjusted to the dark, he became aware of campfires a short distance north. He smelled the smoke, which meant he was downwind. Nate could not identify these men, but he assumed he was safe enough to catch some sleep. The action of this day had been grueling, and he needed rest.

35
An Eye for an Eye

THE MEETING VAUGHN and Ussher attended was not the type where reasonable men exchange ideas. It was a rally intended to infuse focus, purpose, and commitment to those in attendance. Quantrill and Anderson addressed the group of men who held various leadership positions in the militia. Quantrill spoke first in his matter-of-fact fashion.

He informed them of the decision to conduct a major raid on Lawrence, Kansas. He said that it was time to strike greater fear into Yankee hearts. Up to this point, their operations had been defensive and reactive in nature. The 'Hawkers now chose to raise the ante by taking hostages, innocents in the view of the Missourians. A determined response, with a decisive objective, was now necessary.

Anderson interrupted; he stood up and walked around, looking into the face of every man present. "Those 'Hawker-pigs murdered my baby sister. She was only 14 years old. Don't talk to me about being determined and decisive. If you want focus, I'll give you focus. Let me make it clear to every one of you bastards. I want blood, buckets of blood. I want fires in that town that will make Hell look like a holiday. I want so much suffering that mothers will sacrifice their children rather than ever see my face again. Any man who doesn't back me is a limp-dick coward, and I will cut off his balls just before I rip off his scalp."

He glared at the men as he pivoted to make eye contact with each of them. He yelled at the top of his voice, "Do you assholes understand me? There will be no quarter. There will be no man left alive while I still have breath."

"Yeah," yelled Archie Clement as he jumped up and stood beside Anderson.

"We're all with you Bill. It's time for payback."

Ussher looked over at Clement, who appeared in total awe of Anderson. He seemed completely motivated with the idea of inflicting destruction and retribution upon the town of Lawrence and against its civilian population.

Quantrill sought to regain control of the meeting.

"I sent riders out two days ago. We've got militia groups coming in from all over the countryside. They all know what has happened. More important, they all owe Bill and me for past favors, so we are expecting a shit-load of firepower. In two days, we will hit Lawrence at sunrise. There will be a half-moon that night. That should be enough for us to navigate and still have cover until we ride over the top of Hogback Ridge. From that point, we will be riding at full-charge and should be on top of them in no more than a minute."

"What will we do about the Union soldiers? One of the men asked. "They're bivouacked all around the outskirts of the town."

Quantrill allowed one of his few smiles. "Word is that the Yankees don't put out any sentries after midnight. It looks like these Union boys are not the vigilant type. They think that Lawrence is too big a town for us to attack. The combination of the town's size and the military perimeter has given them all a false sense of security, which will work in our favor."

Anderson glared at the man who asked the question.

"Soldiers mean nothing. Cannons, guns, bayonets, bullets by the shit-load, mean nothing. We're going in, guns blazing, with Satan and me in the lead."

Archie Clement remarked, "I'll be right there with you and Satan."

Quantrill looked over at Anderson.

"Bill," he said flatly, "We're gonna' get this done right, but we're goin' to be smart at the same time."

Quantrill looked at the group, "Any questions?"

"Yeah," challenged Anderson, "Any questions, any comments?" He then added sarcastically, "Any objections?"

Vaughn looked at Ussher and saw that he definitely had all three, questions, comments, and objections. He made hard eye contact with Ussher and moved his head in a decisive, negative motion. Ussher understood Vaughn's meaning and its wisdom. Nonetheless, he stood up. Silence fell over the men, as everyone looked his way in anticipation.

Anderson virtually spun around to square up with Ussher. He appeared to be seething at the very thought of any man daring to challenge his plan. Archie Clement also looked Ussher's way. Ussher saw those pale eyes focus as his right hand dropped close to his holster. It did not matter. By standing, he had created this moment. Now, he would have to deal with its consequences.

Ussher said with genuine sincerity, "Bill, I am sorry about your sister. A girl so young and innocent should never die in that manner. I've experienced losing someone I loved and know what it's like to want retribution. We should do everything we can to reckon her loss, but we need to focus on the man responsible.

"Since we're sure that it was Jim Lane, let's go after him. We should be able to get a man or two into that camp unnoticed. I'll volunteer to be one of them. We'll find the son-of-a-bitch and cut his heart out. That will be justice and will send the right message. Going after a whole town means that women and kids are likely to get killed. That just ain't who we are. It will send the wrong message and cause a shit-storm of retaliation from the 'Hawkers."

Although Anderson said nothing, everyone saw anger building inside him as his face reddened.

Ussher continued, "I know how a man feels when only blood can pay for an injury or an insult." He looked around at the assembly. "I've known most of you my whole life. I agree with Quantrill. We have to be smart about this raid. There will be a big 'Hawker reaction. It will be decisive and violent because they will feel obliged to outdo anything that happens in Lawrence. They have already shown they're willing to go after our families, take hostages and wipe out our every source of support. Starvation can work just as well as bullets."

Anderson stood there quietly. The tension within the group was almost painful. Men shifted their weight slightly from one side to the other and carefully looked to their comrades for a reaction, all the while avoiding any eye contact with Anderson.

Finally, Anderson's voice rasped, "Ussher, are you with me or against me?"

Ussher replied, "Bill, I cannot be with you on this raid. It's a mistake. I know you're hurting over Josie's death, but even that can't justify putting the entire Cause at risk."

Anderson walked over and stood directly in front of Ussher. "Once we get back, if you're still in this camp, there will be trouble between us. You've been damn helpful over the past six months. For that reason alone, Archie here ain't removing your scalp at this very moment. But now it's personal, and I take personal right serious."

Anderson turned to Vaughn, "Ussher is your man. I see the two of you together all the time, so I hold you responsible for getting him away from this camp. When we get back, if he is still here, I'm coming after you as well."

Then he turned and pointed to Quantrill, "Don't say a fucking word." Quantrill obliged by remaining silent.

Anderson walked away but Clement loitered for a moment and sauntered past Ussher, keeping more than an arm's length between them. "Nice knowing you, Ussher," Archie said as he quickened his step to catch up with Anderson.

At that moment, a group of riders cleared the outpost guards and came into camp with a prisoner.

36
Nate's Last, Best Chance

NATE DID NOT HIDE as well as he perceived and he was more tired than he imagined. Once awake, he did not look around before he moved. Militia scouts, with two webbed-toed Coonhounds were closer than he realized. Before Nate knew what was happening, the dogs were running in his direction, issuing their baying bark.

Nate did not know these men, and he could not determine if they were friendly or enemy. The scouts shared the same dilemma with identifying Nate, but they were more direct handling the situation. They aimed their rifles and yelled for him to stand still. As the first one ran up to Nate, behind the dogs, he swung his rifle butt into Nate's head, just above his ear. Nate crumpled to the ground. After he regained consciousness, he found his hands tied behind his back and feet strapped securely to Bolt's saddle.

When the riders first entered the main camp area, Ussher gave them a casual glance then quickly took a second look. His attention instantly focused on the horse with the most energy. The long legs and the sleek appearance were as familiar to him as the back of Ussher's own hand. A heartbeat later, Ussher recognized their prisoner. He looked crumpled and injured but was clearly alive. Ussher's chest involuntarily heaved with a sigh of relief. For a moment, the release he felt totally immobilized him. He had been so involved with his anger toward Hawkins and the confrontation with Anderson that the receipt of good fortune was an almost unbearable emotional experience.

When Ussher saw it was Nate, he was relieved and elated. He ran up to him, knife in hand, and cut the restraints. He pulled the kid down from the horse and hugged him like the returning prodigal son. He gave a quick analysis of the bump on his head and the blood around his ear. He shot an intimidating look at each of the incoming scouts. Since Ussher's threatening looks could indeed be menacing, they immediately started to explain the circumstances of how they ran across Nate.

Ussher grudgingly retracted his malice. He understood, full well, the cautions that were necessary out on the trail. He grabbed Nate around the shoulder, with one hand, and Bolt's reins with the other and started to walk away. He stopped suddenly and turned around toward the militia scouts.

"Thanks for bringing my boy back safe," he said.

The scouts nodded acknowledgement.

When Ussher openly referred to him as "My Boy", Nate's spirits soared. The statement proved this man genuinely cared about him. The bond between them elevated to that of father and son. Likewise, Ussher fully grasped how important Nate had become to him. It made him more determined than ever to follow through with his plans

It had taken three and one-half weeks, but Ussher finally received a return letter from his brother. The news was good, and he thanked God for his brother's generous heart. Without waiting any longer, Ussher sat Nate down to tell him what lay ahead in his future.

* * * *

Jack Mingo observed the Missourians camp from behind

cover. He secured his horse a half-mile back and walked the rest of the way to reconnoiter the location. He actually observed Ussher and Nate speaking together. The distance was too great to make a positive identification, but there was something familiar about that man. What was it? Then, part of the picture began to focus for him as he spotted Bolt in the middle of a line of horses. He only saw his hindquarters, but that animal, with those long legs and sleek lines, would stand out in any group.

Mingo remembered the night over a campfire he saw a young Bushwhacker scout spying on his Jayhawker camp. Mingo had been able to get away from the campfire and around behind the scout. He surprised the young man and subdued him with a clubbing from his rifle butt. That horse had been there at that time, and now he was here with this man and a different boy. He would work on it and figure it out. First, he needed to get closer for a better look.

Mingo also noticed the increased number of Missouri militia over the last two days. He figured something big was going to happen soon. You could not hide that many men for too long a time. Mingo actually admired the Bushwhackers more than the Jayhawkers, but it was the Jayhawkers who had the money to pay for bounties. He had always been about the bounties. For Mingo, it was easy money. Men were much easier to track and kill than wildlife. That was something to reconsider and maybe resume in the future, once his need for vengeance was finally satisfied. Reprisal was his first priority. Tradition demanded it as his rightful reparation and the only acceptable currency was blood. Mingo's enemy had dishonored him. Such an affront could never be forgotten.

Grandfather's spirit called out to Mingo. "Remember me. You hold the knife. Settle this thing."

37
Restless

TALBOT HARRIS ACTUALLY began thinking more positively about Tyler from time-to-time. He appeared to be working tirelessly, consolidating and coordinating security around the big house and making an effort to liaison positively with Otto Metzger. This portion of the property had always been Metzger's area of responsibility. Tyler yielded to him whenever there was a difference of opinion and Metzger enjoyed this deference and courtesy.

For his part, Tyler was happy not to go out on any trail as long as Ussher was in the area. With their numbers increasing dramatically, you did not have to be a genius to figure out the Missourians were planning something big. Although there were far more Jayhawkers than Bushwhackers, the Bushwhackers proved themselves to be better at trapping and ambushing. If a patrol did not come back when expected, you had to assume that they might be cornered somewhere in the countryside. This required additional patrols with even greater numbers to locate and save those in trouble. Talbot Harris needed to demonstrate his commitment for finding and rescuing his people in order to get them to venture out in the first place.

* * * *

Vince Harris also reconsidered his situation. He no longer perceived there was any real danger from Ussher. As far as he was concerned, Ussher was a phantom. There had been no actual sightings for more than a month. The fact that someone was using a Henry against his father's men, most likely had nothing to do with him. Anyone could have picked up that rifle. Some other Bushwhacker had probably killed Ussher just to take possession of it. He also looked at it from a gambler's perspective. Even if Ussher was in the area, the chances were slim-to-none he would be in the same place, at the same time, as himself?

What occupied Vince's mind these days was getting away from his father, the cattle, and all the narrow-minded people on the ranch and throughout the countryside. Vince wanted to go to Fort Scott where there were plenty of young, needy, unescorted women. A light gallop could get you there in just under four hours.

Most of the women at Fort Scott were camp followers, who cooked, cleaned, and sewed on a pay-by-day basis. The large number of Union soldiers created an unlimited demand for these services. The men grew weary of Army food and were happy to pay for a meal prepared exclusively for them. Their uniforms always needed repair. Tears required mending, and buttons needed sewing back into place. For many of the young soldiers, getting a chance to interact with women gave them a feeling of being at home and surrounded by the care of their wives or mothers.

This female population included hard-bitten prostitutes. They worked in makeshift brothels, out of saloons or independently from the street. Each woman was at a different point in her experience but all were heading in the same downward spiral. Their situation made them look older than their years and each appeared on the brink of exhaustion. Whatever hope they retained diminished with each passing day. They prayed someone would save them from their existence or when death finally came, it would take them quickly.

The group most intriguing to Vince was the large number of new female refugees. These women had lost their fathers, husbands, and brothers to battle, disease, or medical incompetence. Other women found themselves abandoned by their men after deserting the army to escape the meat-grinder of war. These women were the same sort who worked for Abigail on the Harris ranch.

Vince hated Abigail because she watched over her girls so closely. If she had not been so important to his father, he would have paid someone to cut her throat long ago. The thought was such a pleasant contemplation that he made a mental note to get it done whenever his father decided to cooperate and die.

Vince persuaded two of the youngest cowhands on the Harris ranch, Toby and Leo, to leave their jobs and accompany him to Fort Scott. He promised they would have the time of their life. He said certain women would take off their blouse for a quarter, and if you paid two dollars, you could lay with one for an hour.

At 16 and 15 years old, Toby and Leo were little more than boys themselves. There was never much of anything to do because they had no money. They worked in the stables at the lowest pay and gave all their earnings to their dirt-poor families. The thought of a trip to the infamous Fort Scott sounded very exciting. It was a unique destination, which turned simple stories into campfire folklore. The offer of such an opportunity was simply too compelling to resist. Now, the son of the most prominent man they knew, offered them money and an opportunity for two days and two nights in Fort Scott.

They had heard bizarre stories about Vince but after talking with him, he did not seem like such a dreadful sort. He spoke candidly of his sexual encounters and was graphic with the details, although he failed to mention that his liaisons often proved fatal for the women.

38

An Ending and a Beginning

WEEKS EARLIER, Ussher had written a letter to his brother Benjamin in St. Louis. As was his style, the letter was sincere and direct. He related all the things that had happened, the loss of Darby, the abandonment of the homestead, his reluctant association in the militia, and his concern for his young friend, Nathan. Ussher told Benjamin about Nate's solid qualities and high intelligence. He related examples of the young man's values, insight, experience, and empathy. He asked Benjamin to consider accepting Nate as an apprentice in the law firm, believing both would benefit from such a relationship.

Ussher confessed to his brother that he intended reprisal against Vince Harris for Darby's murder. The price for this justice would likely be his life. He apologized, but stated that after more than a year, this urge was stronger than ever. Ussher told Benjamin that Nate was not aware of his bitter purpose. He asked Benjamin keep this confidentiality to himself. Ussher did not want Nate to feel any obligation to help him and place his own life in danger.

When Ussher informed Nate of his plan to send him to

St. Louis to live with Benjamin, Nate resisted the idea. He had been alone for a year and a half, growing up in an environment of violence and exploitation. On a daily basis, he received the last position in the supper line. Conversely, he was the first to receive assignments for the dirtiest jobs. The clothes he wore were the oversized, damaged, and bloodstained remnants of dead men no one else claimed. At his young age, Nate figured out that a person in his situation should never plan his future more than one day ahead.

Now, after all of his misery, the man Nate admired most of all, had decided to send him away to live with strangers to a place foreign and unknown. He worried that his life of exploitation might continue in the new location as much as in the Missouri countryside.

* * * *

Benjamin was delighted to receive the letter from his brother. It had been over a year since their last correspondence. In that time, Benjamin had sent Ussher letters on three occasions. When two months passed after sending the third letter, Benjamin assumed the worst. All of St. Louis discussed the situation on the border area between Kansas and Missouri. He knew that the Ussher homestead was directly in the middle of all the action. It was virtually unthinkable that so much time would have passed without hearing a word. When he received Ussher's letter, Benjamin was so excited that he closed the law office for the day. He could not wait to get home and share the good news with his wife.

Benjamin happily honored Ussher's request to accept Nate. If this young man was important to his brother, then Benjamin determined that it was his righteous obligation to extend a helping hand. He wrote back that Nate would be welcome, and he would await the details on how they should meet. He assured Ussher that St. Louis was a city of opportunity for those who are willing to learn and work. He closed the letter with a blessing that God would protect Nate during his journey east and protect Ussher as he pursued his path to resolution.

For just a moment, Benjamin thought about trying to talk his brother out of his deadly intention but then decided against that impulse. He had known Ussher for a lifetime. They were of the same blood but not the same fundamental worldview. Benjamin had always been the more intellectually pliant of the two brothers. He could see shades of nuance in situations. For Benjamin, compromise and congeniality were positive attributes. This brought him success, both in the law and in business. Although he maintained high ethical standards for himself, he accepted the idea that individual shortcomings were inevitable in society.

Ussher believed that the only reason a concept, like nuance, existed at all, was that men did not have the courage or the determination to see the truth and deal with it, regardless of the consequences. Although Ussher abided individuals with principles that were less than absolute, he simply felt they needlessly wasted time avoiding reality.

People could have genuine differences of opinions, but that dynamic alone left plenty of room for conflicts in belief systems. If used too often, nuances quickly create dishonesty and distortion. This had always been Ussher's core makeup and his years with Kensington further ingrained the concept into his core. In spite of this difference of personal philosophies, Ussher knew his brother was a good man and would be a superb example for Nate. He did not see a downside to Nate learning different points of view, nuanced or not. Like all men, once he grew up, Nate would have the responsibility to live his life in the way he thought best for himself and his family.

* * * *

Nate stayed quiet for more than two hours. During this time, Ussher spoke to him relating details about his brother and the advantages he expected Nate to enjoy living in St. Louis. He could attend schools and be introduced to new and engaging people. Most importantly, he would be away from the war.

"I'm not afraid of the war," insisted Nate. "I want to be with you. You can teach me what I need to know. I've learned a lot already, you said so yourself."

Nate's voice cracked slightly with emotion as he spoke. There was a long pause as his mind raced to express his feelings. Ussher knew that Nate was searching for something to say. He saw the boy take a breath and then exhale it away. He saw Nate take another breath, hold it for a moment, and then change his mind. After Nate attempted another unsuccessful effort to express his feelings, Ussher simply grabbed and hugged him a moment.

Ussher pushed Nate to arm's length. He paused to steady himself and then made hard eye contact. "After losing Darby, I never thought that I would say this to another human being. Nathan, my boy, I love you as a son and feel as connected to you as if you bore my last name. This is not what I want, but it is something you need to do. Do you hear me?"

Nate thought for a moment and then asked, "Why can't we both go to St. Louis and be together? Why wouldn't you want to get away from this war? If your brother is willing to help me, wouldn't he help you also?"

Ussher smiled, "You are one smart boy. That's remarkably solid reasoning. Here's the truth. I have something to do before I can leave. It's personal. It's private. I hope you can respect that. When it's finished, I will come to St. Louis. As God is my witness, I'll do everything in my power to see you again. Now, answer me. Will you go to live with Benjamin and his family? Will you do this for me?"

Nate paused, reading the sincerity in Ussher's eyes. "Yes," he answered, with an acquiescent positive nod.

Ussher hugged him once again. He told Nate that they were to meet up with Lewis and Emily Randall. They were less than a half-day's ride away. Nate and Ussher would leave first thing in the morning.

In spite of their best efforts, the Randalls decided to give up their farm and move back East near Emily's sister in Cincinnati. To move out of the territory, they booked passage on the Overland stage. Nate would travel with them as far as St. Louis to meet up with Benjamin. Then they would continue on to their final destination.

Ussher actually felt worse about Lewis and Emily losing their land than he did over the loss of his own homestead. After Darby's death, nothing, including the farm, felt essential to Ussher any longer. The farm, in fact, became a place of abhorrence. Every square foot of the entire 12 acres reminded him of his incredible time with Darby. Those days were now gone and unrecoverable.

Ussher and Nate shared a good evening together. They ate dinner alone around their own campfire. Ussher told Nate a few more stories about growing up with Benjamin and the lessons he had learned from his father and Kensington. Nate listened attentively and asked questions as he finished a second plate of beans and bacon. Ussher laughed and commented, "Boy, by the way you're eating, you must be about to go through a growing streak."

They straightened the campsite and packed everything proper for their departure at daybreak. As they settled into their blankets, Nate looked over to Ussher and waited until he could feel his gaze. It only took a moment for Ussher to feel the poignant sensation Nate broadcast in his direction. Now, it was Ussher's turn to look at Nate and wait to see what was on his mind. He didn't have to wait very long. Ussher saw Nate collect himself and ingest a small swallow before revealing his thoughts.

Nate began, "Earlier today, you said that you felt as connected to me as if I bore your last name."

Ussher replied, "Yes, I did say that. I meant every word."

Ussher saw resolve in Nate's face.

"Well, I'd be real pleased if I could introduce myself to folks as, Nathan Ussher from now on."

Ussher choked back his words for a moment. It pleased him immensely to think this young man, who he cared so much about, also wanted to be part of his family. Ussher sat up and extended his right hand for Nate to accept. Nate also sat up and took Ussher's right-hand into his. The older man's words were sincere and resolute.

"Welcome to the family, Nathan Ussher."

Nate beamed with satisfaction, realizing that he was no longer alone in this life.

39
On to St. Louis

USSHER AND NATE left camp just before sunrise. Ussher decided against saying goodbye to anyone, even Vaughn. Although they did not exchange much in the way of conversation during the ride, Ussher noticed Nate had assumed a very positive attitude. Their long campfire discussion the night before, reassured Nate that Ussher's brother was a good man who could help him manage his new life.

The rendezvous with Lewis and Emily took place as planned. The couple rode in a buckboard wagon containing the few possessions they valued most. Everyone exchanged handshakes and hugs. Ussher bear-hugged Nate for a moment, then straightened up and shook his hand.

"Day-by-day is how you do it. Learn all you can as it applies to you. You don't have to mold yourself into something you're not just to please other people. You just need to be the best you can be. That way other people will recognize your worth for the independent man you're becoming. Show the world what Nathan Ussher can do."

Mr. Randall asked, "Did I hear you say Nathan Ussher?"

"Yep," replied Ussher. "This is my boy."

Nate looked exceedingly pleased.

Lewis and Emily Randall exchanged glances and seemed delighted with the news.

Nate went over to the spot where Bolt stood tied. He

walked the horse over to Ussher and handed him the rein.

"I'm guessing that folks don't need lightning fast horses in a big city," he said. "Probably, with his high spirits and all, Bolt and me will just get ourselves into trouble. It will be better if he stays out here in the countryside with someone he already knows."

As Ussher watched them ride away into their future, he realized that Nate, the Randalls and Benjamin were the only people in the world he cared about. At first, it pleased him to think that Nate and the Randalls were leaving this land of war and suffering. Later, in an emotionally conflicted moment, it saddened him to think that he might never see them again. Then, in typical Ussher fashion, he accepted the truth for what it was.

He gave Bolt a quick nudge to start west, the direction of his own destiny. Ussher hollered a warning to Vince Harris, and to the four winds, using the words he remembered from another of his nemeses, Archie Clement.

"Vince, boy, we're gonna' have us some good fun soon enough."

As he focused on the task ahead, Ussher reckoned there had to be some sliver of opportunity that would reveal itself. He just had to figure it out and have the courage to take advantage whenever it appeared. He gave the horse a light kick. Bolt responded by streaking down the trail, causing Ussher to laugh with exhilaration as he surrendered himself to fate.

40
At the Side of the Trail

FOR REASONS UNKNOWN to him at that moment, Jack Mingo thought about the time he had spent in the care of Aaron and Micah Russell. As he rubbed the long diagonal scar across his chest, he marveled how those two fools were able to keep themselves alive. Even though he would have died if they had not found him that day, Mingo still thought them to be irrational with their concept of goodwill.

The war in this part of the country ground the toughest men into dust, let alone well-meaning do-gooders. It made no sense to Mingo to risk your neck trying to connect with the men in this conflict, especially with a ridiculous concept like God's salvation. With opposing militia units in the area, hit and run skirmishing lasted for days. Mingo, too, had come upon wounded men on the trail. It was a common occurrence. He would stop and interrogate the fallen man to collect potentially useful intelligence.

Mingo then evaluated the man's survival possibilities. If death was near, Mingo stopped his suffering and dispatched him with a quick thrust of Grandfather's knife through a neck artery. Next, he gathered anything useful the deceased man might have in his possession. After all, dead is dead, and there is no logic in being wasteful.

* * * *

Mingo heard a horse approaching from a considerable distance. He was hiding out a quarter mile from the Missouri Bushwhacker encampment. The rider traveled away from their camp towards the Kansas border. He could tell that the horse was running flat out and closing the space to where he was holed-up at an impressive speed. In the moment that it took him to pick up his Enfield rifle and begin to sight-in on the trail, the horse and rider flew by much faster than he expected.

It was that same damn horse, but with a different rider. He recognized the man and a strong suspicion about him began to develop. The chance for a sniper shot came and went in an instant. Mingo cursed his inattention. He should have been ready. It was rare for him to miss such an opening. Instead, he was thinking about Aaron and Micah Russell and the foolishness of their pursuit to save men's souls. Lesson learned, thought Mingo.

As he listened to the thunder of Bolt's hooves disappear into the distance, he resolved to be ready for the next time he saw that rider and horse. From the way Ussher rode, Mingo deduced he had some purpose in mind. Experienced woodsman never ride that fast over this terrain without good reason. Mingo mounted his horse, figuring that discovering Ussher's motive would be valuable. Men with purpose are always looking forward. Because of this focus, they are less likely to be looking over their shoulder for collateral danger. Mingo positioned himself to take advantage of that fact. Time was on his side.

41
Planning Infamy

THE ATMOSPHERE in the Bushwhacker camp was electric. They prepared for an attack on Lawrence, Kansas, the heartland of Jayhawker Union fundamentalism. The city was anti-Southern and a base for raids against the militia's friends and family. This raid offered payback for atrocities to injured friends and relatives, especially Bill Anderson's sister, Josie. She symbolized the loss and suffering experienced by all of their families.

It would also be payback for the Jayhawker raid on Osceola and Nevada City. The Jayhawkers executed a dozen Osceola men in front of their families. Word came to the militia that Jim Lane, the architect of the raid against Osceola resided in Lawrence. Lane symbolized barbarity and oppression to the Missourians.

Many of the men agreed that Anderson had the right idea. Successful strategy required that the Missourians elevate the level of aggression and violence. They needed to push the carnage to the point where the Jayhawkers would consider it intolerable to continue this war. The more they talked, the more the Bushwhackers convinced themselves that the raid was necessary and justified. They interpreted their attack as a defensive action intended to deter future aggression.

It did not matter that history had already shown there was no deterrence in this war. There was only continued escalation and retaliation. The focus for the impending attack, with its killing and looting, superseded consideration of potential consequences. Nothing mattered but retribution. Lawrence was open to attack, so attacked it would be.

As Vaughn prepared himself for the coming action, he did so with trepidation. The Jayhawkers were going to pay a grievous price. As he thought about the consequences, he agreed with Ussher. A raid of this size, with its associated casualties and carnage, would elevate this war into an unknown arena. The Jayhawkers knew the general location of the Bushwhacker camp. There were more than enough of them to defeat or drive off the Missouri militia whenever they managed to coalesce and put forth a concentrated effort. Vaughn feared that after Lawrence, they would unite with one another and the area's Union Army forces. The amalgamation would be strategically overwhelming.

Still, there was no turning back. It was going to happen through the sheer momentum of emotion because Anderson demanded it and Clement relished the butchery. Quantrill felt compelled to lead with enthusiasm to maintain harmony with Anderson and credibility with the militia members.

42

Saddling up

AT SUNSET, Bill Anderson walked through the Bushwhacker camp rousing each of the commanders to the task ahead. Most were already preparing for the night's ride. The few who still rested or appeared hesitant received a quick boot kick into their leg or backside. The rude assault quickly stirred them to check their men and confirm they were equipped and ready to move out.

Anderson was restless to get into the attack. For the killing to commence, the Demon needed to be unleashed onto the population of Lawrence. He counseled with the Demon throughout the night. As they drank whiskey, Anderson ordered the Demon to elevate the frenzy beyond all expectation. The Demon was amused whenever mortals consulted him as if they were equals. He was fond of Anderson as an implement of death and promised Bloody Bill that he would have the morning of blood he desired. There would be a harvest of death and bitterness. The hate would grow and thrive to levels never before experienced and beyond all previous comprehension. People would look back at Lawrence and say, that's when the worst times started. That raid was the root of all the sorrow yet to come.

* * * *

The Missouri militia broke camp and headed northwest toward Lawrence. As planned, they coordinated and rendezvoused with other partisan militias along the way. Even Quantrill was surprised how quickly and well synchronized the Bushwhacker troops formed up over the succeeding eight hours. His ranks tripled in a short time to 450 men.

En route, the militia passed through Gardner, Kansas, and the forward scouts spotted two men running away. It was unknown whether they ran because they were frightened or if they were trying to arm themselves in defense. The reason did not matter. They lived in Kansas and were assumed to be Jayhawkers. With whoops and hollers, the Missouri scouts rode them down and shot them multiple times; first blood. After the main body of militia cleared the outskirts of Gardner, ten trailing members of the group set fire to three homes, as a warning to the townspeople, before rushing on to catch up with the others.

The moon disappeared behind an approaching cloudbank creating navigation problems. Quantrill spotted a window light from a small farmhouse nearby. He sent the lead scout and five men to the house to get directions. Minutes later, they returned with confirmed information along with the farmer who supplied it. They repeated this practice several more times during the ride. After new hostages confirmed the accuracy of their route, the militia moved on, except for three. These fighters would restrain the hostage until the main units rode away; then cut his throat to ensure the security of the mission. The trail to Lawrence lay strewn with these sacrifices. The Demon observed and approved.

Close to sunrise, the outer edge of Lawrence appeared just over the crest of Hogback Ridge. The entire Missouri militia paused for its final grouping and coordination. Quantrill ordered Archie Clement to ride to every commander and make sure each waited for the attack signal from his banner. Clement stared at Quantrill and did not move. Quantrill glared back and repeated the instruction with emphasis. Anderson looked at Clement and gave a quick nod as a signal to follow Quantrill's order.

After Clement was out of sight, Quantrill turned to Anderson. "Bill, this may be payback, but it's also military. I don't want women and kids killed. That's an order."

Anderson looked directly at Quantrill.

Quantrill repeated, "We don't kill women and kids. I need

you to tell me you understand."

The rider carrying the militia banner was ten feet behind them. While still staring at Quantrill, Anderson bellowed, "Raise the banner." Then Anderson kicked his horse into action as the banner man moved the flag in several large circular motions. The columns on both sides saw the signal. The tension and adrenaline inside every man released like a rifle shot. "Remember Osceola," a section commander shouted. In seconds, the columns crested the ridge and rushed downward. The town of Lawrence slept as the thunder rolled in.

43

Fort Scott, Kansas

VINCE HARRIS CARED nothing about all the militia activity in the countryside. He and his two young companions arrived in Fort Scott the previous evening. It had been a memorable night indeed. Toby and Leo never imagined that such an exotic place existed. Far from the restraints of their family's values, Vince's money allowed their teenage hormones to explore rarefied pleasures they never knew were possible.

Vince conducted the evening with mastery. He allowed the boys enough whiskey to lower their inhibitions, but not too much, to where their inhibitions turned into inability. He wanted them to be able to enjoy themselves and receive a progressive introduction to the variety of pleasures the whores could offer. They had no problem finding and hiring young women. Vince carried more money than any man they ever knew and supplied everyone with plenty of whiskey and food. Today, Vince was on his best behavior. Tomorrow would be another matter.

The women enjoyed the cabin at the far edge of town. It belonged to a prominent merchant who was a friend of Vince's father. It was clean, well lit, had tables, chairs, and three beds with feather comforters. After plying their trade in back rooms, alleyways, haylofts, and hard ground, they found it to be a welcome upgrade and respite. Each of them hoped that these two young boys and their older friend would stick around for an additional day or two.

Vince held every intention of staying for a while. The boys were already hooked on the experience, the women were content and relaxed, and the cabin was comfortable. It seemed, for the moment, that everybody had whatever he or she needed.

For Vince, the best attribute about the cabin was its secluded location, set far back from the dirt road. It had a small backyard with a well. Behind the backyard was a wooded area where deer and coyote occasionally passed through. The closest building was a saloon; but the bawdy revelry from the drinkers would easily muffle sounds coming from inside the cabin tomorrow night. Vince complemented himself. His plan was coming together.

The women in Fort Scott were unlike any girls Toby and Leo had ever known back in farm country. Their excitement was too high, and their experience too short for them to realize that the enthusiasm the women demonstrated was more for Vince Harris's money than for them.

Vince was interested in seeing which one of the boys had more vitality. He secretly told the women he would pay them two different ways, by the hour and by the tumble. The cabin contained two rooms. One of the rooms was small. Vince claimed that one as his. Since he was the man with the money, no one objected. All the other activity, the drinking, the eating and the sex, took place in the large room where everyone could watch everyone else. No one even bothered getting dressed. The only time the boys put on their pants was when they went outside to get fresh water for the wash buckets.

In one day, Toby and Leo acquired more self-confidence than they had enjoyed in their entire lives. They felt respected, noticed, and appreciated. They joked, laughed, and developed a small strut in their walk. Each was thankful for their incredible luck of becoming a friend to Vince. Both thanked him several times.

"I'm glad y'all are enjoying yourself, but we ain't even close at being done here," Vince responded. "I've got lots to teach you boys. When this here time is over, you ain't never gonna' forget your fun with ol' Vince. Yes, sir, that's for sure."

44
The Harris Ranch

EVERYONE KNEW the location of the Harris ranch, and Ussher headed Bolt in that direction. For someone likely riding to his death, he was supremely calm. Death did not worry Ussher and his focus remained fixed on his purpose, not on the potential consequence of that purpose.

The war had churned around him for years. Even before he joined up as a Bushwhacker scout, Ussher understood militia fighters from either side might ambush or execute him for any reason. He simply became numb to all sensations involving fear of injury or death.

The only concern that ever worried Ussher was that Darby might be hurt or killed in the madness of this war. Since those fears had come to tragic fruition, his mind was singularly set on obtaining justice for her. For Ussher, there was no downside.

When he caught up to Vince Harris, he intended to rip the very life out of his body and incinerate the remains in righteous reckoning. If Vince actually possessed a soul, Ussher knew it would be a dark shroud in the area of his heart. He decided to tear open Vince's chest to locate the blackness and shred it so completely it would be repulsive to the lowest demons in Hell.

If one of the ranch security men managed to shoot Ussher before completing his task, he vowed to stalk Vince into the afterlife. Even at the end of days, Ussher was confident he would find a way to wreak havoc on the bastard. Ussher displayed complete focus and total commitment to the task. Nothing was going to stop his effort. Nothing else mattered. His conscious mind was unable to concentrate on any other purpose. Bolt picked up the emotional force emanating from Ussher. Both horse and man accepted their fate as they streaked toward a precipice of destiny they had no way of resisting.

* * * *

Ussher slipped from the countryside onto the enormous ranch of the Harris cattle empire. He had been here before to snipe at Jayhawker scouting parties and rustle cattle. Those adventures were hit-and-run and always occurred on the periphery of the property. This time he intended to breach deep into its heart and remain as long as necessary. An overcast day was ending and a moonless night looked to be coming. The wind was light and blowing toward him from the direction of the big house, nearly a half mile away. Ussher carried hardtack, bread, and a canteen of water. To conserve energy, he decided to eat just before moving to breach the security around the Harris home.

45
Mingo Identifies Ussher

MINGO EVALUATED all the information and confirmed the identification of his dangerous adversary. There was no longer any doubt in his mind as he concluded that he knew the man who ambushed him that morning without a moment of hesitation. Ussher was the scout who outmaneuvered and almost killed him.

Two pieces of critical information confirmed Mingo's conclusion. After observing the Bushwhacker camp for several days, it was easy for Mingo to identify the leaders. The experienced observer can read the body language of those who lead. There are three main types, and they exhibit particular physical characteristics in their interactions with others.

The first displays bravado and swagger. This was the type personified by Anderson and Clement. Each walked with an air of self-importance. They constantly passed too closely to other men, violating personal space to reassert their perceived superiority.

The second type is the planner or strategist. Quantrill was this sort of man. Mingo noted he engaged other men in conversation, but preferred solitude. He was comfortable accompanied by just the thoughts inside his head. Mingo knew this leadership was crucial but he recognized these men were often preoccupied with the future, which might prevent them from putting forth their best effort in the present.

The best style, commanding the most respect, is lead-by-example. Vaughn was this first among equals type. He never asked a fighter to do a job that he was unwilling to do himself. He walked amongst the men, speaking with encouragement and detailing their readiness before leading them into battle. Too few men exhibited this exemplary leadership style; demonstrating remarkable bravery without ever expecting recognition. If they died in battle, their men mourned quietly and remembered them with reverence.

Ussher was a leader of sorts, but there was more to his character. He was quieter than Vaughn, more thoughtful than Quantrill and possibly more dangerous than Anderson or Clement. Men were not afraid to approach and speak with him but they never lingered. This behavior was indicative of a man who got to the point of a conversation and then got back to the business of surviving the day through vigilance. The man was always busy, caring for his horse, reworking his gear, sharpening a knife or cleaning his rifle. He had the skills and fortitude to outsmart or outwork an opponent. Mingo realized both realities happened to him the morning Ussher shot him. That experience was a first for Mingo.

The weapon he carried was the second compelling clue. Once Mingo got himself a clear look, he had all the evidence he needed. It was a rare, deadly, Henry repeating rifle. No sod-busting Bushwhacker had the money or the connections to own one of those. Mingo knew in his bones it was the one belonging to Old Man Harris.

"Ussher, you son-of-a-bitch," said Mingo. "I know your face and name. It's a name I'll remember the rest of my life."

Mingo watched Ussher travel into an area posing extreme danger. It made no sense, or did it? Ussher did not have to steal to survive. Mingo was fully aware of his capabilities. If he wanted to steal cattle, there were plenty on the fringes of the ranch. There was no reason to travel to the center of the property. For sure, there was a lot more here than met the eye. This was a man on a mission, intent on challenging everything. Mingo concluded that the only reason a careful man, like Ussher, would confront risk at this level would be to cause someone's death.

Mingo thought back to those first days after Tyler hired him. There had been some half-ass story about Harris' spoilt son having his way with some farmer's wife. She ended up dead. The farmer swore revenge against the son but security near the big house provided safety for the insolent fool. The farmer did manage to kill several ranch hands, which thoroughly pissed off the old man. None of that meant anything to Mingo at the time. He did not care what rich boys did to local farmwomen because it was none of his affair, but now it all made sense. Ussher had been the farmer and the woman Vince killed belonged to him. Mingo reflected that she must have been truly exceptional to stir such commitment after so much time.

When Tyler made Mingo the head scout, he mentioned the situation with Ussher casually, almost as an afterthought. He never related that the man was an experienced scout, excellent tracker and stone cold killer. Mingo rubbed his hand along the jagged scar embedded across his chest as all the facts fell into place. He was about to witness the final episode of a life-and-death drama. The forces of Talbot Harris were the odds down favorite because of their numbers. Still, Ussher had a chance to cause some damage because Harris, with all of his security people, had no idea Ussher had already breached their defensives.

Mingo retrieved a small flask with 20 sips of Kentucky whiskey and settled behind cover to observe. Ussher would need to use every trick he possessed to survive. Mingo would take his measure and learn. Grandfather always told him it was better to learn from the experience and mistakes of others than to pay for knowledge with your own blood and sweat.

46
4:30 AM

FRIDAY, AUGUST 21, 1863
LAWRENCE, KANSAS

UNION LIEUTENANT Emmett Blanchard returned to the bivouac area at the edge of Lawrence. Most of the soldiers slept in their tents and the sentries were on stand-down without requesting the authority to do so. Blanchard found this lack of discipline insufferable and made a mental note to dress down Sergeant Carney as soon as he located the son-of-a-bitch.

Blanchard had enjoyed a rowdy evening with a saloon girl. She was new to Lawrence, and he was one of the first to enjoy her company and her favors. He was polite and generous. She was appreciative and responsive. Blanchard actually kissed her hand as he bid her good night to return to his troops. He was exceedingly tired from an over indulgence in poor quality alcohol and above average sex. As he lay back on his cot, he reflected that girls in this part of the country acted appreciative around a man of his caliber and societal status. Before the war, back in Cleveland, Ohio, he was the manager of his family's shipping concern, operating barges on the Cuyahoga River. At 24 years old, he was still unmarried. His social position and occupation allowed him to be a man with resources, able to purchase companionship whenever the indulgence became available.

47

The Harris Ranch

USSHER PLANNED to hole up throughout the night and make his move just before daybreak. He found a few boulders amongst a group of trees surrounded by scrub grass and bushes. He tucked himself into a space behind some shrubs and settled in between a boulder and a tree. Although he saw several guards around the house, he noted that there were far fewer than he expected. Ussher wondered why a cautious man like Talbot Harris would not have more security around the very heart of his empire.

He soon found the answer lumbering inexorably toward him. Tyler and Metzger had decided to move the enormous herd of cattle as close as possible to the big house. With all the reports of militia groups riding and skirmishing in the countryside, there was a genuine concern that cattle rustling might become rampant. As Ussher watched helplessly, the herd of 1,400 Texas Longhorns, along with 25 riders, moved in his direction like a giant ocean wave. The herd flowed up to and then around the trees and boulders where Ussher lay hidden.

Half the drovers rode to the front of the herd to prevent it from getting too close to the big house. The cattle in the rear were initially unaware those in front had halted. The bumping and the pushing caused a powerful reverberation among the animals. Two steers collided into the boulders next to Ussher. In an attempt to escape additional pushing, one of them began to leap over the large rock hiding Ussher. The animal stopped halfway through the jump, with only its front hooves touching the top of the boulder before pulling back. Had it followed through with the move, Ussher would have been stomped by 1,800 pounds of meat and muscle. The event was over almost as fast as it started. Ussher did not allow himself to contemplate this deadly near miss since other dangers required his immediate attention.

As the cattle finally settled down, the drovers stayed strictly on the perimeter of the herd. While individual steers noticed Ussher and stopped and stared at him for a moment, none of the cowhands had any idea he was in their midst.

Mingo's position was well to the rear of Ussher. Because of his elevated location, he was able to see the approaching herd before him. Mingo flanked away from the herd and was able to keep out of sight from the Harris men. He immediately observed that Ussher held a precarious position. He was outnumbered 25-to-1 and surrounded by an entire herd of Texas Longhorns. Those animals could gut a man with one swing of their head.

Mingo could not help a scornful smile at the predicament. No man would ever get himself into such an unfavorable situation intentionally. Mister, you sure got yourself in one Hell of a fix. The unfolding situation would be interesting and dramatic for sure.

48
4:34 AM

LAWRENCE, KANSAS

Lieutenant Blanchard collapsed onto his cot and drifted toward sleep. The rest of the contingent hardly noticed his return. Inside their tents, men stretched out or repositioned their bodies under their blankets. The few soldiers who were awake went about their business at the latrine holes. No one in camp bothered to carry weapons and they hoped the morning would stay quiet. Later, when the shops and saloons opened, they might have a chance to walk around and look things over.

A bright sun began rising in the east over Hogback Ridge. The light was intense and sleepy-eyed young soldiers avoided looking in that direction. A strong southern breeze swirled up dust devils and stoked campfire embers back into flames. A covey of quail suddenly lifted themselves from a stand of prairie grass, and a few dogs barked in the distance.

In spite of his fatigue, Lieutenant Blanchard felt ill at ease. Although sounds around the camp seemed reasonably normal, there was tension in the air that he was unable to identify. Fighting his weariness, he pushed himself up on one elbow and listened more intently. He then realized with clarity what his senses had only perceived. The sensation was not a sound but more of a rumbling vibration. In that same instant, the barking from the dogs became frantic and he heard voices from his men calling attention to riders.

"Hey Sergeant, they sure are coming in fast," a new recruit called out.

"Fast, my ass," yelled another soldier. "That's a full-out fucking charge!"

"Get your weapons, form up, form up," shouted Sergeant Carney, running to meet the enemy with his pistol in hand.

Blanchard scrambled to pull on his pants.

Men ran in every direction. Some readied their rifles while others tried to locate their weapons. The resonance of the charge resembled rolling thunder. The gunfire salvos began. Hundreds of rounds erupted, splintering the air with angry promises of inescapable death. Many of the youngest Union soldiers lost heart, dropped their weapons, and ran in the direction of the town.

Blanchard realized he only had seconds to mount a defense. As he exited his tent, he saw Sergeant Carney yelling at the retreating soldiers and ordering them to stand and fight. He held both his hands up in the air, continually signaling for his men to stop running. Seconds later, he took a bullet in the chest and fell backwards as the Missouri militia crashed through the camp like a tidal wave.

Bullets fragmented the air like anger hornets. A minie ball tore through Blanchard's left bicep, throwing him to the ground. The wound totally incapacitated his arm. Unable to stand, he rolled on his back and prepared to defend himself with his Colt revolver. The pain was excruciating as he maneuvered into a sitting position.

The militia swarmed over the area, neutralizing all resistance presented by these pitiful boys pretending to be soldiers. Blanchard shielded his eyes against the blazing morning sun and tried to analyze his situation through the swirling dust. His evaluation went from grim to hopeless as a looming shadow suddenly blocked the glare. He lowered his hand and looked up to find Bloody Bill Anderson standing over him with the look of diabolical ruin etched into his face.

"It's time for Yankee pigs to die," Anderson announced to Blanchard as he kicked his gun away with ease.

The blow rolled Blanchard over and left him screaming in pain. He was losing a great deal of blood and shock was setting in. Anderson saw the wound and savored the blood. The Demon was keeping his promise. He kicked Blanchard hard in the gut. As the blow connected, Blanchard wheezed with agony and spewed vomit. When the Union officer rolled over, his injured arm flopped uselessly outward from his body. Anderson stomped his boot heel into the bleeding wound. The pain was so intense that Blanchard was unable to utter any sound. His eyes widened and his mouth opened, but there were no words, only disbelief.

Like most soldiers, Blanchard knew this war might cause his death. Those contemplations included scenarios with him dying gallantly in a moment of extraordinary heroism. The end was quick and clean; witnessed by many, admired by all, and historically archived for future generations.

His demise was not to be one where he stumbled about after a night of drinking and debauchery. His men were not supposed to be running away in frantic retreat. Blanchard's ultimate adversary should have been a regular army officer, maybe Bobby Lee himself, not this militia outlaw who beat him with impunity. None of this made sense. How was he going to live his life with only one arm? Blanchard's thoughts suddenly refocused, and his lower jaw dropped, when he witnessed Bloody Bill coming his way carrying a three-pound hatchet.

Anderson acquired his bloody name and fierce reputation through his merciless killing of enemy combatants and unarmed Yankee civilians. He carried multiple handguns, a saber and hatchet. Anderson outfitted his horse with extra rifles and backup pistols. His men followed his example. The handgun was the preferred weapon of the Bushwhacker militia. Many of the men were such excellent horsemen that they could ride, holding the horse rein in their teeth, while shooting revolvers in both hands. The sheer volume of fire they generated would overwhelm troops armed with the standard issue, single-shot Springfield rifle.

As an aficionado of death, Anderson carried an assortment of weapons because certain situations required specialized applications of carnage, and so it was for Lieutenant Emmett Blanchard. As a Union officer, he qualified for a distinctive application of summary justice. Anderson observed and commented later that Blanchard's skull sounded like a splitting melon when his axe cleaved it open.

49
The Harris Ranch

THE PASSING NIGHT was a rough one for Ussher. The drovers pushed the herd of Texas Longhorn cattle as close to the big house as Talbot Harris would allow. Ussher was not able to move from his hidden position under the tree and between two prairie boulders. He understood his location was precarious and briefly cursed his rotten luck. Then he rallied himself to look at the reality of his situation and evaluate his options. If he attempted to move, any reaction from the cattle was likely to draw the attention of the drovers. The inevitable gunfight would cause the cattle to panic. This left Ussher with equally bad choices: gunshot, gored by panicked steers or crushed in a stampede. His death resulted from all of those reactions, leaving Darby's murder unavenged. Ussher did the only thing he could do. He settled in and waited.

Ussher realized he had not actually observed Vince outside. He recognized a house that size contained many rooms. Killing Vince was going to require that he get inside and find the son-of-a-bitch quickly, before security closed in. Maybe, just maybe, all the steers surrounding him served a purpose after all. Waiting a little longer might be a good thing. The logic in his head overruled the passion for killing in his heart. Keep it simple. All he had to do was stay alive and figure out the details. He ate half of his rations and decided to settle in for another day and night.

50

Fort Scott, Kansas

VINCE OBSERVED the whores of Fort Scott and made assessments about their motivation for being involved in the ancient profession. Many women prostituted themselves as a way of life. Their mothers and sisters followed the practice and then they took their turn. Others plied the vocation as a practical alternative to a domestic existence. Still others surrendered the sanctity of their bodies to support hungry children or husbands and fathers disabled from the war. Each had a story for her base existence but there was always another woman whose experiences were even more compelling. Most of the women resigned themselves to their situation and felt fortunate to see the following sunrise.

Vince possessed a practiced eye for identifying character defects, weaknesses, and vulnerability. Two varieties of prostitute especially interested him. The first was the whore who genuinely enjoyed her work for the personal gain it could bring. She knew how to process men through her bed with the least amount of effort and the greatest amount of profit. She enjoyed the lies, deception, stealing, and occasional throat cutting.

Nina Moore was one such woman. She drifted into Fort Scott over two years ago. At that time, she was a hard 42 years old but had the brains, shrewdness, and force of will to know that Fort Scott offered numerous opportunities. Life was hard and it was every woman for herself from Nina's point of view. Soon after arriving in camp, she turned the $15, hidden in her garter, into half-interest in a saloon and a $3,000 nest egg.

Next, she devised a plan to eradicate her saloon partner. The local constable was a frequent customer of Nina's. After her partner's demise, the brief investigation called his death an unfortunate accident. To everyone's surprise, a document soon surfaced leaving the partner's portion of the ownership entirely to Nina. His wife and children, who lived in two back rooms of the saloon, were virtually penniless. Nina demonstrated her version of kindness and charity with a $30 stipend and stagecoach passage, so the family could return back East.

Nina and Vince had met previously and experienced an instant compatibility. He had money and influence. She supplied the other type of woman Vince valued most. These were the women of desperation. They all shared similar characteristics. They were young, naïve, traumatized, and lonely. They all lost their families through death or separation in the whirlwind of war. When they finally found their way to Fort Scott, most were destitute and near starvation.

Nina kept an eye out for these refugees. After escaping the rigors of war and the wilderness, they were exceedingly grateful when she rescued them by offering temporary shelter and three daily meals. The key component of that offer was the condition of temporary. Within a few days, the women faced a grim choice; return to a life without resources, or enter prostitution working 14 hours a day for Nina. All hoped their circumstance would be temporary. As time passed, the futility of hope gave way to the challenges of surviving the long days and nights. Vince lusted for those still retaining shreds of hope.

Vince possessed an exceptionally finite requisite. He sought the ones who most recently accepted shelter from Nina but had not worked the back rooms long enough to be jaded or calloused. He wanted to see these women as their trauma subsided and they began to discern a glimmer of deliverance in their future. These women would suffer the most when they discovered that their perceived salvation with Nina became their absolute ruin with Vince. He found that moment of devastating revelation to be exciting and fulfilling. The enlightened one, the Demon, promised him these feelings were justified. He assured Vince that he was a man of exceptional worth who deserved the complete fulfillment of his fantasies. Tonight, he might be able to realize the satisfaction, denied him over a year ago, when that farmer bitch scarred his face for life.

Nina knew Vince was a dangerous man and was aware the women she sent to him could end up humiliated, tortured, or dead. Knowing this did not stop her from sending them into that risky situation. The most crucial thing to Nina Moore was security for her future. She was getting older and a woman had to take care of herself. She reckoned; if the young women were resourceful, they would figure out a way to salvage themselves. If they were not smart enough to deal with Vince, they would probably die anyway, out in the world on their own. If that was their fate, Nina figured that she might as well receive some benefit in that process.

51

5:00 AM

LAWRENCE, KANSAS

LIEUTENANT BLANCHARD, Sergeant Carney, and 19 Union soldiers lay dead on the outskirts of Lawrence as ten Missouri militiamen rode to the top of Hogback Ridge to guard against any arriving Union Army units. Five Union recruits were still alive. They were either slightly wounded or had surrendered to the Missourians. Archie Clement gave the order to execute them for the crime of being Yankees. The young soldiers hardly had a chance to cry, pray, or beg for their lives before five or more rounds from militia revolvers riddled their bodies.

The lives of men and boys went from cheap to worthless as the attackers rode through the streets shooting everyone they found. Anderson declared that if a boy was old enough to point a gun, then he was old enough to get himself shot dead. Scores of bodies lay strewn throughout town. There was some defensive shooting from townsfolk but return fire quickly silenced all opposition. It was obvious to the militia and the citizens of Lawrence that the town was overwhelmed with surprising ease. For the people, the only question remaining was how terrible would their experience become?

For several hours, there was no sign of rescue on the roads leading to Lawrence. The squads of Missouri sentries guarding the crest of Hogback Ridge were relieved, allowing them a turn at pillaging the town. With overwhelming numbers, the militia first isolated portions of the town and then secured those sections street by street. After they searched house-to-house, they confiscated everything of value for the Cause; at least that is what they told the residents.

A few citizens noticed the militia leaders arguing. The dispute was intense and getting close to violent. Some thought the Missourians would begin shooting one another at any time. The argument was between Vaughn on one side and Anderson and Clement on the other. Quantrill tried to assert authority without noticeable success. Vaughn contended the militia had achieved its goals. The town of Lawrence was defeated. Two dozen Union soldiers and scores of male residents were dead.

Wagonloads of merchandise had been confiscated and thousands of dollars in gold, silver, and Union currency stolen from the bank. It should be time to go. Vaughn saw that things were out of control and the killing no longer served any strategic purpose. Six more civilians died in the brief time that he argued with Anderson and Clement.

Vaughn screamed at Anderson and Quantrill, "Right now you assholes are doing more to unite the Jayhawkers than anything that's been done before. We are taking this raid too far. You're turning a victory into a massacre. Massacres are never forgiven or forgotten and they are always returned in kind."

Anderson stepped close to Vaughn, eye-to-eye. "The men admire you. For that reason, I'm going to let you live but your assignment here is finished. Get your ass up on the ridge and take command of the scouts. We'll take care of finishing things down here."

Anderson totally ignored the fact that Quantrill, who was the recognized leader, stood next to him, and that Vaughn was Quantrill's man.

"If this fucker comes near me the rest of the day," Anderson said to Clement, as he pointed toward Vaughn, "Cut his throat."

Clement looked from Anderson to Vaughn and held his gaze for a long moment. He removed his Bowie knife from the back of his belt for emphasis.

"Yes sir," he said. "I'll cut his throat sure enough. Fact is commander, I'll be happy to cut more than that." Clement pointed the knife at Vaughn's crotch. "You just give me the word and it's as good as done."

Vaughn did not flinch. Not even Anderson and Clement together could frighten him. He had been through too many battles and seen so many men die that death no longer fazed him. Vaughn suddenly stepped back and lowered his rifle in Clements direction. Anderson and Clement reacted instinctively, also stepping back and reaching for their pistols.

At that moment, Quantrill took command and stepped between the three men. "Stand down," he shouted. "Goddamn all of you; stand down. That's an order and I will personally shoot the first son-of-a-bitch who takes this bullshit any farther."

Quantrill's assertiveness worked. All eyes focused on him long enough to allow the killing impulse to lose its edge.

Quantrill turned to Vaughn, "We're gonna' need to split up all the militia units. In a couple of hours, the Union Army is going to have ten times our number trying to track us down. We don't want to be tripping over ourselves as we light out of here. Make sure that the scouts on the ridge get their orders on which way to lead their contingents back to Missouri."

Vaughn stood for a moment, nodded affirmatively to Quantrill, and followed his orders. Quantrill was smart enough to issue a directive to Vaughn, which made strategic sense and appealed to his instinct to protect his men.

Anderson and Clement said nothing. As soon as Vaughn turned away, they returned to join the carnage in the streets of Lawrence. Quantrill looked around and realized that Vaughn was correct and Ussher had been truthful. This raid was a mistake and the Jayhawkers would never forget or forgive their actions. He decided to leave for Texas the following day.

52

Fort Scott

THE CABIN AT THE end of the street, down from the saloon, was quiet, deathly quiet. It was just after daybreak and besides the people in the little cabin, only the birds were going about their business. Vince Harris was angry and on edge. He stood near the doorway, holding a revolver and blocking the only exit from the cabin. He tried to be calm and persuasive but it did not look as if he was going to be successful. The survivors of the night looked fearful with the dread of horrors that might still come.

Toby was dead. Leo was traumatized and crying. Nina Moore tried to appear unafraid but her apprehension revealed itself through fissures in her confident facade. Two of her whores huddled in different locations of the cabin as far from Vince as they could manage. One of them sat on top of a bed comforter with her knees drawn up in front of her body. The other stood in a corner and held a shoe in her right hand. She looked as if she might use it as a club if her situation worsened. Nina's third girl, the youngest, was also dead, lying on the floor of the smaller bedroom Vince had claimed.

Vince did not know what else to say, so he restated his earlier analysis of why things had gone wrong. What he did not realize was that his self-indulgent anger was obvious. His explanation was nothing more than the whiney complaints of a deviant rich boy. Even young Leo recognized this fact.

"I didn't intend for any of this to happen like it did. All I wanted was all of us to have some fun. Fact is, we were having a good time for quite a while. I had this time all planned. The only thing y'all had to do was follow instructions. There was no call for last night to get out of hand or for you not to trust me. I've been more than generous with all of you."

Nina looked around the room. There wasn't anything to do regarding the dead boy and girl. The fact they died so young and violently was a reality not particularly tragic from Nina's point of view. Such things happened all the time in this war. Nina's immediate problem was how to extricate herself and her two remaining whores from this dangerous situation. She decided she would help Vince cover-up what happened the previous night. What else could she do? He was the son of Talbot Harris, one of the richest and most influential men in the territory. Everyone knew that whoever went up against that old man always ended up dead or disappeared.

Nina tried reassurance. "Mr. Vince, put down your gun, honey. Everything is going to be fine. We can get this worked out, no problem. The girls and me ain't gonna' say nothin' about last night. Like, you said, it was all a big misunderstanding. Sometimes… bad things just happen." Nina indicated toward Leo. "There's plenty of room out back. Why don't you and the boy just bury those two in the woods? The girls will clean things up in here and no one will be the wiser. I'm telling you, we don't want problems with you, and we don't want problems with your Daddy. Now, that sounds right reasonable, don't it?"

Nina's words sounded credible to Vince. He stayed quiet for a couple of moments and nodded his head affirmatively. Then, just as he made the decision to trust Nina and follow her instructions, the girl who had been sitting on the bed burst into angry outrage.

Her name was Ella. She entered prostitution unwillingly through desperation six months earlier. The experience had made her a mature seventeen years old. Ella lost count of her number of sexual liaisons after just one week in the trade. They were so numerous that it was all one giant, numbing, ongoing occurrence. There was relatively little diversity in the services required of her. Ella knew her customers would oblige her to be on her back, on her belly, or on her knees. It was the same routine, day after day. If the men were aroused enough, she could start, and often finish the job using just her hands.

Ella was under the impression that she knew everything about men. She had met those who were gentle, those who treated her roughly, and all the ones in between. Vince Harris was distinctly different. She had never encountered a man who possessed such specific and ritualistic needs. Should Vince's instructions be misunderstood or not followed to the letter, he became angry, violent, and punitive.

It seemed that the instructions were purposely convoluted and arcane to ensure that the women would make mistakes and give Vince a reason to punish them. Once the punishment began, his anger morphed into a fiendish sense of enjoyment characterized by his spontaneous, high-pitched, cackling laugh. It unnerved anyone unfortunate enough to be within earshot, except for the Demon, for whom Vince's laugh was melodic as springtime birdsong.

Last night, Vince took the youngest girl, Rachel, into his room. Nina picked Rachel to be Vince's unique diversion for the evening. She met the complete list of Vince's criteria, young, naïve, pretty, lonely, and desperate. The two other girls were company for Toby and Leo.

Nina was there to orchestrate the instructions from Vince. She was also curious to see how events would unfold. She understood that Vince Harris was unique, even for a worldly woman like herself. Nina knew he was dangerous, often brutal, and angered quickly. What she did not know was that Vince voluntarily modulated his frightful personality to suit his disposition and situation. His mood and frame of mind were not understandable as those of normal men.

"You crazy son-of-a-bitch," screamed Ella.

"Stick that rotten gun in your mouth and pull the trigger, you worthless piece of shit. You killed my friend. Rachel was a sweet girl. She never hurt anybody. There was no reason for you to harm her. Why would you kill this poor boy? He was only being kind when he tried to protect me. Who do you think you are, fucking Satan?"

Nina tried to interrupt the outburst. "Keep your voice down, girl," she ordered. Nina kept her own voice calm and steady. For some unknown reason, Ella paid no attention to the fact that Vince held a revolver in his hand.

"Go to Hell," Ella fired back at Nina.

She then turned her attention back to Vince. "You ain't no big man. You're nothing without your daddy's money and protection."

It was clear that Ella's anger now combined with uncontrolled hysteria. While she rebuked Vince, she got up from the bed and stood in front of him, pointing her finger in defiant reproach.

Vince just stared at Ella. No woman had talked to him in such a disrespectful manner since that farm bitch, who he shot-dead over a year ago.

Again, Nina attempted to reassert herself into this critically dangerous situation. She positioned herself between Ella and Vince and once again sought to reassure him that everything was going to be fine.

"I'll take care of this one," Nina said confidently to Vince. "There's no reason to worry. You just holster that gun now, Mr. Vince. I'll handle everything. You and I have been friends for a long time. There ain't no reason why we can't continue to be good friends."

* * * *

Earlier, in the bigger room, Nina drank whiskey as she watched Toby and Leo cavort with the two girls. She laughed at their inexperience. They thought they were quite the roosters and her girls convinced them they possessed the strength of heroes. The boys were animated, loud, and full of vitality. The girls were accommodating and encouraged the boys to keep coming back for more. Toby and Leo were having the time of their lives for the second evening in a row. They were starting to feel confident that Vince Harris genuinely liked them and enjoyed their company. Individually they made the decision to do anything he might ask. It turned out that anything was a much larger commodity than they could ever envision and assessing Vince's motivation was far beyond their youthful abilities.

Nina began to notice what sounded like muffled distress coming from the small room where Vince was lying with Rachel. At first, she dismissed it as the release of sexual tension, but there was more to it. The stress in the woman's voice had the presence of anxiety, evolving into fear. Nina was aware that interrupting a man at such a time often created problems, so she did nothing. She rationalized that everything was under control and no one was in danger. Over the next few minutes, the sounds of apprehension from the girl heightened and then gradually subsided, all the while accompanied by grunts from Vince in his final moments of sexual rut.

Vince emerged from the room looking wide-eyed and fully invigorated. Nina could see Rachel's bare legs and feet through the door opening. They were stone still, spread embarrassingly apart and lifeless. Nina didn't need further confirmation to know the girl was dead. The contradiction was disquieting. Rachel lay motionless on the floor while Vince was totally energized and animated.

Vince looked around the room and then walked over to where Toby and Ella were lying on their bed, embraced in each other's arms. Vince ordered Toby to get up because he was going to take Ella away from him. Toby hesitated long enough to evoke Vince's anger.

"Get up. I'm taking this bitch."

Ella looked frightened. Toby saw Ella's fear. He then looked to Nina and saw apprehension.

"Mr. Vince," challenged Toby. "This is my girl. We've been together for the last two days."

Vince's anger surged. He grabbed Toby by the hair and pulled him sideways out of the bed.

"You don't talk back to me, you little shit. Everything and everyone here, belongs to me."

Toby rolled onto the floor. Ella let out a small scream combining fear and shock. Vince ripped the blanket back partially covering Ella. As she sucked in a breath to scream again, he slapped her with all his strength on the left side of her face.

Young Leo and the other girl tried to stay clear of the conflict. Leo hoped that things would just settle down. The girl looked about the cabin. From her vantage point, she could not locate Rachel, and she assumed the worst. It was not much of a stretch to figure out that after Vince was through with Ella, she would be next.

The girl turned to Leo and pleaded, "Please baby, don't let him hurt me."

Toby recovered quickly from the assault. He was on his feet and angry. He squared up on Vince and yelled at him.

"Mr. Vince, get away from my girl. I swear to Jesus, I will beat you to death if you hurt her."

Even though Vince was older and outweighed him by 30 pounds, Toby's blood was up, and he had the protective instincts of a righteously raised young Christian man. Two days of debauchery, even Fort Scott debauchery, was not enough to offset 16 years of training in upright, protective values.

Young, inexperienced men often mistake lust for love, and after two days with Ella, Toby thought he was in love.

"Mr. Vince, I appreciate everything you've done for us but you're not taking Ella from me. You stay away from her. She's my girl. If we need to fight, then let's do it, I ain't scared of you."

Vince thought the confidence he saw building in the boys over the past two days was entertaining. What he never saw coming was the possibility one of them might bond emotionally with the girls. That was exactly what happened with Toby and Ella and now that confidence surfaced to protect her and oppose him.

Vince looked at Toby for a long moment. He knew that he could whip the boy in a bare-knuckle fight, but he also remembered the pain he suffered, from two dislocated fingers, after punching that hardheaded farm bitch.

Once again, things were not going Vince's way. Rachel died too quickly, but the experience was good enough to motivate Vince to want more. The next woman, closest to the type he liked, was Ella, and now she was being protected by a sod busting, ingrate farm boy.

Vince's demeanor changed so quickly it took Toby entirely off-guard.

Vince smiled with genuine understanding. "I'm sorry boy, I got carried away. You're right; this here is your girl, sure enough. Y'all just keep on enjoying yourselves." Pointing to Nina, he said, "I'll just take that one for myself."

Vince got up and walked toward his room where Rachel lay dead.

Toby sat down next to Ella and put his arm around her. He pulled her close, and she responded by holding onto him. In that moment, Ella felt that someone genuinely loved her. This 16-year-old boy made a statement proclaiming she had genuine value worth defending. No one had ever shown her that kindness. No other man had ever claimed her as his own and risked his life to punctuate that fact. "Toby, she whispered, "Thanks for caring about me."

He embraced her closely and whispered back, "When we leave, I want you to come home with me. This here ain't no place for you anymore."

That statement became the kindest and most fulfilling occurrence of Ella's young life.

Suddenly, Vince emerged from the small bedroom, pistol in hand. Nina saw the gun, as did Leo and the other girl. With Toby's back turned, he never saw Vince approaching. Ella's head was sideways against Toby's chest with her eyes closed. Before anyone was able to utter a sound, Vince buried the gun barrel into Toby's back and pulled the trigger. The muzzle blast seared Toby's clothing and flesh as the bullet tore a hole through the center of his heart. The ballistic shock of the impact thrust Toby's body against Ella, causing both of them to fall back on the bed. Toby's eyes never closed as he lay half on top of Ella.

She extricated herself from under the dead boy and glared at Vince with disbelief and hate. Vince backed up defensively against the front door and contemplated his next move.

* * * *

Ella continued her verbal assault, not caring if she died as a result. For her, it was important to show defiance as a sort of punishment toward Vince for the sins of the past night.

"I hate you, you low-life son-of-a-bitch. You've got no right to be with real people. I want you to die. I curse you and your bastard daddy who made you."

Standing between Ella and Vince, Nina turned on Ella and slapped her hard in the face. Ella stepped back startled. Nina moved forward and slapped her again, this time with both a forehand and backhand. She was stronger and more experienced in fighting. She broke up many battles between whores, quickly stopping the conflicts to protect her investment in them.

Nina pushed Ella by the throat into a wall and held her there for a long moment. She looked into Ella's eyes and yelled, "Now, you will shut that cussed mouth of yours, you hear me?"

Ella became emotionally overwhelmed, tears welled up, and she started crying hysterically. As Nina let go of her hold, Ella sank to the floor defeated by the evening's brutality.

Vince thoroughly enjoyed the moment. The violence from Nina and the humiliation and grief from Ella struck a note of satisfaction inside him. The incident gave credibility to Nina's promise she could handle problems in Fort Scott, and he could return to the Harris ranch without concern.

Vince indicated toward Leo, "You can keep him for the burying duties. He's not welcome back at the ranch." He looked directly at Leo. "If I ever see him around the ranch, I'll make sure both he and his whole damned family disappear. We've got a specific place back there for troublesome types."

53
The Harris Ranch

TALBOT HARRIS SENT orders for Tyler to report to the Big House for an update. Otto Metzger sat to his right, both men facing Tyler. "There's been no information or sightings of Ussher for two weeks. What's going on with him?" Talbot asked.

Tyler did not have any credible new information but attempted a broad answer to sound actively involved. "No one has seen or heard anything about him. It's as if he dropped off the face of the earth. Some of the men say they think he might be dead."

He immediately sensed displeasure for compensating the lack of tactical information with an unsupported remark. For Harris and Metzger, the only thing worse than a report using conjecture was relating a rumor containing second hand conjecture.

Tyler quickly preempted any potential rebuke from Harris by quickly stating, "I'll double my efforts, sir, and get you hard facts right quick."

Harris stated flatly, "Get to it" and Tyler immediately left the room.

Once Tyler was out of ear shot, Harris said to Metzger, "He's not right for this job and he knows too much. It might be better if he disappeared, once this Bushwhacker problem is settled."

* * * *

From his hidden location, Ussher caught sight of a rider coming in from the West at full gallop. It was obvious he was not a practiced horseman or else he was drunk. He lacked the ease of a man who spent much of his life in the saddle. Poor riders do not keep their body centered and balanced, causing the horse to adjust continuously. Over the course of a long ride, this places extra stress on the animal and tires him out. This horse was laboring to the point of exhaustion as it passed close by to where Ussher was hiding. Ussher immediately recognized the rider and leaned forward to confirm every detail of his appearance. He was the same man Ussher caught spying on Darby and himself back at their homestead. Over a year had passed, but the face remained indelibly etched in Ussher's recollection.

"Hello, Vince boy," Ussher intoned. "Now I know for a fact that you're back home with daddy. Later tonight, let's set aside some time to get reacquainted, just you and me."

* * * *

Mingo noted Ussher's reaction to the incoming rider. He watched Ussher observing other cowhands tending the herd. On those occasions, Mingo noted he looked at them in a manner that simply assessed each man's capability. When Ussher saw this rider, his focus was intense and stayed on the man from the time he first observed him until he arrived at the house. The rider was clearly someone important, as attendants met him and took charge of his horse. Mingo knew the rider well enough. He was the self-center aberrant son of his former boss. Now he had the next piece of information needed for a full understanding of the situation.

* * * *

Tyler was the first one at the house to realize Vince had returned. In a voice loud enough for everyone to hear, he directed one of the stable hands to feed and wipe down Vince's exhausted horse. Tyler offered his right hand and said, with as much sincerity as he could muster, "Glad to see you Mr. Vince. We've all been real worried about you."

Vince looked at Tyler's extended hand but did not move to accept it. He simply stood mute, looking blankly at the gesture. The rebuke made the moment uncomfortable and Tyler drew back. Vince allowed the attendant to take his horse and then turned to Tyler. "Tell that bitch, Abigail, that I'm hungry. I'll be back down to the kitchen in 20 minutes after I see my father."

54
9:30 AM

LAWRENCE, KANSAS

The last of the Missouri militia had finally departed Lawrence. After four hours of Hell, the citizens realized the raid was actually over. A nine-year-old boy climbed the church tower and confirmed that the Bushwhackers appeared to be gone.

Two hours later, more riders appeared on the eastern horizon pulling wagons. To the relief of everyone in town, the riders were friendly. They were neighbors from Eudora, a town about 12 miles away.

The Missourians passed by Eudora after the raid. The town's lookouts saw the large group approaching and raised an alarm. They recognized the riders came from the direction of Lawrence and correctly assumed the worst. They rallied the citizens in time to muster 50 rifles and handguns, sending out a staccato of shots that caused the militia to veer around their settlement.

The smoke from the burning town was visible for miles in the mid-morning sky. The neighboring townsfolk brought relief wagons to Lawrence loaded with food, medicine, blankets, and most importantly, guns and ammunition.

The condition of the survivors was grim. Some were in silent shock while others cried uncontrollably. The dead were everywhere and no one could make a decision as what to do first. Finally, one of the townswomen declared to several others, "We all have family to care for. We've got to identify the fallen and see to their needs before burial. Pass the word." She pointed to a couple of surviving boys, "You two, bring a team of horses with a wagon and be ready to help."

Under the woman's leadership, the people of Lawrence drew in a collective breath and set themselves to the task of preparing proper Christian burials. They dug graves, recited the Psalms, and cursed the "Black soul of Quantrill" 182 times, for each of their beloved dead.

55
The Harris Ranch

AS THE SUN BEGAN to set, Ussher readied himself. The moment he pictured in his dreams had arrived. The night that preoccupied his existence for over a year was at hand.

In the course of the day, he gathered a bundle of dry twigs and grass. Using his knife, he cut several cloth strips from the end of his shirt. He tied the bundle into a sheath of tinder with the cloth strips and used the remainder of the material as a long tether cord.

Although the cattle pressed close to where he lay hidden, they became accustomed to his presence, and his minimal movements no longer drew their attention. Ussher selected one of the larger longhorns for his diversionary plan. He was a powerful animal, weighing well over a ton. Ussher noted that other cattle yielded extra space to him, even as he settled his hulking frame onto the prairie grass for the night. His resting place was just beyond Ussher's reach.

The wind shifted and blew toward the big house.

Ussher brought along a small pouch of his dark leaf tobacco. He mixed gunpowder into the pouch and buried the mixture deep inside the tinder sheath. After tying a slipknot lasso on the remaining end of the tether, he was ready to begin and let Fate decide tonight's outcome.

Checking for the proximity Harris riders, Ussher left his hiding place and crawled cautiously behind the big animal, not wanting to risk a kick. Other longhorns looked passively his way but did not react. He rechecked the tinder sheath to make sure he bound it tightly. Carefully, he looped the slipknot over the tail of the big steer and cinched it tight. The burly animal did not seem to take notice. Ussher struck a wooden match, briefly brightening the area and then touched the match against the sheath. As the dried bundle began burning, he scrambled back behind the boulders.

* * * *

In the big house, Vince Harris sat in the kitchen eating a meal prepared from dinner leftovers and slab bacon, earlier set aside for breakfast. The reheated coffee was slightly bitter but cream smoothed out the taste. In spite of Abigail's best effort, given the short notice, Vince showed complete dissatisfaction with the offering. At first, he ate hungrily but after he was sated, Vince pushed the plate away with an air of contempt.

"This food ain't fit for the man of the house," he yelled to the four walls. Vince was alone in the kitchen, but Abigail and the cook heard the remark from the adjacent pantry room. She used a small table in a corner of the room to plan the activities of the household staff.

Vince yelled out again, "I want a fresh cooked, man-sized steak. You hear me, Abigail? Get your ass in here when I'm talking to you."

Before Abigail had a chance to respond, Talbot Harris entered the kitchen. Vince heard someone approaching and assumed it was going to be Abigail or one of the household staff. He allowed his ill-tempered demeanor to surface so they would be immediately aware of his displeasure. He inhaled a deep breath with the intent of vilifying whoever entered. When Vince saw it was his father, the pent-up breath coughed from his throat as he tried quickly to readjust his bad-mannered behavior. Although the senior Harris heard Vince's abusive remark to Abigail, he made no comment.

"It's good that your home. There's a lot going on in the territory that we need to talk about with Captain Metzger and Tyler first thing in the morning. We also have Army procurement officers stopping tomorrow to finalize a new deal for the herd. I need you to be ready and looking like you know what's required to run this ranch. Do you understand me, son?"

Vince said nothing as he walked to the walnut counter, where an open bottle of cooking Brandy sat. He picked it up, took a long pull on the contents and slammed the bottle back down. He pursed his lips to indicate he did not like the taste. He was about to comment on what his father said, when both men became aware of commotion outside the house. It was a thundering sensation combined with the panicked yells of men. Talbot Harris immediately guessed the source of the uproar. Vince noted the look of trepidation on his father's face as the senior Harris turned and walked decisively from the room.

* * * *

Out by the herd, the cowhands had settled in for the evening. After working many long hours, they hoped for a quiet night. Of those who were actually on horseback, most were napping while still sitting in their saddle.

The tinder sheath caught fire quickly. The big steer immediately spotted the flames, jumped up and lumbered away. With the bundle tied to his tail, the flame followed him. He quickly moved his stocky frame against and around other cattle as he tried to retreat from the burning mass. He turned franticly in circles but the movement did not shake the bundle loose. Instead, it actually swung outward and then back underneath his backside. The bellowing from the steer sent a menacing warning across the grassland into the entire herd.

The fire burned into the pouch of tobacco and gunpowder and started to hiss and smoke. This created a thunderous panic with the steer who bellowed even louder. All the animals closest to the burning bundle ran to escape the violent bucking. Crackly sparks spewed from the tinder sheath and within two minutes panic turned into pandemonium.

* * * *

As Talbot Harris opened the front door and stepped onto the porch, hundreds of cattle stampeded by the perimeter fence. He couldn't see anything but chaos. By the time the big steer shook the burning tinder loose, panic and dread flooded through the entire herd. The wailing of the terrified animal was so genuine the cattle perceived there was an insidious threat from which they needed to escape. The Longhorns reacted defensively and ran from the source of the panic. A giant dust cloud arose as thousands of hooves beat against the earth. The combination of night and dust made visibility nearly impossible.

The mounted cowhands responded to the situation with alarm and panic. Without any time for coordination, all they could do was ride with the running cattle until exhaustion forced the herd to rest. The remainder of the drovers ran to their horses to help the others. The horses, sensing the fear created by the stampede, pulled wildly against their reins attempting to free themselves. Most of the cowhands were able to mount their terrified horses but two pulled free of their tethers and raced away. Their riders impulsively chased them on foot into the onrush of the herd. Each disappeared beneath hundreds of hooves and fell trampled into shapeless demise.

* * * *

Jack Mingo watched the chaos from his safe location. Fortunately, none of the stampeding animals ran in his direction. From his vantage point, he was not able to identify the source of the chaos, but he guessed Ussher orchestrated the bedlam. Mingo was impressed and a wry smile crinkled involuntarily. With all the odds against him, Ussher figured a way to create a diversion and give himself a fighting chance.

All Mingo could make out was the hazy illumination of the big house in the distance. He figured he needed to prepare himself for whatever was about to happen. If Ussher's success continued, there might be an occasion for Mingo to capitalize on the moment. If Ussher did not succeed, Mingo might have to withdraw quickly to await some future opportunity. Either way, preparation and readiness were essential for success.

56
Confrontation

USSHER SAW A Harris cowhand riding toward his direction. The man did not notice Ussher; he was only concerned with staying in the saddle to avoid the stampeding cattle. Ussher looked around to judge the flow of the herd and figured he had just seconds to make his move.

The man's horse passed at half-gallop. Ussher sprang up and ran along the left side of the horse. Using the barrel of the Henry rifle like a club, he hit the rider across the base of his spine. Fractured vertebrae set waves of pain through the man's body and down his legs. Continuing to run, Ussher transferred the Henry rifle to his left hand and reached up to the cowhand's belt with his right, pulling with all his strength. The rider fell backwards over the horse and onto the ground. His pain subsided almost instantly as the hooves from two Longhorns ravaged his body. One of the animals stepped on his lower back, crushing through his rib cage and lacerating a kidney. The second steer trampled across his neck, severing his spine from his brainstem, killing him instantly.

Ussher continued to run alongside the horse as he transferred the Henry back to his right hand. He only had one chance to saddle up. If he missed the mount, he would also fall and likely die from the rush of the frenzied Longhorns. With the rifle in hand, Ussher threw his right arm over the seat and snagged the front lip of the saddle with his first and middle fingers. At the same time, he grabbed the saddle horn with his left hand, pulled up and slipped his toe into the stirrup. The combination of a push with his left leg and a pull with his right hand finally placed him atop the horse.

Ussher allowed the horse a loose rein. In this situation, the horse's instincts were likely superior to his own reactions. He was better off trusting the horse to save itself, and him in the process. He was eventually able to maneuver out of the main flow of the stampede. Inside the camouflage of dark and dust, he moved in the direction of the big house. Ussher took his time and tried to take on the appearance of a Harris cowhand to avoid attention. Sweat and dirt caked his face.

As he drew closer to the house, the profile of the porch, illuminated by several lanterns, became clearer. Ussher saw two large men mounting horses brought by a stable hand. Both men began riding in his direction. Ussher tried to circle wide but they veered directly toward him. It was none other than Talbot Harris flanked by Otto Metzger. Ussher tucked the Henry under his leg on the right side of the saddle and positioned himself so the left side of his horse faced the oncoming men.

Metzger took the lead, "Where in Hell are you going?" he demanded.

Neither Harris nor Metzger had any idea it was Ussher. Tyler was in charge of all the hiring. New cowhands came in all the time and neither Harris nor Metzger cared much about learning names or establishing relationships. They assumed Ussher was a malingering worker who needed his butt kicked to get him back on the job. Once Ussher realized they did not recognize him, he adjusted to his good fortune and continued the subterfuge.

"My horse has gone lame, Boss, Ussher said, "He can't cut to the right. I was just going in to get me another mount. Ten minutes and I'll be back out doing my job for y'all."

Metzger gave Ussher a hard stare, followed by a considered lookover of the horse. Metzger recognized that the horse appeared exhausted and it was possible some of the stress was the result of a leg or hoof injury.

"Make it fast or I'll have your ass on a pike," Metzger sneered.

Ussher responded, "Yes, sir, I'll be back out right quick."

As Ussher rode toward the big house, Harris and Metzger moved out to evaluate the progress of controlling the herd.

Harris watched the interaction between Metzger and Ussher from a short distance. The dust and the darkness prevented him from seeing Ussher's face but two aspects nagged at him regarding this cowhand. The first was the tone of his voice. It was steady and direct. It did not contain the deference or fear that Harris was used to hearing when men spoke with either Metzger or himself. The second was that this man appeared to hold steady eye contact with the much-feared Captain. These observations troubled Harris as he and Metzger rode further onto the prairie.

* * * *

As Ussher rode up to the main door of the barn, he watched for any sign of Vince Harris. He decided to use the exchange of horses as a diversion to slip away and get inside the ranch house. The first of two stable hands approached him.

"I need a fresh horse," announced Ussher. "This one has gone a little lame."

The stable hand had worked on the Harris ranch for seven years, and he knew every cowhand employed there. "I don't know you," he said flatly.

Ussher remained calm. "The boss sent me in and now I've got to get back on the job right quick; so stop the bullshit and get me a new mount," Ussher stated with feigned authority.

The first man eyed the other. The second man moved around a post and picked up a long set of collaring tongs from one of the anvils. "Around here, we don't call the boss, Boss. We call the boss, Captain. If you were actually one of us, you would know that fact."

With that, he yelled and rushed at the face of Ussher's horse while waving his hands wildly. This caused the horse to rear up, throwing him backwards. Ussher did not resist the momentum. As soon as his reflexes assessed that a fall was unavoidable, he concentrated on how to handle the upcoming trauma to minimize potential damage to his body. Ussher was able to push away in the same direction the horse was moving. The thrust threw him back and over to his left. As he landed, the momentum caused him to roll back and over at an angle but he quickly recovered his footing. As he came up, Ussher's knife appeared in his hand.

The two Harris men rushed toward him. Ussher dispatched the closest one by ducking under his lunge and stabbing the man with a backhand slash as he passed by. The cut went deep over his right kidney but was not deadly or immediately disabling. The second man, with the tongs, stopped and squared up to fight. He started to circle Ussher, looking for an opportunity to strike a blow.

His wounded partner pulled back from the fray and screamed, "Invader, invader! Get us help! Invader, invader!"

Ussher initially drew the knife hoping to settle things quietly, but the yelling no longer made that possible. Circumstances forced him to settle things quickly. He un-holstered his revolver and shot the man holding the tongs in the center of his chest. His opponent dropped with a groan and did not move. The first man kept yelling until Ussher's next bullet struck him just below the fifth rib and finished him.

Ussher's horse ran into the stable to escape the conflict. Ussher followed him and retrieved the Henry rifle from the saddle holster. There was work to do.

* * * *

Like Ussher, Jack Mingo mounted his horse in the darkness and attempted to blend in as a Harris cowhand. He saw the run-in between Ussher, Harris, and Metzger. Again, he was impressed that Ussher seemingly spirited his way through a dangerous encounter. Now, as Mingo came up onto the edge of the grounds around the big house, he heard the two gunshots. He was near an old tool shed. Mingo dismounted, secured his horse and proceeded cautiously on foot.

* * * *

Ussher re-emerged from the stable and ran to the porch, intending to enter right through the solid oak front door. He guessed everyone near the house must have heard the gunshots and it might be only a matter of minutes before riders returned to investigate. He needed to find a way inside the house quickly and when he found the door locked, he cursed his bad luck. Ussher knew that climbing through a window could make him an easy target, so he circled the house to find another possible entry.

The home's large kitchen was at the back of the house. Under one window was a small door leading to a root cellar. Ussher pulled the door open and the rusty hinges screeched their protest. A faint moist scent emanated from the dark opening. With no time for caution, he inhaled a calming breath and ducked inside.

* * * *

Abigail heard the first stable man yelling about an invader. When she looked out the window, she could see he was bleeding and holding his back and side. She also saw a second man facing off with Ussher. As she gathered the women of her household into the pantry room, Abigail heard the shooting. She grabbed a butcher knife from a carving block to defend the women and herself just before going inside. She then pulled the door closed and latched it top and bottom.

* * * *

When the stampede began, Vince watched his father and Captain Metzger go off to supervise the reorganization of the herd. The stampede did not concern Vince. He had just returned after a hard ride from Fort Scott and felt no obligation to help gather any damn Longhorns. That kind of work was for common people, like cowhands and dirt farmers. It was not for men of his caliber. His father and the Captain always felt they needed to set an example for the men by going out and appearing to give a damn. "Why should I give a shit?" Vince thought.

He did not care about appearances. In his opinion, cowhands should be satisfied to do their job and risk their lives for the simple fact they received payment to do so.

He grabbed his half-empty bottle of Old Crow and returned to his room.

* * * *

Talbot Harris continued to experience a nagging feeling regarding the cowhand he and Metzger talked with earlier. He believed in the wisdom of his gut; it had served him well for many years. With only two stablemen to provide security, Harris ordered Tyler and three cowhands to ride back and make sure things were under control at the house

Tyler was happy for the chance to ride back to the big house. The assignment got him away from the risk, dirt and stench of the herd. Once they arrived, he and his men would take their time thoroughly searching the house, barn, and bunkhouse. If things worked out right, Tyler would not have to return to the dangers of the roundup. Truth was, when he reached the big house, he intended to down a man-size portion of whiskey from a bottle stashed near his bunk.

* * * *

Ussher figured it right; the root cellar contained a ladder, which rose up through a trap door and onto the floor of the kitchen. There was no latch and Ussher opened it slowly, anxious someone might be waiting in ambush. He could see a little on three sides but the fourth side, with hinges, was blind from view. Throwing caution to the wind, he threw open the door and propelled himself up the ladder. As the trapdoor flew back, it landed hard against the side of the pantry, causing a loud bang. The noise frightened a couple of women inside and they sucked in an audible breath. Ussher heard the collective gasp and identified its source. He stepped to the side, pulled on the door handle and discovered it locked.

Outside, he heard horses galloping as Tyler and three drovers rode up to the front porch. Tyler ordered the men to check the house. He headed for his bunk and the bottle.

The door to the pantry room had a fence-gate style latch. Since Ussher could not get into the pantry, he wanted to make sure no one could get out. He twisted a fork, jammed it into the latch and pushed the freestanding cutting block up against the outside.

A quick look around did not reveal anyone else on the lower level. As he started up the stairs, the three cowhands started pounding on the front door.

57

Moments of Truth

AT THE TOP of the stairs, Ussher saw two doors on the right. The first was close to the head of the staircase, the second was farther down the hallway. Suddenly, a shot rang out followed by another. The bullets whistled past his head. Halfway down the hall on the left, a semi-intoxicated Vince Harris ducked back into a doorway. He reappeared, pistol in hand, and fired another four rounds. Ussher ducked behind the top two stairs for cover. The cowhands heard the shots and yelled for someone to open front door. One of the three ran to look for Tyler while his partners pounded frantically on the frame; one started to kick the latch. The cowhand searching for Tyler passed the blacksmith shop and found the two dead stable hands.

Ussher ran down the hall toward the room where Vince was holed up. A locked, solid oak door blocked his entry. After kicking it several times, he lowered his rifle and fired two quick rounds into the latch. He kicked it again. When the door held solid, Ussher knew it had slide locks as well as a latch. He fired three more times, high and low, sending splinters through the door and down the hallway. At that moment, the drovers began shooting at the lock on the front entrance of the house. Ussher returned to the top of the staircase, reloading his rifle as he moved. He was in position just as the two cowhands burst in.

Ussher scored a kill with his first shot but missed with the next. The second cowhand returned fire, and his bullet grazed Ussher's left side, opening a deep cut and cracking a rib. Pain shot through Ussher's body as he involuntarily buckled to one knee. The man missed with the next two bullets and then pulled back. Ussher heard him yelling for Tyler and the first cowhand to come to his assistance.

Ussher spotted a towel sitting under a vase on a small table. He grabbed it, tumbling the vessel to the floor where it shattered into pieces. He quickly folded the cloth and placed it against his wound, holding it in position with the inside of his elbow. He recognized the wound was not severe but knew the loss of blood would weaken him and send him into shock. Walking determinedly back down the hall to the room hiding Vince, he gave the door another two kicks. The first made it shudder; the second caused it to fly open and crash against the adjoining wall. He immediately stepped into the room, looking left and right, but saw nothing. Leading with the barrel of the Henry, Ussher searched behind furniture, under a table, and inside a closet. The open window to the rooftop provided the answer to his quandary.

Vince Harris was many things but he was not stupid. In his security meetings with Tyler, Metzger, and his father, he heard reports about Ussher's effectiveness as a killer. Vince did not give that problem its proper level of concern because he never envisioned a circumstance allowing Ussher to penetrate the security of the ranch. Now that the son-of-a-bitch was here, Vince was terrified to the point of panic. There was no telling what a man of Ussher's capability could accomplish. The reality of his situation seized control of his nervous system and tested the management of his urinary function. Fact was; he never had to piss so badly in his entire life.

The cowhands located Tyler at the back of the property. They reported the loss of the two men from the stable and the rider. They also informed him that Ussher was inside the big house and shooting was going on. Tyler instructed the men to go to opposite corners of the house so each could watch two sides of the structure. Tyler announced he would ride back to report the situation to Harris and Metzger because he owned the fastest horse. The cowhands hesitated until Tyler shouted to get their asses moving and follow his instructions. At that moment, all three men heard Vince Harris screaming for salvation, as he perched at the edge of the rooftop.

"Help me, god-damn-it. There's a son-of-a-bitch up here shootin' at me. I think its Ussher. Get me down. Watch the doors and windows and kill that bastard as soon as you see him. Get me down, get me down now."

Tyler knew immediately there was no choice but to stay and help. If word ever got back to Old Man Harris that he abandoned his baby boy in a time of need, Harris would have Metzger eviscerate him in The Meadow for damn sure.

As Tyler and his men ran back to the front of the big house, Ussher was just beginning to exit through a window. All three men fired at Ussher with their revolvers. The bullets shattered the glass and splintered the window frame, forcing him to duck back inside the upper room. The reverse movement caused extreme pain to his wound but he quickly rallied to continue the fight.

* * * *

Out on the prairie, the cattle herd was nearly back under control. The Harris men were reconsolidating the animals about a mile and a half further from where the stampede originated. Although exhausted, the herd was still agitated and the steers bellowed and complained loudly.

The increased distance and the incessant din of the Longhorns prevented the cattlemen from hearing the conflict around the big house. Harris decided he and Metzger would stay awhile longer to thank the men individually for their efforts before heading back. At half-gallop, it would only take a short time to return to the big house.

* * * *

Tyler retrieved a ladder from the barn and placed it against the roof of the house. The two cowhands trained their guns on the window where Ussher had tried to exit as well as the lower windows and doors.

Tyler yelled to Vince, "Climb down the ladder. We'll make sure Ussher stays inside."

Vince hesitated, searching the area for his pursuer. "How do I know he won't shoot me on my way down?"

"There's three of us", Tyler snarled, "and when you get down here, there'll be four. We should be able to handle one man without a problem. Come on, get your ass moving." Vince nervously looked around to reaffirm conditions were safe.

Tyler became agitated. With a man like Ussher so close, he did not want to be in the open any longer than necessary. "Vince," he shouted, "I'm telling you for the last time, get your ass down here right now or I'm gonna' leave you on your own. You hear me?"

Tyler's tone of authority made Vince react. He holstered his revolver. "Hold the ladder tight," he called out as he turned and started to descend the rungs to safety. Just five steps down, Vince froze in place, traumatized by the sound of rifle fire from the Henry.

Ussher did not bother trying to use a window or door to reenter the fight. He exited the house the same way he entered it, via the root cellar. The root cellar was something Tyler never considered. For him, it was a worthless little entrance used by the household staff for purposes he never bothered learning. Now it provided Ussher with a conduit for retaliatory surprise.

Ussher fired two rounds in quick succession, killing the closest man on Tyler's left. Tyler never attempted to return fire. He reflexively ducked and then abandoned the ladder, running with jackrabbit speed toward the bunkhouse. Unnerved by the sudden gunfire and the sight of Tyler's cowardly retreat, the second man fired several wild shots toward Ussher. When his next trigger-pull fell on an empty chamber, he wasn't sure if he should run or try reloading. Ussher used that moment of indecision to focus and fire from the hip, hitting him low in the belly. As the man's knees buckled, Ussher aimed and fired a fatal second bullet through his forehead.

* * * *

The leading edge of the sun split open the horizon and the area in front of the big house loomed vast and lonely for Vince Harris. The action below his position took place with such violent efficiency that he never thought to draw his revolver to defend himself. Two stablemen and three ranch hands lay dead, Tyler had run away and he was alone, making Ussher more dangerous than ever. Vince clung breathlessly to the ladder, stomach muscles bound tightly and mouth agape, hoping Ussher would not look up and discover him.

Ussher watched the fallen men for a moment, confirming they were no longer a threat. As he walked closer, he released the spring tensioner and reloaded the Henry. Vince watched in immobilized silence as each of the deadly rounds dropped into place. Ussher slowly scanned the area and horizon and saw no immediate threat. He stood in place, as if gathering himself in a reflective moment, while looking down at the Henry. Vince saw his hand flex against the rifle stock as his gaze leveled ahead. Finally, Ussher turned forcefully around and deliberately looked up and into the traumatized face of Vince Harris.

Vince gazed downward to witness Joseph Ussher, dirt farmer, militia scout, and loving husband to Darby, in the most menacing stance imaginable, holding that damn rifle. A small stream of urine followed gravity down Vince's leg. For a moment, he actually thought he heard the amused laughter of the Demon.

Vince held the ladder with his left hand and extended a shaky right hand, palm out.

"Don't…don't shoot. Please mister, don't kill me. I don't want to die out here in the dirt. We can work this out. I can give you anything you want. I'm rich and I'll make you rich too. Don't kill me. I'm begging you, please don't kill me."

Vince continued down the ladder until his feet were four rungs from the bottom. He started crying and actually experienced a clear understanding about the impact and shock of helplessness and fear. Although begging never worked for the victims, he and Andy Hester tortured and murdered, he hoped it would work for him.

Then, from the deep recesses of his devious mind, Vince came up with his version of a can't-miss idea, which he thought to be truly inspirational. He quickly gulped a breath to fight his anxiety and regain composure.

"Mister, listen to me, besides money, I can give you something amazing that I know you ain't never experienced." Inside this here house, we got us a genuine French Creole housekeeper with a beautiful ass. I'll give her to you. You can do anything you want with her, anything at all. Her name is Abigail."

Vince looked at Ussher and waited for a sign of approval.

Ussher hesitated. It's strange how recollections can surge through your mind in times of extreme stress. He looked around the porch of the Harris house. Once again, there were dead men all about him. He suddenly realized how tired he was of the hate, the fighting, and the killing. He thought about Nate. He was exceedingly relieved and grateful that boy was safe in St. Louis with Benjamin. Ussher prayed that Nate's early life experiences would not change the goodness inherent in his soul. That boy was going to turn into a fine man with the ability to accomplish great things in his life.

Ussher then thought about himself and his own chances for salvation. After all the things he caused to happen with ambushing and killing, was there any possibility of ever receiving forgiveness?

Ussher pointed the Henry away from Vince and up toward the sky. "Come all the way down," he said simply.

Vince sucked in a gulp of air and then let out a long breath as he struggled to compose himself. Gradually, he began to appear hopeful. A half-smile of anticipated salvation appeared on his face as he descended the final rungs. Reaching the ground, he straightened himself and half tucked his shirt into the waist of his pants.

Vince stood facing Ussher and assumed the man had reconsidered and accepted his remarkable offer. He reflected with satisfaction that he had saved his own life and was about to rid himself of Abigail, all in one brilliant move. His father would be devastated and furious over losing the woman he loved and respected so very much, but Vince didn't care. He was already devising a story to shift all the blame to Tyler because the bastard ran away. The old man would order Metzger to rip Tyler to shreds. Vince might even offer to assist. As these thoughts coursed through his mind, he suppressed a smile as he waited for Ussher to tell him how much money he would demand. When Vince noticed Ussher's eyes divert briefly, he figured the man was calculating the monetary amount he considered satisfactory.

Ussher was at peace with his decision. Everyone wants

change, but it is always a desperate struggle to be the first to back down and even more difficult to forgive. The circumstances of this damn war made that which is difficult, nearly impossible. If change was ever going to be achievable, it had to start with someone making the first gesture.

Peacefully extending the olive branch to adversaries was a necessary first step, regardless of the offense they previously committed. Ussher decided that he would be that man and leave this life of violence and death behind him. For the remainder of his days, he resolved to follow a path searching for tolerance and understanding of human weakness. There might still be time. A determined Joseph Ussher could demonstrate the ability to rise above the frailties of his past and use his talents to promote benevolence and compassion.

Ussher needed to decide the timeline when his transformation from fighter to man-of-peace would commence. Yes, change would surely come and his outlook and life intention would transcend. Yes, he intended to achieve a higher plane of humanity. Yes, he wanted to be an example to demonstrate the benefits of temperance. However…conversion and commitment would require delay until…TOMORROW.

Ussher looked at an increasingly reassured Vince Harris, now standing calmly just a few feet away, probably planning his activities for the rest of this day.

His focus ultimately riveted on the bite scar embedded into Vince's cheek. He thought of his sweet Darby and the totality of her love surged through his heart. He felt humbled with gratitude for her bravery that saved his life. Pain and emptiness immediately followed these sensations as he recollected her violent and senseless loss. Ussher's gut seized tightly and acid boiled into his throat. Adrenaline surged through his muscles and his brain hard-wired back to his core purpose.

Vince instantly recognized the transformation. His eyes widened in direct proportion to the way Ussher's eyes narrowed. Ussher lowered the Henry and targeted the center of Vince's body. He chambered a .44 caliber round into the Henry with emphasis. The lever action returned a satisfying metallic sensation as the deadly round rotated and settled into place.

Vince heard the unmistakable sound and knew Ussher had rejected his offer. His body shook once again as fear of impending doom solidified. The tremors were so intense they became paralytic and urine soaked his pants. He tried to resume pleading for his life but could not think of anything more to say, so he reached out in a gesture of pathetic desperation.

"Mercy," he appealed with the most imploring tenor his voice could devise. His retching sobs continued to send shudders of dread down his spine. He started repeating his pleading but Ussher cut him off mid-sentence.

"My wife's name was Darby," Ussher's voice thundered.

Vince tried to back away, but the ladder stopped his movement.

"My wife's name was Darby," Ussher repeated with even more intensity.

"YOU violated our home. YOU punished her without cause. YOU took her from me, you low-life piece of shit."

Ussher's tone quickly rose from anger to deadly threat. Vince half-turned and placed his foot on the first rung as if he might try to climb back up the ladder. His foot slipped over so that he now straddled the rung. He turned back toward Ussher, both hands raised in a gesture of desperation. He opened his mouth to speak, but no words vocalized as he stared into the blackness of the Henry's cold steel barrel.

"Say her name," Ussher raged as he walked closer to Vince.

Vince's mind went blank with dread. "What?" I don't understand…which name…who are you talking about?" He looked around the area as if expecting to see someone standing nearby.

"Darby! Say her name…say Darby," Ussher screamed in his face.

"Da…Darby," Vince stammered fearfully.

"Tell Darby you're sorry you murdered her. Say it!"

Vince looked into Ussher's burning eyes and realized he was about to utter the last phrase of his life. The only words he was able to stammer out were, "I'm real sorry."

Ussher pulled the trigger of the rifle. The report from the Henry had never been as loud or sharp when the fatal round blasted out the barrel. Vince's body jolted as the bullet passed through his chest below his sternum and exited through his back, shattering vertebrae. Dust and wood splinters jumped from the boards as the bullet crashed into the side of the house.

Pain surged through Vince's nervous system as his spinal cord severed and his body lost all communication with his brain. Ussher chambered another round and fired again. The transfer of energy from the second bullet slammed Vince's torso against the ladder and snapped his neck backwards across a rung. His frame rebounded off the ladder and his legs started to collapse.

Before Vince's body fell all the way to the ground, Ussher fired a third round. The bullet shattered his collarbone and seemed to lift him upwards and spin him around. Vince's body deflated into a vacant remembrance of a man. His lifeless frame lay sprawled and discarded, leaving his arm dangling over and clinging to the lowest rung on the ladder.

Ussher looked at the vestiges of the man who caused him so much pain and suffering. For over a year, Vince Harris was his obsession and now his enemy was dead. The feelings he experienced manifested relief, retribution, and compensation, but there was no satisfaction. Ussher thought it unfair that his enemy died so quickly. He wished he could somehow revive the bastard to extend his suffering and kill him again.

This moment of reckoning left Ussher's mouth with the taste of bile and bitterness. Surprisingly, the confrontation also left him with an inordinate sensation of emptiness. Avenging Darby closed the loop of justice owed to her and released Ussher from his self-imposed obligation. What he never anticipated was that, although release brought closure, closure meant there was nothing more he could do for Darby. Although her memory remained as strong, their connection now drifted and reinforced the harsh reality that she was gone forever.

The truth and clarity of this moment caused expressive power to surge between Ussher's heart and brain stem. Shutters of energy cascaded through his body and conflicted emotions strained his sanity to the breaking point. The only release Ussher could engender was to look up to heaven and scream out his frustration. He nearly collapsed from the exhausting ordeal.

58
Mingo Settles the Score

USSHER COLLECTED himself, taking a last look at Vince Harris. The pain from the wound in Ussher's side was tolerable and the bleeding had stopped.

Unexpectedly, he glimpsed a man's profile to his left and turned to face the threat. It was Tyler, running from the bunkhouse to the back of the property to hide. Even though Tyler carried a loaded revolver, he hesitated to shoot at Ussher. He figured if he missed the shot, the report would give away his position and condemn his survival. He ran from building-to-building seeking an advantage or a place to hide, each time looking back to see if Ussher was following.

Ussher moved in the same direction to ensure Tyler could not shoot him as he left the Harris property. Since he did not encounter opposition, Ussher arrived at the last building at almost the same moment as Tyler. The location offered an almost tragic, poetic climax to the trials of this past night and early morning. It was the torture barn where Vince Harris and Andy Hester spent countless hours perfecting their technique for torment, degradation, and death.

Ussher saw Tyler as he opened the swinging door and ran inside the barn. As Tyler turned, Ussher stood inescapably close, with the Henry rifle at the ready, prepared to finish this day's work. Tyler first looked fearful, then with a sideways glance, his eyes widened as if he saw a ghost. Ussher saw Tyler's reaction just seconds before losing consciousness.

He was out-cold for a half minute from the head blow of Mingo's rifle stock. That was long enough to be completely disarmed. When Ussher came to, he was lying on his belly. As he attempted to get up, Mingo pushed downward fiercely with a boot heel, and placed his rifle barrel against Ussher's ear.

"Well, just what do we have here?" he said, looking at the wound under Ussher's tattered and blood-soaked shirt. "So, tell me Bushwhacker, how does it feel to get a bullet crease across your body, and then get knocked down to eat dirt?"

Ussher did not attempt an answer, better to say nothing than to make a stupid or provocative remark. As he thought through the situation, he wondered why he was still alive. Mingo had taken a risk walking up so closely, considering all the dead men lying about the property. A prudent scout would normally shoot first in this circumstance.

Tyler was aghast and celebratory at the same time. He kept looking at Mingo with incredulity. He had seen Mingo get shot-down by this redneck dirt farmer, who now lay unarmed and helpless between the two of them, and now he looked as healthy and strong as ever.

Tyler kept laughing in nervous disbelief at his perceived good luck and almost mystic salvation from certain death. Old Man Harris was going to be uncontrollably angry over the loss of his son. Now, Tyler had a good chance of claiming that he was responsible for subduing and capturing Vince's killer, and the most hated man in this part of Jayhawker territory.

He remembered that Mingo had no taste for dealing with powerful men who considered themselves superior. Whenever they came back from patrolling the perimeter of the ranch, Mingo always stayed with the men. He never sought to interact with either Talbot Harris or Otto Metzger. This left Tyler to explain situations in any manner he wished. He could take credit for the good and heap blame on the dead whenever it suited his purpose, without fear of contradiction.

"Mingo, you crazy son-of-a-bitch," Tyler finally blurted. "I can't believe you're here. I can't believe that you're alive and still in the fight. This is fucking amazing. I'm going to make sure that you get the biggest bounty of any man in this whole territory. Harris is going to skin this asshole alive. I mean, literally, he will skin him piece-by-piece, strip-by-strip, down to the bone. He's going to turn Metzger loose to inflict so much misery on this piece-of-shit, that dying will look sweeter than bagging your first virgin."

Mingo watched Tyler as he walked around Ussher.

Then Tyler taunted Ussher. "You hear me boy? By the time we get through, you won't know the difference between Hell and the Garden of Eden. You're going to promise to eat your guts raw, rather than live another minute on this earth."

Tyler heard Mingo cock the hammer on his Enfield rifle as it pointed toward Ussher. He quickly put up both hands with a stopping motion in Mingo's direction.

"Hold on. We want to keep Ussher alive. He's worth a lot more that way. Harris and Metzger are gonna' want to rip him apart. I know I can get you a much bigger bounty if we turn him over alive. Just imagine how much fun Metzger will have irritating that wound in his side. He's probably gonna' cover that gash with fire ants and allow them to eat right through to his liver. It's going to be great. You and I can be part of this. This is gonna' make us big time. We'll look back on this day and think about how this dirt-bag brought us the fortunes we deserve."

Mingo looked at Tyler for a long moment. As the hammer

remained cocked on his rifle, he raised and redirected the barrel, centering his aim on Tyler's chest.

Tyler was instantly startled, took three steps backwards, swallowed hard and tried to regain his composure.

"Mingo, let's not fuck around," he said, "We have to take care of business here. Old Man Harris is going to be back any time now. He will expect things to be under control and moving back to normal. You're going to get a pile of money for helping me out today."

"I am taking care of business," Mingo replied, "my business."

Tyler's mood changed from jubilant to fearful as he tried to understand Mingo's actions and motivation.

"What are you talking about? Why are you pointing the rifle at me? You and I are on the same team. We have always been on the same team."

Ussher remained absolutely still. He could detect the strong dynamic between Mingo and Tyler. As he listened to their words, he sensed the tension between the two men was genuine and dangerous.

Mingo revealed a contemptuous half-grin. Though his lips drew slightly back, his eyes did not crinkle to complement the smile. The resulting sneer fully revealed the hatred he held against Tyler.

"So…you don't know what I'm talking about, eh? I'll tell you what I'm talking about. My reason for pointing this here rifle at you, Mr. Boss Man Tyler, is because I intend to shoot your ass, right here and right now. You're right, at one point we were on the same team, but you changed all that."

Mingo paused and repeated, "YOU changed all that."

Tyler began to panic. "What the Hell are you talking

about? For months, we patrolled together and hunted bounties. I always took care of you, made sure that you were paid before anyone else."

Mingo did not respond, which frightened Tyler even more.

"Why are you so mad…what do you have against me… why would you want to shoot me instead of killing Ussher? This asshole shot you down for God's sake."

Mingo answered with a tone of explanation and revelation.

"Of course Ussher shot me; why wouldn't he? Hell, I don't hold that against him. I was gonna' kill him if I would've gotten the chance."

Pointing at Ussher, Mingo continued, "The only thing this man did was defend himself. That, I understand. That, I completely respect."

Tyler had always been good at talking himself out of tough situations and searched for the magic of a plausible reason to make Mingo reconsider his decision.

"I still don't understand. What did I ever do, to make you want to kill me?"

Mingo shouted, "Ussher may have shot me, but you abandoned me. You left me behind like a piece of worthless discarded scum. You never fired one bullet in my defense. I watched you today as you ran away, never firing one bullet in the defense of our badass rich boy, Vince Harris, either; same Tyler, same chicken shit reaction, same fucking result."

* * * *

For Mingo, killing Tyler was a matter of dignity. The Pawnee would never abandon a warrior in battle. If one of their people fell in combat, it inspired the surviving men to fight more ferociously. They wanted to fight for their people as well as recover their fallen brethren. For proper burial, a man must be wrapped in a buffalo robe and receive the prayers of his relatives before transport into the afterlife was possible. Mingo never knew a Pawnee warrior who was not faithful to that covenant. Mingo carried lifetime scars of honor from wounds received fighting to recover fallen brothers. As his Grandfather knew and noted, Mingo's heritage might be half-breed, but his warrior instinct, prowess as a fighter and belief in traditions were pure Pawnee.

Tyler was not ready to give up his defense. An excellent rationale came to mind, and he felt a surge of optimism as he anticipated Mingo's reaction. Then, just as Tyler took a quick breath to continue his argument, Mingo pulled the trigger. The heavy .58 caliber Enfield bullet hit Tyler in the lower abdomen. As his heart pumped out the last of his life's blood, his brain attempted to rationalize how circumstances got away from him.

"Fuck it," he said with ultimate acceptance to no one in particular, "I always figure this shit out in the end." Then he died.

* * * *

Mingo removed Tyler's revolver and walked back to Ussher.

"Get up," Mingo instructed.

He continued, "I've been watching you Bushwhackers for weeks. I know about that kid you sent away and I've learned many things about you. The one thing I really know for sure is, after today, you have to disappear…forever."

Ussher remained quiet, keeping his eyes focused on Mingo. Mingo noticed Ussher's hesitation and said with assurance,

"I ain't gonna' kill you, unless you make me. You need to leave the territory and Old Man Harris needs to believe you're dead. He'll dedicate his life to hunting you down if he thinks you're still alive. With a man like that, the smart money will bet on him and against you. That's the way I see it."

Ussher got to his feet. Now Mingo stayed focused and alert. Ussher asked. "You got an idea for me?"

Mingo explained, "No, I've got an idea for myself that just might also benefit you. Talbot Harris wants you dead and he wants his Henry rifle returned. The man who figures out how to do that job earns one big ass bounty. See what you think about this…"

He reached down and pulled Grandfather's Pawnee knife from his belt. He walked over to where Tyler was lying face down and straddled his lifeless body. Mingo looked over to Ussher and declared, "Death to all these fuckers."

He pulled Tyler's head back by the hair and placed his boot on the back of Tyler's neck. He cut a deep semicircle gash across his forehead and jerked hard with a backward motion.

As Tyler's scalp tore away and separated, Mingo spoke to the dead man, "Yeah! Now that's the way you do it," mocking the words Tyler used when he mutilated Jimmy.

He stood up, spit on Tyler's corpse, and then wiped the blade clean against Tyler's shirt.

Mingo walked over and picked up the Henry rifle. He held it up in his right hand and said, "I've got this."

With his left hand, he held up Tyler's scalp and stated, "And, I've got this. The rifle and the scalp are an inseparable set. This scalp is you. You are officially dead, and I am about to earn enough money to get myself out of this war."

Pointing to Tyler, Mingo instructed Ussher, "Take his

weapons and get your ass moving. You probably have less than half an hour before Old Man Harris gets himself back here, likely surrounded by ten or more men. I figured out where you hid that crazy fast horse of yours. Goddamn, but I sure would have liked the chance to ride that animal for a while. I ain't never seen one that quick. I've got him tied in a shallow wash, alongside my pack mule, about a quarter mile south of here.

Mingo went over to a corner of the barn and picked up a shovel. He motioned, indicating Tyler. "I'm gonna' drag this dirt bag out back by the ravine and throw some dirt over him. Once I'm finished, you better be gone from here, in case I change my mind about collecting that bounty."

Mingo looked down at Tyler. He prodded the remains, kicking with the toe of his boot, and asked sarcastically, "Well, Mr. Tyler, are you ready to get your sorry dead ass planted?"

Uncharacteristically, Mingo seemed amused with his quip. He felt whole and justified that the insult to his honor was resolved. Grandfather would have been pleased. Still smiling, he looked back to see if Ussher showed any reaction. The smile changed to surprise when he realized Ussher was already gone. A shadow seemed to flicker for a moment near the door, but he couldn't be certain. For the final time, Mingo was impressed with Ussher's wilderness skills.

I hope I never run into that son-of-a-bitch again, Mingo thought, extending a full measure of respect and admiration for a brother-in-arms.

59
August 22, 1863

LAWRENCE, KANSAS

The morning after the Bushwhacker raid, the town of Lawrence was under protection from 250 disciplined and veteran Union troops. They patrolled the streets and perimeter of the town. The soldiers walked through the streets in groups of four. One of these patrols discovered a disoriented outsider hiding in a stable stall. It was Charlie Hawkins.

The day of the raid, Charlie did his share of killing civilians. He especially enjoyed mocking his victims, using coercion and ridicule, before executing them. The murderer stole money, smashed windows, and destroyed family relics. He also took time to molest women and threaten little girls, sending them running and screaming in terror. It had been a good day for Charlie.

The event got even better, or so he thought, when he found a half-full, white Oak barrel filled with apple-flavored whiskey. It was 50 percent distilled corn alcohol and 50 percent sugar mixed with apple juice. The brew was so sweet and smooth that Charlie consumed a pint of it before he realized his head was spinning. He drank another pint and then passed out, which lasted the rest of the day and throughout the night. By the time he awakened, the town of Lawrence was in recovery and Union troops were everywhere.

Charlie was not a good liar and a search of his pockets

revealed money and jewelry he stole from the citizens. The Union troops marched him into the street with his hands tied behind his back. Several of the women recognized him as one who murdered their son, brother, or husband. Anger sparked through the residents like lightning. The women rushed up to Hawkins striking him with fists and kicks.

A Union officer rode up to investigate all the tumult and listened to the impromptu testimony of the women as they screamed their accusations and damnation at Hawkins. Eight more soldiers arrived to observe the cause of the commotion.

Hawkins tried to deflect the punishment while screaming for mercy and advocating his innocence.

"Y'all are dead wrong. I never hurt no one," Hawkins pleaded, when a blow from a broom handle connected with his temple.

"I was just passin' through last night. I got in late and decided to get me some sleep in the stable," he lied...as two women grabbed his hair, pulled him backwards to the ground and started kicking him.

Without further contemplation, the officer pronounced the verdict and issued his order. "Hang the Fucker."

He pointed to a beam extending from the roof of the livery stable and began riding off, then paused and amended his order. "Let the women have him while y'all get the hanging rope ready."

It took the soldiers less than five minutes to find a rope. In that short time, Hawkins received hundreds of blows from the angry mob. With his hands tied, there was little hope of protecting himself as they punched and kicked him to near unconsciousness.

The soldiers finally pushed through the angry women

and picked Hawkins up. They dragged him over to the livery stable, threw the rope over the beam, and placed the noose around his neck. The officer could see Hawkins was trying to say something. He instructed one of the soldiers to listen to what Hawkins had to say.

As they tightened the loop, the soldier reported to his officer. "He wants a minute to pray."

The officer thought for a moment and responded, "Nope, I don't think so. There will not be any prayers for this one. He followed the devil, now the devil can have him."

With that, three soldiers pulled on the rope and hoisted Hawkins high enough so his feet were just six inches off the ground. For the next minute and a half, his feet danced in the air, his face went from red to purple, and his eyes bulged from his head. Hawkins fought strangulation to no avail. Asphyxiation shut down his brain before Charlie Hawkins went comatose.

There was only minor twitching followed by total stillness. His hands remained clinched even after death. The women watched every moment of the drama. His punishment was their just due but his suffering represented a pittance of compensation for their unspeakable losses. Now it was over but it was not near enough. No amount of reprisal could compensate for the suffering they endured the previous day. Several women continued to punch Hawkins' swinging body or throw rocks at him. The officer instructed the soldiers to let him hang until the women finally tired of inflicting their revenge.

* * * *

Union General Thomas Ewing received word of the massacre at Lawrence from an Army express rider. Although he possessed no military experience before the war, he used political savvy to move up in the Army chain of command. In March 1863, he received a promotion to Brigadier General, tasked with keeping control over the Kansas - Missouri border. He failed to achieve his mission through indecisiveness, failure of leadership and never learning the difference between winning the war and keeping the peace.

The attack and massacre on Lawrence changed all need for nuance. Concern over the application of authority was no longer a worry for General Ewing. Quantrill made his decision easy, Anderson made his decision obvious, and Clement made his decision compelling. A decisive defeat, such as Lawrence, needed answering through overwhelming reprisal. Ewing made his most far-reaching decision of the war. He struck back for the suffering of one Union town by inflicting wholesale punishment on four Missouri counties. He avenged the misery of the 1,645 residents of Lawrence with almost unthinkable retaliation against 20,000 Missouri citizens.

Ewing issued Military Order #11. It gave an immediate eviction notice to all people in the Missouri counties of Jackson, Cass, Bates, and Vernon who could not prove their absolute loyalty to the Union. Eventually, Ewing's decree virtually wiped out the population of the entire area. Massive numbers of cavalry entered the region to enforce the evictions. There were no grace periods or exceptions. Suspected Bushwhacker sympathizers, meaning virtually all residents, were given mere days to evacuate their homes and abandon their ancestry.

Overwhelming numbers of Union soldiers burned every building and summarily crushed any resistance. They executed many men and drove the women and children off the properties. The evictions took place just before the harvest. Few Missourians had enough food for more than a week. Thousands died quietly and undocumented on hillsides and in the deep ravines of the countryside.

* * *

Bloody Bill Anderson obtained satisfaction for the death of his sister, Josie, but thousands of Anderson's supporters reaped unbelievable sorrow, resulting from his vicious overreaction and Quantrill's inability to control the militia. Anderson never felt responsible for their fate. For him, they died for not fighting viciously enough to save their own lives.

60
The Days that Followed

When Talbot Harris and Otto Metzger returned, they discovered Vince still draped over the ladder rung. Talbot's only visible emotion was silence until he went inside the big house where he raged with anger and swore unspeakable revenge against Ussher.

During the fighting, Abigail and her girls managed to force open the door of the pantry room. They peered out a side window in time to hear Vince offer to sacrifice Abigail and then beg for his life to no avail. They saw his urine soaked pants leg and witnessed Ussher firing the fatal rounds into his torso.

Each looked on as Vince's body jolted violently with the

impact of each Henry bullet. They felt no emotional loss as blood spewed from his wounds and saliva spilled from his mouth. After a minute of watching Vince hang limp and lifeless, Abigail shuffled everyone back to the pantry room to wait for Talbot to return.

Later, as they related the report of what they witnessed, the women exhibited compulsory sorrow, invented regret, and feigned condolences over the violent loss of his vile youngest son.

Harris ordered Vince's body cleaned and his wounds sewn before placing him in a simple wooden casket, which sat inside the house for two days. During those two days, he had Vince's torture barn torn to the ground. The wood was set aside for winter kindling used in the bunkhouse. Harris directed Vince's remains be buried in the cleared location where the barn once stood. His grave was marked with a simple headstone.

Harris then ordered the rest of the ground plowed, raked, and planted with flowers. In spite of the gardener's best efforts, none of the flowers survived and no one planted more. During the winter, when the cowhands placed wood from Vince's barn in the fireplace or Franklin stove, they commented it was the hottest burning tinder they ever used.

* * * *

Jack Mingo waited three days before riding back to the Harris ranch. Harris and Metzger had received word he was coming in with results. The men stood on the porch of the big house discussing ranch business the morning Mingo arrived. He dismounted and walked up carrying a trophy.

Mingo presented Harris with Tyler's scalp and told him

that it belonged to Ussher. He kept his story simple. Mingo stated he came upon Ussher's campsite while hunting. He knew about the bounty, it was common knowledge throughout the territory. He said that while Ussher sat on the ground eating beans from a cook pot, he shot him twice, once in the chest and the other in the forehead.

Harris appeared genuinely pleased with the news. Mingo went back to his horse and pulled the Henry rifle from inside his blanket. Metzger reached out, took the rifle from Mingo, and passed it to Harris. He looked at the serial number. It was one digit higher than its mate, which sat inside a gun rack awaiting this reunion. Harris looked at Metzger and nodded, confirming its authenticity.

"Because of what's happened here," Harris said, "I'm going to award you $3,000 in gold and a job for life."

Mingo nodded his understanding but countered, "I'll settle for the $3,000. As far as needing a job, no thanks, I work for myself."

* * * *

Months later, at the height of his wealth and power, Talbot Harris unexpectedly died.

Abigail heard him tap his walking cane on the floor. The summons echoed loudly through the ceiling and into her apartment. Dutifully she bathed and prepared herself to attend to him for the evening. Just before ascending the staircase, she heard the tapping repeated. It was uncharacteristic for Talbot to be so impatient. She exhaled mild exasperation, proceeded up to his room, and opened the door. Abigail found Harris sitting alone, his dead eyes staring into the emptiness of a cold fireplace. The spilled remains of his Old Crow whiskey lay pooled on the floor.

Harris always wore a two-pocket vest; each pocket exhibited a gold chain. The one on the right secured a gold Swiss watch and the other a key. The key opened a heavy floor safe where Abigail discovered $14,000 in gold and currency. Before booking stagecoach passage, she mailed the key to Evelyn Harris along with a note of condolence and thanks for allowing her many years of employment.

When the oldest Harris son, Morgan, arrived to settle his father's estate, he discovered an ivory cameo pendant along with the gold and money, still inside the safe. The keepsake was part of a real estate foreclosure collected years earlier. Harris gave it to Abigail, claiming he purchased it exclusively for her. She sensed the story was fictitious but wore it every day to please the big man. Abigail always knew she would never be Talbot's wife so she chose to discard anything that might induce worthless nostalgia.

61

Purging the Poison

AFTER LEAVING the Harris ranch, Ussher located Bolt, secured next to Mingo's pack mule just as he had promised. The faithful horse was happy for a reunion with someone he trusted but he sensed an unsettled spirit inside Ussher.

Man and mount departed swiftly down an unmarked path for a mile and then followed a more frequently used trail. Bolt's tracks blurred and finally vanished with scores of others. Despite sensing Ussher's discomfort, Bolt was full of energy and confidence He knew instinctively that if danger came near and all else failed, he held the best option of all. He could run.

Ussher faced crisis almost immediately from the gunshot injury he received during the fight at the Harris ranch. The crease wound in his side became seriously infected. The problem turned chronic and even cauterization did not help. He cut drainage incisions in the wound several times with his knife, but within a day, it refilled with seepage and inflammation. The pain was severe. It prevented him from riding, hunting, or sleeping. As exhaustion and weakness became increasingly oppressive, Ussher smiled cynically and contemplated the incredulity that he might die from a virtual scratch after all the adversity he had overcome.

He was nearly out of food, and with the infection sapping his energy, Ussher decided to yield to the inevitable and rest by the campfire to await the Grim Reaper. He removed the saddle and bridal from Bolt and let the horse wander as it pleased him. He thought of his Darby. Even in this time of waning vitality, her memory was a comfort to him. Ussher was confident that she was waiting to greet and embrace him as he crossed over from this life.

Inside his restless sleep, Ussher became increasingly aware of a humming resonance. He attempted to ignore the reverberation but it continued and amplified. Within his fever and exhaustion, he pondered if there was any benefit in struggling to awaken so he could identify the annoying sound. Finally, an agitated horse's whinny persuaded him to open his eyes, He observed Bolt running in circles, turning and shaking his head left to right. It required a minute for Ussher to realize what was happening.

The bees were agitated and let the horse know he had gotten too close and stayed too long. Ussher stared straight up and identified the problem. When he first lay down atop the saddle, he never noticed the hive. Suppressed adrenaline roused his mind as he recognized a possible pathway back to health.

Ussher rallied his strength and gathered several smoldering sticks from the campfire. He shook off the burning ends, created a smoking bouquet, held the smoke under the beehive, and let nature take its course. The bees reacted defensively but not aggressively. Evolution conditioned the insects to believe the smoke is from a fire about to destroy their hive. The stress prompts them to gorge on honey in preparation for abandonment of their home. This focus disrupts their natural aggressiveness and allows the knowledgeable to charm the honeycomb from the hive.

Ussher's smoke and bee-charm worked successfully. The bees left the hive without attacking him in the process. He first consumed some of the honey for energy. Again, he cut the wound and drained the pus. After irrigating the area with water, he let the sun bake his skin dry. He applied a poultice of raw honey liberally on the wound. Then, with his last ounce of energy, he fell back on top the saddle, pulled up his blanket and fell asleep for two days.

When he awakened, the infection had not returned. The natural ability of raw honey to fight germs and bacteria worked flawlessly. A small amount of honey remained in the comb, which Ussher consumed hungrily on the spot. The reunion with Darby would wait a while longer.

Bolt was standing nearby as Ussher awakened and began to

move about. The horse danced impatiently and snorted, what sounded like disapproval, over Ussher's lengthy hibernation.

"Yeah, yeah," Ussher retorted wearily, "Don't go getting your tail in a knot. I'll get myself going soon enough for sure."

62
Gospel in the Wilderness

AARON AND MICAH RUSSELL continued to work tirelessly for the Lord and the salvation of souls through the example of their ministry. They labored eighteen hours a day setting up impromptu worship camps, caring for the needy, and preaching the Word before moving on to the next location. Their thin frames were testimony that they shared nearly all their food and never concerned themselves about their next meal.

The men were fearless, often coming upon deadly skirmishes between Kansas Raiders and Missouri Militia. They never hesitated to ride into the middle of the action, holding their hands out, palms up, seeking supplication of the Lord for the deliverance and protection of all combatants. For Aaron and Micah, there was no Jayhawker or Bushwhacker. All men, regardless of political persuasion, geographic location, ethnic heritage, or skin color were God's children and needed deliverance.

As the degradation of the fighting increased, so did the passion and fire of the sermons delivered by Aaron Russell. He was determined to tell the truth at all costs. When he witnessed actions of greed, barbarity, and evil, he courageously defined the acts and indicted those responsible. He never searched for words that were allusions of the facts. There could be no substitution for legitimacy.

Crowds flocked to hear Aaron speak as people hungered for the refreshing clarity of his intellect and insight. When their suffering from the war seemed intolerable, Aaron taught the benefits of forbearance. Whenever oppression neared victory, he espoused perseverance. He succeeded in countering all the negative circumstances of their existence and demonstrated that through God's hand, subsistence was tolerable and transcendence would be their reward if they retained the faith to endure.

People brought their sick to these revivals; hoping faith would bring healing to their lives. They dedicated their children with baptism and prayed they would live long enough to become adults. While listening to Aaron's words, his followers held each other's hands, sang songs of praise, and honored God's presence with choruses of "Hallelujah."

At the end of the night, the collection plate often returned empty. Income did not matter because they did not conduct God's work for money. The few coins they occasionally gathered provided food and medicine to supplement those in need, and need was everywhere.

* * * *

One Thursday evening, late in August, the faithful gathered near a quiet grove on a small, deserted homestead farm. Many were hungry but still happy with the anticipation of listening to the inspirational words of Aaron Russell. The sermon was everything they expected. It was forceful and uplifting, containing clear ideas and well-defined truths. He opened their minds as well as their hearts, providing focus and perspective on the issues of highest importance.

While Aaron's message thundered into the uplifted souls of the assembly, Micah distributed two buckets, each with ladles, containing sweet, cool water. Several of the worshipers took a second sip after tasting the first. Many commented the water exhibited a most remarkable and pleasing flavor, leaving them thoroughly restored.

The water came from an artesian well, which bubbled happily, as it gave forth its refreshing gift. The area, overgrown with prairie grass and wildflowers, felt warm and welcoming. With sunset, the light gave way to long shadows that blended softly down the curve of the hill running back toward the stream.

Few noticed the old gravesite, about 25 feet up from the artesian spring. The headstone had fallen to one side. Sediment obscured most of the engraving, except for one word near the center. It read simply, "Beloved." None of the good people in attendance knew the occupant of the grave or the circumstances that made the gravesite necessary.

At the end of the evening, the crowd slowly dispersed. Most stopped by the artesian spring to fill canteens and jars with the sweet water. In families, couples, and individually, they carried renewal and revival back to their homes. After a few short days, their world would once again be oppressive and they all hoped for another chance to see Aaron and Micah. They thanked God for sending these disciples and prayed the gospel circuit would include their location when it came around the next time.

* * * *

Two dozen lighted torches usually outlined the area where the crowd assembled to listen to Aaron. At the end of each service, after everyone returned to their homes, it was Micah's assignment to retrieve the torches and pack them into their wagon. One evening, when all was quiet at last, Aaron looked up and observed Micah standing motionless, peering into the illuminated space about a stone's throw from their campfire. The young man was looking at the silhouette of a late visitor standing at the far, outer edge of the lighted perimeter. The man looked both tentative to approach and yet compelled to linger.

Aaron walked over to Micah. The distance and the fading twilight prevented the men from recognizing the individual in the flickering illumination. The frogs and crickets piped their songs and serenaded one another beneath the waxing half-moon. The warmth of the day yielded to a pleasing coolness as a light breeze refreshed the evening air and shuffled through the prairie grass.

Aaron stepped forward and called out, "Come into the camp, my friend. This is a safe haven on holy ground consecrated by prayer. Here, everyone is welcome."

Although hesitant at first, the man approached at an easy pace into their camp. Drawing nearer, his footsteps quickened as if releasing a lifetime of burdens. When he removed his hat his face was completely revealed. From twenty steps distance, Aaron and Micah smiled widely. The workings from the hand of God always provided remarkable moments for those privileged to stand as a witness.

Smiles and handshakes proved insufficient as Jack Mingo stepped into the lighted perimeter surrounding their campsite. Aaron and Micah hugged him as a returning brother. He was unarmed. His eyes were wide open and absent their suspicious squint. He looked relaxed, comfortable, and unafraid. There was a glow from his face exceeding the mere reflection of campfire and torchlight. Aaron and Micah quickly diagnosed the blessing. Jack Mingo was at peace with himself and ready to accept the will of destiny and Aaron Russell as his teacher.

63

Colorado

OVER THE NEXT several weeks, Ussher made his way to Colorado. He followed the map drawn on the coyote hide given to him by Kensington. The rough drawing indicated the location of a mining claim that Kensington shared with another miner. The map was good enough to get him close. From that point, Ussher rode in crisscross grids searching for the man Kensington often mentioned as his trusted friend. He came across several wary and protective miners working their claims and made certain his approach was easy and apparent. No need to startle a man and invite a gunshot in his direction. A few of the men ordered him away but most helped with directions when asked.

Ussher finally located the claim of Kensington's partner, Carlos Rocha. Although they had never met, Rocha welcomed Ussher like a long-lost friend. Kensington had talked about Ussher many times and Rocha could tell that his old friend thought of Ussher as a son. Rocha was just finishing a meal, and there was enough food remaining for an extra plate, which Ussher accepted with thanks.

Rocha and Kensington were partners for many years. They were close as any brothers. Rocha spoke of a great service Kensington once performed on his behalf. He did not give details and only said he would be happily indebted to Kensington for the rest of his life. Rocha commented he always knew that one day Ussher would find his way to Colorado so they could finally meet.

The difference between Rocha and Kensington was that Rocha was a worker and Kensington was a roamer. Rocha found satisfaction in his work, probing the hillside and working the streams searching for gold. Kensington worked the claim long enough to accumulate traveling money and then would disappear for months. This time, it had been a year since Rocha last saw his good friend. The nature of their partnership was simple; whatever gold you found, you kept. Since Rocha worked the claim virtually nonstop, he had become quite wealthy. He talked about one day returning to his native Brazil, but then again, maybe not.

After a day of rest, Rocha invited Ussher to work the claim to accumulate a stake. He told Ussher that possessing the coyote hide map was Kensington's way of conferring partial ownership.

Working the claim helped both Ussher's mind and body. It did not trouble Rocha that Ussher would go for days without saying a word. He knew the man was recovering physically and spiritually. He gave Ussher time and allowed him to work out his grief and anger. At night, Rocha would speak to Ussher, never concerning himself about a response. He told Ussher of the various adventures he enjoyed with Kensington and often shook his head and laughed aloud about the many narrow escapes they once experienced. Eventually, Ussher asked a few questions and slowly the men began to have genuine conversations. Most importantly, they learned to trust one another.

Ussher finally revealed the details of his journey through love, conflict, hate, retribution, and regret. These were the most painful of the discussions. Ussher experienced bitterness over Darby's loss and continually second-guessed many of his actions.

"It is my fault she was killed. I was pig-headed and refused to leave the homestead. I had put so much damn time and effort into that worthless twelve acres of dirt that I was blind to the fact danger and death were everywhere. All the people in that part of the country had gone crazy with killing. It was plain stupid and careless of me. We should have left and found another way to earn a living."

Rocha just listened.

"Darby never complained or worried because she believed in me. She had faith that I could protect us both, and that trust got her killed. I should have realized how big the problems actually were and taken her back East."

Ussher also confessed the nature of his inner man and questioned the possibility that he could change for the better during the last half of his life. Time would tell all.

Rocha reflected on Ussher's story and then one evening shared his insights. As the men sat quietly over campfire embers, Rocha related his interpretation of Ussher's experience.

"Joseph," Rocha began, "What you are experiencing is natural, but you are not considering the entire picture. It is very well to grieve for your Darby. It is actually necessary in order to heal. She was truly a unique woman and an incomparable friend. I understand that you will carry her loss in your heart forever, but the fact remains, you are not responsible for her death. You cannot allow regret, caused by the evil of another man, to afflict the remainder of your life."

Ussher looked at Rocha but before he could interject a word, his friend continued.

"It was not you who caused Darby's death, it was Vince Harris."

Rocha restated that last sentence with emphasis.

"It was not you who caused Darby's death. It was that soulless bastard, Vince Harris. That fact is an undeniable truth. The reality that you and Darby were so happy and content with each other is a testament to the fact that you were living your life correctly. Where you lived, as well as how you lived, contributed to the bond you shared. That mixture was a necessary element of your happiness as a couple."

This last thought made Ussher reflect on the honest veracity and depth of Rocha's insight.

Carlos continued, "I will tell you truthfully, Darby's death was not tragic in her own eyes. She made a choice to protect you. She carried out her decision without regret and without hesitation. Her love fed her bravery, and her bravery reflected her love. Both emotions combined into a magnificent display of unselfish commitment to the one she cared for most…you. How many people love so fiercely that they would sacrifice everything? How many people experience the privilege of such a glorious death? Her actions reflected her thanks to you for the life you both shared. I assure you the moment her soul passed away from her body it entered into heaven."

Tears rolled down Ussher's cheeks as he stared into the fire's ash.

Rocha continued, "You did what was necessary. You destroyed the evil that injured your wife. That evil does not deserve any additional attention. Its last hold on you is regret and that is an emotion of emptiness. Deny the evil its nourishment. Fill that vacancy. Move forward with your life by taking a positive outlook. That is your nature."

Ussher listened intently.

Rocha continued, "Allow me to explain. There is only one way to honor such a splendid woman. It is not regret, and it is not remorse. The only suitable way to pay homage to Darby's memory is to be thankful for every moment you shared together. Even though your time together was short, what you shared are treasures to keep. Chisel every recollection of her into your mind. Open your heart to remember every detail about her. Most importantly, permit yourself to smile with every reflection. Allow Darby to live inside you. Always remember what the two of you shared was honest, exclusive, and authentic."

Ussher remained motionless and silent as Rocha quietly pulled up his blanket and settled in.

After about half an hour, Ussher began to talk once again, this time about Darby. Rocha got up to place two more logs on the fire. He retrieved a flask of homebrew from his pack, sat down, and leaned on one elbow to listen quietly. The men shared the contents of the flask as Ussher shared his memories.

He told Rocha about their orderly home, the wild flowers she gathered and how beautifully she sang her songs. He spoke of Darby's faith and her dedication to tending their farm.

Ussher confessed how her beauty left him weak, and her sensuality stirred his blood. He closed his eyes and recalled how much he loved kissing the line of her neck where it flowed into her shoulders.

Finally, Ussher laughed as he related those times of playful banter. He told Rocha about her fierceness, as she scolded him for alleged misbehavior or laziness. Rocha laughed loudly as Ussher displayed a loving mimic of Darby placing her hands on her hips and arching her left eyebrow for emphasis. The evening drew to its end with both men enjoying reflective silence. Each drifted leisurely into sleep. For the first time in recent memory, Ussher's rest was peaceful.

* * * *

Rocha could read the signs. After his time with Kensington, he knew when a man was becoming restless. After nearly two years, Ussher was again strong and healthy. The mountain air cleansed his body, and the solitude cleared his mind. Rocha could see he was ready to use them both to move his life in another direction.

One evening, as they ate there dinner, Ussher confessed, "There's something I've got to do back East."

"So do it, my friend. When you're finished, you will always be welcome here."

Ussher looked at Rocha and nodded with purpose and affirmation.

The next morning Ussher saddled Bolt early. He rode by Rocha on his way out of camp, stopping at the location where the old prospector was working in the stream.

"Thank you," Ussher said, "you are a true friend."

Rocha looked back, nodded acknowledgement, and returned to his work.

64
Homecoming in St. Louis

NATHAN USSHER WAS a happy young man. No one called him Nate anymore, and he was pleased with that fact. Nate was his name from another time and a different place where he barely survived as a boy. Nathan was a name with added character and was more appropriate for the man he was becoming.

Nathan just turned seventeen and since moving in with Benjamin had grown four inches and gained twenty pounds. He was a fine looking young man and the young women took notice. Nathan was articulate, spontaneous, and funny. Whenever he spoke with them, he lingered for an appropriate time and always found something positive or complimentary to say. He never sounded condescending or insincere because it was his nature to look for the best in people. When he departed to resume his business, the young women chortled excitedly with one another as they gauged their chances of attracting more of his time and attention.

Several prominent mothers identified Nathan as a prized candidate for their daughters to marry. He received numerous invitations to family dinners, Sunday barbecues, and lemonade socials. Benjamin's wife, Christine, took it upon herself to filter these invitations. She developed a strong fondness for her adopted nephew and wanted to make sure Nathan finished his education before one of these society raptors swooped in to capture him. Nathan actually found it slightly amusing as well as comforting that Christine was so protective.

Joseph F. Dwyer

The associates and clients of Benjamin Ussher could see that the young man was going to do well in the family's law practice. He seemed mature beyond his years, and with the high intelligence he possessed, his interpersonal attributes would continue to improve.

Nathan was aware of all the attention but did not allow it to go to his head. He knew the origin of his roots. He came from nothing and always acknowledged that fact. He had cared for horses and shoveled manure for the opportunity to eat the scraps that other men threw from their plate. Nathan could not remember how many times he went to bed hungry, only to wake up even hungrier. He knew how fragile life could be and how lucky he was to be part of this family. Nathan cared for Benjamin almost as much as he cared for his adopted father. He decided to succeed because Ussher's protection made this new life possible and Benjamin's generosity gave him the chance to achieve and excel.

* * * *

Tuesday morning introduced a blazing sunrise sending dappled streaks through the lace curtains on the kitchen windows. Nathan rose early and brewed coffee from fresh ground beans. He took his cup outside to sit on the front porch steps and enjoy the quiet. The street appeared deserted except for a solo rider far in the distance. He looked away for a moment but something drew his attention back to the approaching man. The rider's profile revealed a lean, agile build, and the way he sat astride the saddle was unique and familiar. The horse he rode was next to draw Nathan's attention. It was tall and spirited.

Nathan squinted for better focus and realized the rider was returning his gaze. The man nudged the horse into a gallop as Nathan put down his cup and stood to welcome an event everyone assumed was hopeless. After a two-year hiatus, Ussher was indeed safe and reunited with his family. As Nathan stepped off the porch, Ussher reined Bolt to a halt and dismounted in a single movement. The men bear-hugged each other, Ussher kissed Nathan on the cheek and pushed him to arms-length for a father's appraisal.

"Boy, just look at you. Good God, you've grown taller than me. That home cookin' sure does agree with you."

Tears and smiles demonstrated the happy emotions of both men. Nathan exclaimed with incredulous realization, "I can hardly believe you are really here. We've sent dozens of inquiries for any word about you. The only thing we ever learned was that you simply disappeared and folks assumed the war had found a way to take you."

From the kitchen window a voice thundered, "Praise God."

Benjamin ran outside, followed closely by Christine. The entire family shared hugs, laughter, and joyous tears. As Nathan watched his family celebrate, he received a nudge in the back. Bolt remembered Nathan as someone who genuinely cared for him. Nathan returned the affection with a neck pat and ear scratch.

After this celebratory welcoming, the Ussher clan enjoyed an extended breakfast and further reestablished their family bonds. Finally, Benjamin and Nathan expressed regret and explained they had business commitments to honor. Ussher stated he would like to clean up and sleep for a couple of hours. Benjamin suggested he join them for lunch to discuss additional details regarding Nathan's progress.

Before the two left the house, Ussher grabbed Benjamin by the arm. "The kid looks great," he acknowledged. "I don't know how I will ever repay you."

"Nathan is the best thing that's ever happened to us, Benjamin replied. "We love him as our own. He will do well here in St. Louis. He learns quickly and retains everything he observes and hears. He is always studying and works long hours without complaint. I can't wait to show you some of the things he is doing."

The lunch went well as did the three weeks that followed. Ussher observed the many aspects of Benjamin's and Nathan's legal practice and social life. Nathan attended tutored lessons in English, history, science, and mathematics. The rest of his schooling came from his work at the law office. Benjamin's family entertained friends and received a steady stream of invitations themselves. It was obvious Nathan found genuine satisfaction living and working with Benjamin. He was enthusiastic, positive, and best of all, confident. Ussher felt pleased and proud of this young man, whom he claimed as his son.

Ussher listened to Christine talk about the girls whom she thought were plotting to snare Nathan as a husband. She acknowledged they were all women of quality from excellent families and each could become a fine wife. She simply thought it improper that the girls of the day were so forward and obvious with their desires. "I simply don't know what's happening with this younger generation," she said with bewilderment.

Christine checked the proximity of other family members and then added in an almost confidential tone, "He doesn't say anything, but I think Nathan has his eye on someone. It vexes me so; I've asked him if there is anyone special, but I just can't get him to say who it might be." With a tone of mock disdain, she quipped, "You Ussher men are so tightlipped. It's just not polite to constantly keep a lady guessing."

That evening, Nathan announced he was going outside to take the air and asked Ussher to join him. They walked down several streets and turned a corner. After passing three houses, Nathan paused. This area of St. Louis was not as professional and aristocratic as where Benjamin resided. The houses were simple but solid. The yards appeared well kept and ran deep, allowing the residents to grow large gardens behind their homes. These gardens supplied highly valued vegetable and fruit supplements for variety in their meals throughout the winter.

"I want you to meet someone," confided Nathan, as he walked up three creaky steps onto a small porch and knocked on the door. A beautiful, slim 16-year-old girl answered. Ussher could see her mother standing a few feet back from the door, far enough to respect her daughter's privacy, yet close enough to identify with whom she was speaking.

The older woman peered out and called, "Evening, Nathan."

"Evening, Ma'am," Nathan replied, Gesturing to Ussher, he said, "I'd like you to meet my father." Annie's mother looked at Ussher and gave a polite nod, which he returned in kind.

Nathan then looked at the girl, smiled widely, and said happily, "Hey Annie."

Annie was a lovely young woman with a pretty face, dark hair, dark eyes, and a luminous smile. What made her especially interesting was the spark in her personality. There was duality in her every interaction. She was sweet and yet impish, polite but not always proper, demure and yet strong and confident. Annie was direct when she spoke to you. Her intellect was obvious and her sense of humor a joy to experience. Ussher smiled to himself. She was an almost perfect contradiction to keep a man off balance and interested.

As the three of them sat on the steps of Annie's home, Ussher felt an immediate bond with this young woman. The ensuing two hours of conversation made time fly by. Annie was a great listener as well as an engaging chatterbox. When she spoke, her eyes danced back and forth between the men. She constantly found excuses to touch Nathan's arm or nudge his shoulder. She brushed phantom dust particles from his shirt and poked his side as she teased him with playful banter. She often flushed slightly while doing this but quickly regained her composure by straightening her posture and playing with a strand of her long silky hair.

During this first evening together, Annie decided she would love Ussher. Meeting him helped her identify the source and mixture of the positive aspects in Nathan's character. Nathan was his own person, and that part of him was the core of Annie's affection. He possessed his uncle's gift of interpersonal ease. This attribute was apparent in the way he seamlessly engaged one individual and then the next, in all situations, impressing men and charming women; but there was more.

Nathan was protective and exhibited strong, quiet courage. He possessed a muted edge, which could intone a subtle admonition to a rival. The message stated that a line existed which could not be crossed without consequence. Meeting Ussher allowed Annie to understand it all now. She determined that this merger of qualities made Nathan the man she would claim for herself.

Just before sunset, Ussher announced he was going to head back to Benjamin's home. He wanted to allow Nathan and Annie some personal time. Annie protested at first and then said to Nathan, "Well, if your daddy is leaving, then the least you can do is walk me down the street a bit before mama makes me go back inside."

Nathan mocked irritation and replied that he was too tired to go for a walk. Annie pretended she never heard his objection. She walked a few steps over to Ussher, raised herself on her toes and gave him a kiss on the side of his cheek at the line of his chin. The kiss was sweet and gentle. She then threw her arms around him and hugged him tightly, placing the side of her face against his chest. Annie lingered for a moment and then whispered in his ear.

"I'm totally in love with your son. Can you tell?"

As she asked the question, she shivered slightly with excitement. Behind that emotion was an appearance of confidence that the two of them would be a perfect match for each other. Ussher hugged Annie in return.

"Yes, I can tell. I think Nathan is a lucky young man to have someone so special to love him. Of course, you need to keep him a little humble in the process."

Annie's eyes sparkled. "Of course," she agreed.

She released Ussher from her embrace but kept a fingerhold of both his sleeves. While still looking at Ussher, she gave a shout out to Nathan, pretending exasperation.

"Nathan, are you going to take me for that walk or not?"

She glanced over her shoulder, turned the long line of her neck toward Nathan, and flashed her mischievous eyes in his direction. She then hollered out with feigned attitude, "Boy, I do not believe that you want to get on my bad side. Am I wrong?"

When Ussher saw Annie move and speak in that manner, his heart skipped to a joyous flashback of his time with Darby.

Annie let go of Ussher's sleeve and walked back to Nathan. She pulled on his arm coaxing him to follow her instructions.

"Come on Nathan. I want you to walk with me down the street and hold my hand. I think we should pass by some of them big houses where those fancy girls live. Can you imagine what a fuss that would cause?"

As Annie asked her question, her fingers meandered softly across the back and side of Nathan's neck, stirring his blood and weakening his resolve. Nathan knew that he would eventually concede and walk the neighborhood with Annie. Still, he enjoyed the good-natured teasing and mild annoyance he was causing by not surrendering to her wishes immediately.

Annie played her part of the game to perfection. She was confident she would ultimately prevail. Success was just a matter of time. She was fully aware that Nathan cared deeply for her and that his affection was progressing steadily toward love. Because of those feelings, it made their playful interaction all the more enjoyable.

"Nathan Ussher," Annie said sternly, "I insist that you take me for a walk and hold my hand. A lady needs to be escorted properly by her gentleman." As she spoke, Annie placed her arms demurely to her side and turned slightly, one-way and then the other. Then she stopped and looked toward Nathan to assess his reaction.

He revealed a half-smile in Ussher's direction. Ussher looked away in amusement and waived off Nathan with both hands, lightheartedly indicating he did not wish to take sides. Nathan folded his arms across his chest. He set his lower lip indicating mock willpower, looked Annie in the eye, and sat down with resolve.

"No Ma'am, I don't think so. That ain't gonna' happen tonight, 'cause this man ain't movin' another muscle."

Annie stepped boldly in front of Nathan. She stood as straight as she could to make her bearing as tall as possible. Annie placed her hands on her hips, exhaled a long breath and revealed an exaggerated pout. Her antics disclosed purpose spiced with amusement. She shifted her hands from her hips to Nathan's shoulders. From there, she slid them together on either side of his face, tipped his head backwards and bent down to kiss his lips. As she lingered, her thick, dark hair cascaded a caress over Nathan's cheeks. When she slowly drew backwards, he looked up into her lovely face, unable to form a coherent thought. He sat motionless and transfixed with his lips slightly agape, trying to gather his composure.

Annie smiled as she sensed Nathan's fortitude weakening but Nathan had learned a thing or two about the way Annie responded in situations. He understood that Annie enjoyed a certain level of complication in her interactions and this was certainly one of those moments. He also recognized that handling that complication correctly could be very rewarding. His best move would be to exhibit body language that confessed impending surrender while concurrently verbalizing the inflexibility of his position. Nathan looked upward toward Annie but purposely avoided eye contact.

"I am very sorry, Miss Lady," he stammered mischievously, "My feet are hurtin' and I am just plain tuckered out. I don't think there is any chance of you getting your way, so you just gotta' get yourself used to that fact. Besides, when a man says no, a woman has got to learn her place and accept the situation."

He looked a little sideways and shrugged his shoulders slightly, indicating there was nothing else to say.

Annie retorted, "Oh, I understand the situation just fine."

Again, she stood tall and moved close to where Nathan sat. She gently but firmly pulled his face in against her firm stomach and massaged the back of his head with her fingertips. The fragrance of clean cotton wafted from her summer dress. Nathan pushed his face into that scent and moved his head side-to-side to gather more of the caress from her fingers. Annie looked up from Nathan and over to Ussher. Flashing those beautiful dark eyes, she suppressed a muted smile.

Looking Ussher's way, she arched her eyebrow slightly and declared, "Well, sir, I'm thinking this boy and me had us a real problem but now things appear headed toward a right proper resolution."

Annie glanced downward at Nathan. He was saying something, but with his lips pressed against her mid-section, his response was barely audible. In the next moment, Nathan gathered himself and rose to his feet. He placed his arm around the lovely young girl, hugging her firmly. He looked at Ussher and then back to Annie as if just struck by a transcendent revelation.

Nathan said brightly, "Hey Annie, I have a wonderful idea. How 'bout you and me take us a nice long walk. You know, before your mama makes you go back inside."

Annie didn't miss a beat, "Why, Mr. Nathan; that is a wonderful idea. I would certainly be delighted." Would this walk include holding my hand?"

Nathan reflected for just a moment, "Yes, Ma'am, I do believe it does. After all, a lady needs to be escorted properly by her gentleman."

Ussher displayed a thoroughly satisfied smile. The three walked together awhile, at ease and jovial with the evenings banter. Ussher was at peace that all was well in Nathan's life. At the next corner, he hugged Nathan and Annie and split off to return to Benjamin's home.

* * *

The time together with Nathan and Benjamin proved insightful. It allowed Ussher to gain perspective toward setting a course for his own future. St. Louis was the perfect place for Nathan. It had a rhythm and heartbeat that was wonderfully predictable. People followed schedules that dictated daily activities, coordinated their efforts, and marshaled collective resources. There were rules and etiquettes and the citizens judged each other regarding how well each adhered to the expected codes of behavior. These protocols were the lubricant of the social engine driving this highly organized society.

Ussher felt positive he could adjust to this civilized existence over time but a persistent nagging in his gut kept his focus to the West. Months had passed and he wanted to check on his aging friend Carlos Rocha. Ussher needed to make sure the hard-working miner was safe and would live to enjoy the fruits of his labors. He even thought about suggesting to Rocha that he retire to the safety of St. Louis to live out his years in comfort, among friends. Unknown to Ussher, his apprehension revealed itself in solemn moments of vacant disquiet. His concerned thoughts furrowed his brow and his everyday actions predicted he would soon be on the move.

Nathan read the signs with intelligence and coherence. "You're leaving soon, aren't you?" he stated to Ussher one afternoon. Ussher found himself taken back by Nathan's perception. At this point, he had not fully acknowledged his restlessness to himself.

"How did you know?"

The young man answered with a woodsman's situational acuity. "You're too quiet. There are no sounds around you. Although you appear comfortable, your focus is away from here. I also noticed that after your clothes are washed, you place them back in the mule pack instead of the chest of drawers you were given. Lastly, I am your son and your student. You taught me to read signs and interpret their meanings according to the situation. Who would know you better than me?"

Ussher reached out and grasped Nathan around the back of his head. He pulled his son's forehead toward him until it touched his own.

"You are just too darn smart," he said. "You're reading me perfectly. I do need to go back West on some unfinished business but after that I will come back and, if you will have me, I'll stay."

Nathan hugged his father. "I understand," he said. "Wait another day or two and then get yourself going. The sooner you finish your business, the sooner you will be able to return to your family."

* * * *

Ussher left St Louis on a Friday morning.

Although a mature mount by this time, Bolt displayed unmistakable excitement. When he saw the pack mule loaded with supplies, he sensed a long ride was ahead. That was just fine with him. The noise of the city was not particularly to his liking. Ussher promised the family he would return soon, springtime at the latest. Since he was a man of his word, everyone felt confident with happy expectation for that future reunion. Benjamin, Christine, and Nathan watched and waived as Ussher turned Bolt around and departed westward.

* * * *

After a moment, Benjamin said to his wife, "There's a very nice home for sale near the law office. It's small and needs some work, but I think it would suit my brother perfectly. Let's buy it and have the problems repaired for when he returns."

"That's a wonderful idea," answered Christine. She absolutely loved projects where she could demonstrate her decorating talents "I'm sure I can get a couple of my friends to help with details." She was already thinking about two very fine women she knew from her church. In her opinion, either of them would be an excellent wife for Ussher.

Benjamin gave her a long, semi-serious look and said, "Details? Please keep in mind this is my frontiersman brother we're talking about. We should keep the woman's touch to a minimum."

Christine revealed displeasure with Benjamin's observation and replied with a mild huff in her voice, "I'm quite aware for whom we are doing this. I know your brother's nature after all, so please give me the credit for understanding the measure of the work to be done."

She continued with a peeved intonation. "And just what is wrong with a woman's touch?"

Benjamin tried to let the comment slide unanswered but it was too late.

"Tell me Benjamin, what is it you don't like about the way our home is furnished and decorated? Just what do you want changed? How would you improve my woman's touch?"

"Stop," Benjamin stated with authority. Then he added with a firm and respectful tenor, "We'll discuss the project tonight after dinner; over a glass of wine, in our beautifully appointed living room; where I promise to listen and be open to all your ideas."

Christine inhaled a quick breath to punctuate another thought and then allowed her vexation to evaporate. Hearing the acknowledgement in his voice was just as satisfying as having the last word. An air of normalcy quickly filled the room and she seamlessly changed the subject to news about one of the neighbors.

Nathan witnessed the entire exchange between his aunt and uncle. He looked over to Benjamin and whispered to himself, "Very well played."

* * * *

Bolt's long legs set a fast pace. As Nathan watched his father's silhouette recede into the distance, he experienced a compelling moment. His earlier life flashed by for a split second as he recalled all the events that led him to St. Louis, Benjamin's family, and Annie.

Once on his way, Nathan knew Ussher would not look back. It was not his style. Forward was always his direction and focus. Continually the vigilant scout, he was already studying the horizon for warning signs and planning response tactics. Survival was, after all, a full-time occupation. As Ussher turned the next corner, he nudged Bolt and dust kicked up as his stride quickened. Man and mount dissolved into the crowded street.

Nathan and Benjamin exchanged a brief glance and then

turned back for a final look at Ussher but it was too late, he was already gone. The future swallowed him whole as Destiny reappeared to frustrate his purpose, redirect his intended course and deny him the peace and rest he hoped to find. The winds of discord stirred and blew just enough to obliquely alter his path.

Leaving St Louis a day later would have removed all imperatives and hastened his return. A rider with less endurance or sitting atop a slower mount would have left the revelation hidden and undetected. A man of just average insight and intelligence would have overlooked the small details that indicted those culpable. Someone without courage would have assumed the circumstance was beyond recovery and avoided the consequences of further involvement.

None of these nuanced traits, parsed qualities or situational distinctions meant anything to Joseph Ussher. The interpretation of the facts was obvious and he recognized what tasks were required to resolve the matters at hand. Hesitation spawned from jeopardy was never an option when those he respected or loved were involved. He reacted decisively and paid the full measure for that response.

Three years passed before Ussher's family received word confirming his fate and approximate location. The messages came through a trusted, impeccable source. This information chronicled incredible trials, detailing his exceptional legacy, but left the family uncertain he would ever return to them.

CHARACTERS

Aaron Russell
FICTIONAL

Abigail
FICTIONAL

Andy Hester
FICTIONAL

Andy Morton
HISTORICAL

Annie
FICTIONAL

Archie Clement
HISTORICAL

Benjamin Ussher
FICTIONAL

Big John Harper
FICTIONAL

Bloody Bill Anderson
HISTORICAL

Bolt
FICTIONAL

Carlos Rocha
FICTIONAL

Charlie Hawkins
FICTIONAL

Christine Ussher
FICTIONAL

Darby Prichard Ussher
FICTIONAL

Doc Jennison
HISTORICAL

Ella
FICTIONAL

Emily Randall
FICTIONAL

General Tom Ewing
HISTORICAL

George Todd
HISTORICAL

Henry Rifle
HISTORICAL

Jack Mingo
FICTIONAL

James Lane
HISTORICAL

Jimmy (Our Jimmy).
FICTIONAL

Joseph Ussher
FICTIONAL

Josie Anderson
HISTORICAL

Kensington
FICTIONAL

Raid on Lawrence, Kansas
HISTORICAL

Raid on Osceola, Missouri
HISTORICAL

Raid on Nevada City, Kansas
HISTORICAL

Leo
FICTIONAL

Lewis Randall
FICTIONAL

Lieut. Emmett Blanchard
FICTIONAL

Little Bill Hooker
FICTIONAL

Maggie Pritchard
FICTIONAL

Mama and Pa Pritchard
FICTIONAL

Mary Anderson
HISTORICAL

Mary Elizabeth Prichard
FICTIONAL

Micah Russell
FICTIONAL

Nathan Ussher (Nate)
FICTIONAL

Nina Moore
FICTIONAL

Otto Metzger
FICTIONAL

Pawnee Battle Knife
FICTIONAL

Pawnee Grandfather
FICTIONAL

Rachel
FICTIONAL

Sgt. Carney
FICTIONAL

Talbot Harris
FICTIONAL

The Meadow
FICTIONAL

Toby
FICTIONAL

Tyler
FICTIONAL

Vaughn
HISTORICAL

Vincent Harris
FICTIONAL

William Quantrill
HISTORICAL

The Demon
ALIVE & WELL

A NOTE ON THE AUTHOR

JOE DWYER WAS RAISED IN ALSIP, ILLINOIS, a rural community with 1,200 citizens, known for its farms, brick making and numerous cemeteries. Neighbors looked after one another and emergency help came without needing to ask. The majority of the children walked to school and only entered after the custodian pulled the rope to ring the old bell. Each of the four classrooms accommodated two grade levels with the teacher alternating instructions between each group of students.

Boys as young as 14, were happy to work for 50 cents an hour harvesting tomatoes, cabbage and cantaloupe. Ancient Potawatomi arrow heads were sometimes found in the dirt of the plowed furrows. Children referred to their parents and elders as "ma'am and sir" and performed chores around the farms from their earliest memories.

His working class parents instilled in him the importance of God, family, country and self-reliance. While growing up, borrowing tools for chores was common in his cash poor community. Along with the customary thank you, the borrower insured these implements were always clean and sharp when returned to their owner. Borrowing money from a neighbor was only considered in desperate situations and debt repayment carried the reverence of a sacred oath.

Joe married his high school sweetheart, Christine, one year after their graduation. While working and raising a son and two daughters, Chris helped Joe to finish college and earn both a bachelors and master's degree. For six years of this period Joe served as a full time police officer. They are blessed with six grandchildren, all girls.

Joe always enjoys the storytelling part of history and has developed a deep interest in the cause and effect of the events linking the past to the present. From that perspective his interest progressed to studying the impact these changes exert on individuals and groups. Through research, assessment and introspection, he evaluates these dynamics to assess the course they may impose on a community or society.

Harvest the Bitter Root tells several stories set within the brutality of the American Civil War. The conflict presented both fortune and jeopardy, quickly separating those prepared and adaptable from those who were not. To the survivors fell the task of using their experience to educate succeeding generations in the art of inclusive governance. The events from the end of that conflict until today stand as witness to that progress or lack of it.

The author hopes that citizens will educate themselves and raise up leaders who study the lessons of history and seek justice for the people they serve before personal gain and political motivation.

Today Joe works for a hand tool company in charge of manufacturing and engineering. He and Christine live in a home which sits at the end of a quiet street adjoining forest preserve land. Their backyard receives frequent visits from coyotes, raccoons and deer, who enjoy eating Christine's flowers at every opportunity.

www.ingramcontent.com/pod-product-compliance
Lightning Source LLC
Chambersburg PA
CBHW032028290426
44110CB00012B/715